Workers and Utopia

Gerald N. Grob was born in New York City and studied at City College, Columbia University, and Northwestern University. He has edited *American Ideas* and *Interpretations of American History,* and his articles have appeared in several scholarly journals. He is now Professor of American History at Rutgers University/Douglass College, New Brunswick, New Jersey.

Workers and Utopia

A STUDY OF IDEOLOGICAL CONFLICT IN THE AMERICAN
LABOR MOVEMENT 1865–1900

Gerald N. Grob

Quadrangle/ The New York Times Book Co.

First QUADRANGLE PAPERBACK edition published 1969 by Quadrangle/The New York Times Book Co., 10 East 53 Street, New York, New York 10022. Manufactured in the United States of America.

Second printing, March 1976

International Standard Book Number: 0-8129-6088-2

FOR LILA

Preface

౿ IN RECENT YEARS the role and function of organized labor in the United States have become increasingly popular topics of debate. Scarcely a day passes without some comment on the labor movement. Business and union leaders, prominent political figures, government officials, scholars, journalists, and the general public all have joined in the discussion. Partisans of the labor movement seek to justify its ideas and practices, proclaiming its virtues in enthusiastic terms. Opponents of American unionism, on the other hand, attack its alleged monopolistic and arbitrary powers, as well as the seemingly endless inflationary push given by continuous wage demands. Still others attempt to follow a middle path, looking toward the public interest as their point of reference.

My purpose in this study, however, is neither to justify nor condemn the American labor movement. Nor am I studying its past history to find clues that would help to resolve present problems and issues. Instead I have attempted to assess from a historical point of view the development of the ideology of organized labor as an integral part of American society and culture. For American unionism is more than simply an economic movement. Like other institutions, it tends to reflect the dominant standards and values of American culture. One of my basic assumptions has been, therefore, that unions are simply a microcosm of a larger whole, and I have tried to show why American unionism has developed in its own peculiar manner. After all, unions in America have evolved in a very different fashion as compared with those of England and Western Europe. Why has this been so? My answer, briefly stated, is that American unionism is simply a response to the values which American culture emphasizes. Functioning in a materialistic, acquisitive, and abundant environment, unions have derived their goals and orientation from society at large.

In writing this book, I have profited from a large number of studies by other students, most of whose contributions are acknowledged in the bibliographical essay at the end of the volume. In particular, however, I should like to single out the classic work on American labor by the late John R. Commons and his associates (*History of Labour in the United States,* 4 volumes, New York, 1918–1935). This work, which gained instantaneous recognition as being the authority on the history of American

ix

labor, became the point of departure for all future research, a position that it still retains. Indeed, it would not be too much to assert that all studies since the *History of Labour* (with some exceptions) have been little more than elaborations of its basic theme. While this work still remains as the single most important one in the field of labor history (and justly so), scholars have come to question some of its interpretations. Written by men trained as economists rather than historians, the *History of Labour* frequently treated labor developments apart from the general milieu, and almost completely neglected the influence of leadership. Since its publication, moreover, a large mass of manuscript and printed material has become available, shedding much new light on the labor movement and substantially modifying our understanding of the Knights of Labor and the American Federation of Labor prior to 1900. When I have disagreed with the approach and interpretation of the Commons' school, however, it has only been with great reluctance and careful consideration. My debt to this group of scholars, despite my disagreement with some of their interpretations, is evident throughout.

I should like to emphasize that I have not attempted to write a history of organized labor from the Civil War to the turn of the century. The history of the Knights of Labor, of many national and international unions, of local and regional developments, still remains to be done. Instead I have chosen two themes that seem to me to have dominated the labor movement in the nineteenth century—the concepts of reform unionism and of trade unionism. I have attempted to explore the ideology and development of these forms of unionism, culminating in their polarization in the 1880's. Above all, I have attempted to explain the success and triumph of trade unionism over reform unionism during these years. Whether or not I have succeeded, of course, is for the reader to determine.

Finally, I should point out that I have to some extent ignored a chronological narrative, largely because of the difficulty in tracing ideology within a narrow time sequence. Rather I have endeavored to describe first the program and tactics of the National Labor Union, then that of the Knights of Labor, then the conflict between the Knights and the trade unions and its ultimate resolution, and have concluded with two chapters on the organization and early development of the American Federation of Labor, the organization founded by the trade unions in response to the challenge laid down by the Knights in the 1880's. As a result of this approach, the chronological evolution of organized labor has been subordinated, although I hope that the exposition has followed a clear and logical sequence.

It is now my pleasant duty to acknowledge my obligations to those individuals and institutions who so generously aided me in the preparation of this study. I would like to thank Mr. William Schnitzler, secretary-treasurer of the A.F. of L.–C.I.O., for permission to use the records of the A.F. of L. prior to 1900, and Father Henry J. Browne, formerly of

Catholic University of America, for his help in searching through the Powderly collection. The limitations of time and space prevent me from naming the many individuals at various libraries who offered freely both their time and help. I would, however, like to thank the officials of the following libraries: New York Public Library, Library of Congress, United States Department of Labor Library, Wisconsin State Historical Society, John Crerar Library, Newberry Library, Chicago Public Library, Boston Public Library, and the libraries of Northwestern University, Columbia University, Catholic University, Harvard University, Johns Hopkins University, and Clark University. The editors of the *Journal of Economic History, Mid-America, The Review of Politics* and *Labor History* have graciously permitted me to reproduce material which first appeared in their respective publications.

Professor Ray A. Billington of Northwestern University, and Professors Morris H. Cohen and Marc Raeff of Clark University were generous in their comments and criticisms. I would also like to thank Professor Richard M. Brace and the Committee of Northwestern University Studies in History for their aid in publishing this book. I owe my greatest debt to Professor Arthur S. Link, who has guided this work through all of its stages with patience, tact, and friendship. Much of whatever merit it possesses is due to his unfailing help. My parents through the years have been a constant source of encouragement. Last, but not least, I wish to thank my wife, Lila K. Grob, whose help and encouragement is far greater than she realizes.

Contents

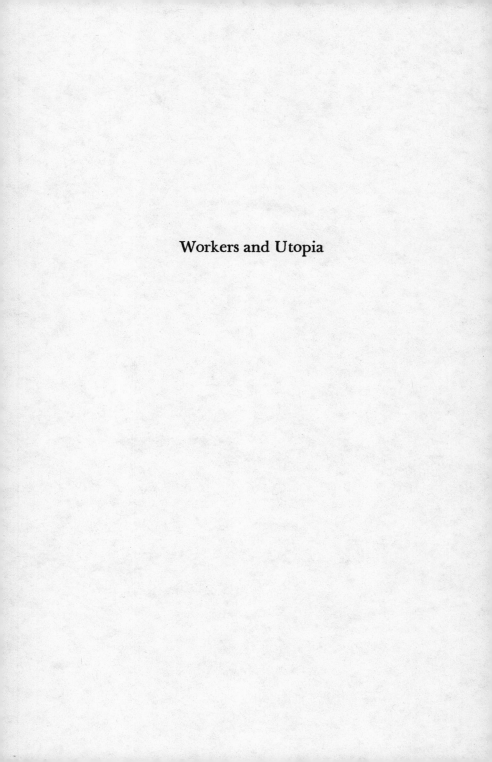

Workers and Utopia

CHAPTER ONE

Introduction

✌ ON THE MORNING of December 5, 1955, delegates representing the affiliated unions of the American Federation of Labor and the Congress of Industrial Organizations ratified a document healing the schism that had divided labor's ranks for two decades. Scores of prominent figures, from the mayor of New York City to the President of the United States, joined in paying homage to the power of organized labor. For the American worker it was indeed a climactic moment, symbolizing the importance that his unions had come to exercise in almost all walks of life.

Yet, as Adlai Stevenson so eloquently told the assembled delegates, there lay behind "a century and a half of preparation, of building, of upward struggle, of fighting for a liberty no working man could win alone, but only in company with his brothers." [1] There had been a time when labor organizations were regarded by many with suspicion, when employers refused to bargain collectively with their employees, and when the immense powers of the state and national governments were arrayed against organized labor. History was indeed a compelling witness to the notable transformation that had occurred in the century and a half preceding that fateful morning of December 5, 1955. From its minute and obscure origins the American labor movement had at last come of age.

The process of growth and development, however, had been slow and arduous. During the colonial period there was little need for working-class organization because of the relative lack of distinction between employer and employee. This era was, in the words of one historian, "the age of the individual entrepreneur, who, in such industries as the workshop crafts, performed the labor as well as put up the capital for the venture himself." [2] With the gradual expansion of industry, a development made possible by a revolution in transportation and communication, the traditionally close relationship between master and journeyman underwent a significant change. The increase in the size of the industrial unit and the introduction of machinery enhanced the master's position, while at the same time it reduced the journeyman to the status of a paid and dependent worker. The pressure of increased competition induced em-

[1] *American Federationist*, LXIII (January, 1956), 42.
[2] Richard B. Morris, *Government and Labor in Early America* (New York, 1946), p. 38.

3

ployers to attempt to hold down wages, increase working hours, and seek
new sources of cheap labor.

The changes in industrial organization presented an ominous threat to
the favored position held by the skilled craftsman, and it was he who took
the lead in uniting for self-protection. The first unions probably originated during the last quarter of the eighteenth or in the early nineteenth
century. Many were at first fraternal or mutual aid societies, but implicit
in their formation was the incipient hope of protecting members against
forces menacing their economic and social status. Combinations were
especially evident among printers, cordwainers, tailors, carpenters, coopers, and shoemakers.[3] These early bodies, although local in character
and small in membership, represented the first concerted efforts to maintain and preserve the status of the workers.

The first major expansion of labor organizations resulted from the improved economic conditions following the panic of 1819, and many local
trade societies came into existence. More significant than the formation of
such isolated bodies, however, was the Mechanics' Union of Trade Associations. Conceived in 1826 and formally organized in Philadelphia in
1827, this was one of the earliest bodies to bring together workers of different crafts. Although intended mainly as a medium for political activity,
the Mechanics' Union of Trade Associations was motivated primarily by
the hope of arresting a growing capitalism and substituting in its place a
society based on the small producer where the journeyman artisan would
retain a respected place in the community.[4]

The organizational activities of the 1820's demonstrated that the position of the skilled artisans was deteriorating as a result of industrial and
technological changes. Initially their reaction had been to form trade
societies to offset such disturbing developments, and then to expand these
societies on a regional basis to meet the competition that had followed the
improvements in transportation and the appearance of a market that
transcended local geographical lines. The fraternal, social, and mutual
aid aspects of these early unions tended to disappear as their members
became more and more conscious of the widened gulf between the
journeymen and the masters, especially since the latter were becoming
employers rather than workers. The skilled artisans, therefore, began to
transform their organizations into fighting bodies whose object was the
preservation of the older patterns of work. As a result of their efforts, the
labor movement came to an early, although short lived, maturity.

By the late 1820's and early 1830's many unions were turning to politics

[3] John R. Commons, ed., *History of Labour in the United States* (4 vols: New York,
1918–1935), I, 104; William A. Sullivan, *The Industrial Worker in Pennsylvania 1800–
1840* (Harrisburg, Pennsylvania, 1955), pp. 86–87.

[4] See Louis H. Arky, "The Mechanics' Union of Trade Associations and the Formation of the Philadelphia Workingmen's Movement," *Pennsylvania Magazine of History
and Biography*, LXXVI (April, 1952), 142–76.

in an effort to remedy the lot of their members. Joining hands with farmers, professionals, and small businessmen, they formed "workingmen's parties" in about fifteen states, ultimately winning some minor victories. Eschewing interest in purely economic goals, these parties were primarily concerned with the extension of public education and the abolition of imprisonment for debt. This political agitation, however, did not represent either a class or a modern labor movement. Workers were confused and baffled by the impersonal forces at work and were as much concerned with social position as economic conditions. Combining a curious blend of humanitarian and business motives, labor aspired toward employer status while simultaneously denouncing aristocracy. Enthusiastically attacking special privilege, these skilled workers did not limit themselves to strictly union activities, and they included in their program, in addition to their major political goals, such diverse objectives as the ten-hour day, restriction of child labor, abolition of contract convict labor, temperance, prohibition of private banks empowered to issue currency, abolition of the militia system and lotteries, and an end to licensed monopolies.

By 1833 the strictly political aspect of the labor movement was in the process of decline, although the workers had by no means abandoned their interest in politics. Nevertheless, after 1833 the craftsmen began to avoid organized political action and emphasized instead the formation of trade unions that had as their primary function the extension of mutual aid during disputes with employers. A natural consequence was an increased contact between various local organizations of the same trade. Furthermore, as a result of the efforts of the New York General Trades Union, the National Trades' Union, one of the first federations to transcend state boundaries, was founded in 1834. Never more than an advisory and agitational convention, the National Trades' Union concerned itself with general demands rather than the problems confronting individual trades. It failed, however, to survive the panic of 1837.

In one sense the early flurry of organizational and agitational activity during the Jacksonian period had been premature. For the fact remains that these early labor societies did not include either the common laborers or the rising factory workers. Rather they were composed largely of skilled mechanics, craftsmen, and artisans, each of whom was a relatively independent individual refusing to think of himself as a member of a permanent and distinct working class. This group regarded themselves as the producing class and therefore the only legitimate group in the community. Their animus was directed toward the aristocratic and wealthy elements of society. Ardent supporters of the democratic and equal-rights philosophy, these workers were not anticapitalistic, for they aspired toward the status of independent producers.[5] It was during these years, when an expanding capitalism was destroying old and established patterns, that

[5] See Edward Pessen, "The Workingmen's Movement of the Jackson Era," *Misissippi Valley Historical Review*, XLIII (December, 1956), 434.

the ideal of a peaceful, idyllic community based on the small productive unit began to develop.

The panic of 1837, however, brought to a close this first chapter in the history of organized labor. And when a new movement arose in the 1840's, it functioned under vastly different conditions. By then the impact of the rising tide of immigration was making itself felt. The Irish were especially prominent among the new groups, providing a major source of cheap and abundant labor. Frequently they came into direct conflict with native workers, whose places they took, thus preventing any consolidation of labor's forces. The substantial reliance upon women and child labor, and the disturbing impact of mechanization on the skilled trades, also hindered the emergence of a bona fide labor movement.

As a result of the divisive forces at work within labor's ranks, the disappearance of the Jacksonian labor movement, and the bewilderment unleashed by an ever-quickening industrialism, the working class began to become closely involved in the middle-class humanitarian movements of the 1840's. Such movements as land reform, temperance, abolitionism, communitarianism, utopianism, and others provided a natural habitat for those workers disillusioned with earlier experiences in labor organization, as well as a means of escaping from reality through supporting a comprehensive program of social reform that would introduce, if not the millennium, then certainly a form of utopia. Many workingmen, therefore, grasped eagerly at the varied panaceas that appeared to offer such glowing hope for the future, and in the 1840's the labor movement was nearly absorbed into the middle-class humanitarian movements. The latter's adherents made determined efforts to capture labor support, and they often descended in droves upon labor meetings and conventions. The meetings of the New England Working Men's Association in 1844 and 1845, for example, called initially to consider plans for establishing the ten-hour day, were attended by such prominent figures as George Henry Evans, Albert Brisbane, George Ripley, Robert Owen, and Horace Greeley, none of whom were bona fide workers.[6] Generally speaking, such individuals approached the problems of the working class from the outside, since they were largely philanthropists possessing a sense of social responsibility toward the less fortunate. And yet there was a basis for the *rapprochement* between workers and reformers, namely, the hope of the former of improving their condition and the vision of the latter of transforming society.

Consequently the labor movement of the 1840's came to emphasize the ideals of the middle-class reform movements. Associationism, propounded by Albert Brisbane and Horace Greeley, land reform, led by George Henry Evans, the widespread and influential co-operative movement of this period, all competed for the allegiance of workers. Especially appeal-

[6] Commons, *History of Labour*, I, 537–38.

ing to labor during this decade were the land reform theories of Evans, who led a national movement designed to develop rank and file support for his program. Basing his ideas on a natural rights and equalitarian foundation, Evans argued that only the abolition of land monopoly could solve the pressing problems facing American workers. Thus he advocated both a limit on the amount of land any individual could own as well as the free distribution of public lands to actual settlers only. Evans believed that such a system would result in the reduction of the labor force, thus raising wages, and also permit workers to become independent themselves. Actually the central aim of the land reformers was the establishment of independent townships, where farmers and craftsmen-mechanics would produce and exchange their products in simplistic harmony. The ideas of Evans and his followers were of major importance in the 1840's and afterwards, since they offered to the workers the hope that their position of independence could once more be restored and monopolistic institutions destroyed.[7] As a matter of fact, they were destined to influence the labor movement until the 1870's and 1880's, contributing significantly to the thought of those labor leaders who insisted that only a fundamental reform of society could improve the depressed conditions of American workers.

The legacy of the Jacksonian labor movement and its successor in the 1840's, therefore, was an ideology of reform unionism. By the middle of the nineteenth century those workers, whose instinctive reaction had been a fierce rejection of industrial society, had articulated a program designed to overcome the difficulties that they faced as a result of the rapid transformation of America. Wedded to a democratic philosophy of liberty, equality, individualism, and progress, they looked with fear and uneasiness at developments which seemed to be the very antithesis of their ideals. Having taken as their norm the vision of a past society (perhaps one that existed only in their own minds) where the independent artisan combined in his own person both employer and employee functions, they could not understand the divisions between rich and poor, worker and employer, that were becoming integral features of the environment. The only legitimate division that they recognized was between the producing and the nonproducing class, the former being given the stamp of legitimacy and the latter marked for obliteration. The end objective of reform unionism was the creation of a society where all would belong to the producing class, and the individual would combine in his own person both worker and employer functions.

These reform unionists, moreover, were also disturbed by the changing nature of the work process. Originally a means of self-fulfillment as well as a means of subsistence, the significance of work was undergoing a

---

[7] See Helene S. Zahler, *Eastern Workingmen and National Land Policy, 1829–1862* (New York, 1941), *passim*, and Norman J. Ware, *The Industrial Worker 1840–1860* (Boston, 1924), pp. 180–84.

subtle metamorphosis as a consequence of the change from a pre-industrial to an industrial technology. Many artisans, however, still retained a pride in their skill and workmanship that resulted from seeing a product through its development from start to finish. But when placed in the midst of a technology where specialization, reliance upon machine labor, and large-scale production were reaching unprecedented extremes, these artisans found that they were rapidly becoming the raw matrial for a dispossessed working class that was divorced from any responsibility for the completed product. Such a process of alienation was foreign to these individuals. Unwilling to accept their new status despite the possibility of greater material rewards that might conceivably result from the changes in the productive process, they fought instead to return to an earlier period when the individual entrepreneur supposedly dominated the productive process. In the 1840's, when various forces served to divide the labor movement, these artisans were joined by other workers to whom the hope of improvement through a fundamental reform of society was indeed an attraction.

The appeal to the past was thus the outstanding characteristic of the reform unionists. In their eyes the primary function of the labor movement was the restoration of the independence of the working class, and they constantly sought to develop appropriate means for this purpose. Their end objective was the constant; the means to achieve it, however, were considerably more flexible. They could be ardent supporters of cooperative techniques in order to bypass the "monopolists" who were slowly coming to exercise arbitrary control over the productive process. They could at times demonstrate a proclivity for political action and at other times reveal a deep and abiding hostility toward politics, depending on the degree to which this means had proven successful or unsuccessful. They could be simultaneously hostile and favorable toward capitalism, depending on whether it was defined in post- or pre-industrial terms. They could oppose organization along trade lines and yet look askance upon industrial unionism and collective bargaining, largely because these would not affect the basic difficulties facing the working class. In short, the reform unionists attempted to use whatever means at their disposal in an effort to restore the individual entrepreneur to a commanding position. And if one technique did not prove successful, a different and even an opposing means could then be tried. But whatever the method, the objective would remain constant.

At the same time that the reform unionists were developing a comprehensive program to achieve their ideal, there was emerging in the labor movement in the decade prior to the Civil War a rival ideology that received its institutional expression in the form of the local and national trade union. Appearing initially with the upturn of the economic barometer in the 1850's, these organizations developed a much more limited and narrow program that revolved principally around the job and the conditions of work. The National Typographical Union, for example, organized formally in 1852, spent most of its early years discussing such problems as the adoption of a national price scale so as to eliminate wage differentials between areas, the desirability of recognizing union membership on a national scale in order to provide for traveling members, the establishment of a "just" wage scale, the issue of apprenticeship, and the like. Although this as well as the other early national trade unions were little more than advisers to sovereign local bodies, they nevertheless formed the nucleus of the centralized craft organizations that came to dominate the labor movement after the 1880's.

The trade unions of the 1850's differed in several important ways from their predecessors. Not only had their members begun to minimize benevolent and fraternal functions, but they had also given up the hope of becoming masters and regaining a self-employed status, thus implicitly recognizing that the growth of the factory system had rendered this goal futile. Perhaps accepting unconsciously the permanence of their wage-earning condition, they began to develop the economic functions of unionism in order to gain recognition and engage successfully in collective bargaining. Though weak and immature, the trade unions of the 1850's provided the basis for a nationwide expansion of labor organization in the late nineteenth and twentieth centuries.

While it is true that on the surface there were some superficial similarities between the reform unionists and the trade unionists, there were in actuality fundamental differences that proved in the long run unbridgeable. The trade unionists, unlike their opponents, were little interested in plans for social reform. Indeed, they argued that it was virtually impossible to return to a pre-industrial technology. Emphasizing that the direction of industrial evolution was irreversible, they attempted to formulate a program that would be in harmony with the changing conditions that they faced. Implicitly acknowledging the permanence of capitalism and industrial society, they spent most of their time in efforts to devise common programs of immediate economic objectives. Most of the early trade unions were composed of skilled workers belonging to the same trade. Unlike the reform unionists, however, these workers had emancipated themselves from the idea that their interests were identical with those of their employers. They also began to stress their own welfare rather than the welfare of their class, and they accepted the loss of status involved in the changes in industrial organization.[8]

The trade-union ideology was thus much more limited and restricted in terms of its basic objective than the reform union ideology. In a sense it represented a tacit *quid pro quo* between labor and industry. In return for labor nonsupport of revolutionary theories, industry promised the worker a rising standard of living and a respected though subordinate position in the community. Confined at first to the skilled workers, such a program was capable of indefinite expansion, and by the middle of the

[8] Ware, *Industrial Worker*, p. 227.

twentieth century had been accepted by nearly all of organized labor.

After the Civil War the quest continued for an answer to the new problems that had arisen as a result of technological change and the nationalization of competition. The difficulties facing the workers were becoming ever more acute because of the postwar acceleration in the rate of industrial expansion. This growth was accompanied by a large increase in the number of workers dependent upon others for their means of support. Between 1870 and 1900, for example, the number of individuals employed in manufacturing, construction, and transportation and other public utilities, rose from three and a third million to nearly ten million.[9] Indexes of industrial production showed an even more startling rise because of the greater reliance upon machine rather than hand labor.

In these years of industrial expansion workingmen, heirs of a long tradition of the self-reliant individualism so characteristic of agrarian America, found that their hitherto respected status in society was being rapidly downgraded and that they no longer possessed their cherished dream of independence. More and more they found themselves at the mercy of an impersonal corporation. Threatened with periodic unemployment because of the vagaries of the business cycle, disturbed by their lack of authority in determining wages and conditions of work, and resentful of the conditions of urban life, they began to seek ways and means that would enable them to have greater influence and responsibility in determining their own destinies. To such men, as well as to the large number of immigrants who had come to America to better their lives, passive acceptance of their status was unthinkable. So, despite the fierceness with which employers received their efforts, workers continued to seek a *modus vivendi* that would result in a better and more equitable adjustment to the problems of industralized society. During the last part of the nineteenth century the working class became engrossed in a search for techniques that would accomplish its aims.

In 1865, however, following four years of war and turmoil, American labor was still undecided as to its path. Its choice, as a result of the experiences of the previous four decades, had been narrowed to two major types of unionism—reform unionism, which looked to an earlier society for inspiration, and trade unionism, which involved an acceptance of industrial society and American culture and an emphasis on collective bargaining goals. In the succeeding quarter of a century the labor movement was destined to be drawn into various political crusades, participate in numerous reform ventures, and flirt briefly with socialism and other radical ideologies. By the end of the century, nevertheless, the trade-union ideology had triumphed over the reform-union ideology and was in the process of becoming institutionalized. How this came to pass is the subject matter of this history.

[9] U. S. Bureau of the Census, *Historical Statistics of the United States 1789–1945* (Washington, D. C., 1949) , p. 64.

CHAPTER TWO

Reform Unionism: the National Labor Union

I

℣ AT THE END of the Civil War the American labor movement was still divided along ideological lines. Despite these differences, however, there was near unanimity on the necessity for organization on a nationwide basis to strengthen labor's hand. The establishment of the national trade unions, commencing in the 1850's, was one manifestation of this belief. Equally significant was the movement to organize a national labor federation. This movement reached fruition in 1866 with the establishment of the National Labor Union, the first truly national federation of labor in the United States.

The germ of the idea for such a federation had been planted at the beginning of the Civil War when the International Union of Machinists and Blacksmiths adopted a resolution calling for the formation of a committee "to request the appointment of a similar committee from other national or grand bodies (of Trade Unions) to meet them, fully empowered to form a National Trades Assembly, to facilitate the advancement of the interests of labor." [1] In 1864 the International Industrial Assembly of North America held its first convention, but the failure of the unions to send delegates was fatal, and no further meetings were held. There were also other proposals for national organization, none of which resulted in any concrete action.[2]

It was not until 1866 that plans were set in motion to organize a national labor federation. In February of that year William Harding, president of the Coachmakers International Union, met with William H. Sylvis, president of the Iron Molders International Union. Their conference led to a meeting the following month with other leaders, who decided to hold a national labor convention in Baltimore on August 20, 1866. Upon objection by the Workingmen's Union of New York City that

[1] International Union of Machinists and Blacksmiths, *Proceedings*, November 1861, reprinted in John R. Commons and others, eds., *A Documentary History of American Industrial Society* (10 vols: Cleveland, 1910–1911), IX, 117 (hereinafter cited as Commons, *Documentary History*).

[2] *Fincher's Trades' Review*, August 13, October 15, 1864, December 16, 1865.

the officers of the national unions were assuming unwarranted power in calling for a "National Convention of Trades," a compromise was reached whereby organizations such as eight-hour leagues, which included individuals sympathetic toward labor but not themselves workingmen, could send representatives.[3] This decision ultimately permitted diverse reform groups to send delegates to the annual congresses of the National Labor Union.

From this modest beginning the National Labor Union quickly rose to a prominent position. The *Chicago Tribune* in 1869 estimated its membership at 800,000, and Sylvis himself put the figure at 600,000. Both estimates are undoubtedly exaggerated, but it is apparent that the organization represented a substantial proportion of the nation's laboring force and numbered at its peak perhaps between 200,000 and 400,000.[4]

At the beginning the National Labor Union was composed of relatively homogeneous groups. Seventy-seven delegates were present at the first congress, representing fifty local trade unions, thirteen trades' assemblies, five eight-hour leagues, and two national trade unions. The representation of the latter group, however, was stronger than it appeared, for all presidents and secretaries were given invitations to attend with the right to speak but not to vote. Actually, ten national unions were represented at the first congress.[5]

At subsequent conventions, as the National Labor Union took on more and more of a reform character, the delegates began to form a heterogeneous group. By 1867 there were in attendance delegates from antimonopoly associations and land and labor leagues. The following year representatives from local "labor unions" began to make their appearance. These bodies were essentially workingmen's organizations formed for purely political purposes. By 1870 it was obvious that the exponents of political action were gaining in strength. Fully seven state and eighteen local "labor unions" were represented. The national trade unions, unhappy at the direction in which the National Labor Union was pointed, began to disaffiliate, and after 1870 the political and reform elements were in control. At the time of its demise in 1872, these diverse groups were the preponderant elements in the National Labor Union.[6]

[3] James C. Sylvis, *The Life, Speeches, Labors and Essays of William H. Sylvis* (Philadelphia, 1872), pp. 64–65; Boston *Daily Evening Voice*, March 30, 1866; Commons, *Documentary History*, IX, 126–27.

[4] *Chicago Tribune*, February 16, 1869, cited in Philip S. Foner, *History of the Labor Movement in the United States* (2 vols: New York, 1947–1955), I, 376–77; Commons, *History of Labour*, II, 126; Richard F. Hinton, "Organization of Labor: Its Aggressive Phases," *Atlantic Monthly*, XXVII (May 1871), 549, 557.

[5] Chicago *Workingman's Advocate*, September 1, 1866; Commons, *History of Labour*, II, 96–97.

[6] For the composition of the National Labor Union see the Chicago *Workingman's Advocate*, September 1, 1866, August 24, 1867, September 4, 1869, August 27, 1870, August 19, 1871, September 21, 1872; Commons, *History of Labour*, II, 96–97, 115, 126–27, 133, 144.

The National Labor Union, aside from its mixed character, was also weakened by the fact that it had no integral structure of its own. Composed of sovereign constituent organizations, it could do little more than agitate, pass resolutions, and offer advice. The most pressing need of the 1860's—the formation of a closely-knit, widely-organized, and financially solvent labor movement—was neglected. Little progress was made in organizing subordinate labor unions and, unlike the Knights of Labor and the American Federation of Labor, the National Labor Union did not found even a single national trade union. The few locals that were organized were more political clubs than labor unions. The National Labor Union was never a bona fide labor movement from the bottom up; it was more the instrument of a few hard-working individuals.[7]

Another major barrier standing in the path of the National Labor Union was the lack of an adequate revenue. Although the Executive Board was given the power to levy an annual per capita tax of twenty-five cents upon all members, its officers encountered troubles in collecting the money because of the difficulty in determining who were actually members.[8] Following the adjournment of the congress of 1866, the *Iron Molders' Journal* colorfully remarked: "The fact is, the Convention met, held a five days' session, built a splendid railroad track, placed upon it a locomotive, complete in almost all its parts, provided an engineer and numerous assistants, placed them upon the foot-board, told them to go ahead, then suddenly adjourned without providing wood and water to get up steam, and there the whole machine will stand until the third Monday in August, 1867." [9] Subsequent attempts to place the National Labor Union on a solvent basis and provide salaries for its officers also ended in failure, for more often than not the lack of funds hindered compliance with the law. In 1870, financially its most successful year, the National Labor Union collected a little over two thousand dollars, while expenses were nearly double receipts.[10] The perpetual lack of money was a determining factor in the inability of the National Labor Union to push successfully the work of organization.

II

These are, however, only the bare facts of the rise and decline of America's first national labor federation. As we will see, the National Labor Union was more a reform movement aimed at preventing monopoly, preserving equality of opportunity, and strengthening democracy,

[7] Terence V. Powderly, *Thirty Years of Labor. 1859 to 1889* (Columbus, Ohio, 1889), p. 70.

[8] Chicago *Workingman's Advocate,* September 1, 1866, August 24, 1867.

[9] *Iron Molders' Journal*, n.s. vol. I (September, 1866), 177.

[10] Chicago *Workingman's Advocate,* August 24, 31, 1867, August 27, 1870, August 19, 1871.

than a modern job- and wage-conscious phalanx. Moreover, it drew more from the humanitarian heritage of the ante-bellum period than it contributed to the development of a modern labor ideology.

The basic character of the National Labor Union was in large measure determined by the background and ideological orientation of its leaders, most of whom had been born and had grown to maturity during the reform and antimonopoly crusades of the 1830's and 1840's. The career of William H. Sylvis, undoubtedly the dominant personality in the National Labor Union, is perhaps typical. Born in Pennsylvania in 1828, he was apprenticed in a foundry in 1837 following his father's failure as a wagon maker. Easily shifting from the status of journeyman to part proprietor and then back to journeyman, Sylvis' experiences were typical of the labor movement as a whole. Growing to manhood in an era of ferment, he retained the political and social reform philosophy that was such an integral part of the ante-bellum labor movement. To him the primary purpose of the labor movement was the abolition of an impersonal and degrading wage system, which would be replaced by a co-operative society based on the dominance of the small individual producer.

Yet Sylvis, oddly enough, was also the most brilliant and constructive trade union leader of his generation. Like many other individuals active in the labor movement, he saw no inherent contradiction between his actions as a trade unionist and his reform ideology. It was because of his efforts that the Iron Molders International Union was founded in 1859. Elevated to the presidency of this organization in 1863, Sylvis proceeded to build it into one of the most successful unions in the country. Also active in the National Labor Union, he was elected president in 1868, and was responsible for a large measure of its success. His sudden death in July, 1869, at the age of forty-one, seriously affected the National Labor Union, which disappeared three years later.[11]

The presence at the annual congresses of delegates like Horace Day, a prominent reformer of Brooklyn, New York, and Susan B. Anthony and Elizabeth Cady Stanton, feminist leaders, also serves to illustrate the heterogeneous background of the leaders of the National Labor Union. Including not only working-class representatives, but land, currency, feminist, and utopian reformers, the National Labor Union faithfully reflected the trade and reform traditions of the ante-bellum labor movement. Even Richard F. Trevellick, Sylvis' successor as president of the National Labor Union, was as much a reformer as he was a labor leader. Although English by birth, Trevellick espoused many of the causes so dear to American workingmen, including such diverse objectives as land,

---

[11] The best study of Sylvis is Jonathan Grossman's *William Sylvis, Pioneer of American Labor* (New York, 1945). There is also much information not obtainable elsewhere in James C. Sylvis, *Life . . . of William H. Sylvis.* Charlotte Todes, *William H. Sylvis and the National Labor Union* (New York, 1942), calls attention to some neglected aspects of Sylvis' life.

tax, and currency reform, women's rights, labor political action, a large public works program, inflation, and co-operation.

Yet the leaders of the National Labor Union were not unrepresentative of the social and economic thinking of the labor movement of the 1860's. A trade-union mentality, emphasizing practical and immediate objectives, was as yet in its infancy. Hence men like Sylvis and Trevellick saw no fundamental conflict between their ideal of reforming society and their actions as leaders of unions having more restricted goals. Even those advanced trade unionists who were in disagreement with certain aspects of the program of the National Labor Union stood ready to submerge all differences in the hope that a successful national federation would result in a more thoroughgoing organization of the working class.

At the first congress in 1866, therefore, representatives of diverse groups appeared to unite harmoniously in the formulation and adoption of a platform. The logic employed by labor leaders in 1866 resembled closely the Jacksonian labor movement's analysis of the causes of workers' difficulties. To labor in the 1860's the chief threat to equality of opportunity seemed to be the development of large-scale organization, even monopoly, in industry, transportation, and finance, a trend encouraged, workingmen thought, by the monetary policies of the federal government. But if monopoly were fostered by political policies, it could also be destroyed by political measures, specifically by a currency reform that would reward industry and deny undue privilege to the few. The idea of currency reform had been raised earlier by Edward Kellogg, a New York City merchant, who began to study the problem after he lost his fortune in the panic of 1837. Believing that the degradation of labor inevitably ensued when bankers were permitted to create and to lend money at high rates of interest, Kellogg argued that the lowering of the interest rate was of fundamental importance. This he proposed to achieve by the establishment of a federal "National Safety Fund," which would issue paper money based on real estate and bear a fixed rate of interest of 1 per cent per annum. As competition would force private agencies to lower their interest rates, abundant and cheap credit would be made available to all persons. Thus the producing classes (defined by Kellogg as "agriculturists, manufacturers, mechanics, planters, in short, all who wish to earn a support by honest industry") would receive the just fruits of their toil.[12]

Kellogg's ideas were taken up in turn and extended by leaders in the National Labor Union.[13] On the surface it might appear that the demand

---

[12] Edward Kellogg, *A New Monetary System* (New York, 1861), pp. 274–76, 307–24. This work originally appeared as *Labor and Other Capital: the Rights of Each Secured and the Wrongs of Both Eradicated* (New York, 1849). Kellogg's views were disseminated in the 1860's by Alexander Campbell's widely-read pamphlet, *The True American System of Finance* (Chicago, 1864).

[13] Chester M. Destler, "The Influence of Edward Kellogg Upon American Radicalism, 1865–1896," *Journal of Political Economy*, XL (June, 1932), 338–39, 344–48.

for monetary reform was a reflection of the currency agitation that was sweeping the country at the time.[14] Actually, the idea of labor spokesmen went far deeper than mere inflationism; their larger purpose, to be achieved in part through currency reform, was a complete revamping of society through the organization of economic life on the basis of a large number of small producers.

Briefly stated, the National Labor Union's political economists argued that all wealth and property were products of labor, and that workers would receive most of the fruits of their own toil under a just monetary system. The real cause of labor's distress, they contended, lay in the fact that workingmen were receiving too little and "nonproducing capital" too large a share of the national product. Since the interest rate determined the respective proportion of production awarded to capital and labor, Congress was to insure a just division of production through close regulation and supervision of the interest rate.[15] Sylvis did much to publicize this theory. Not an original thinker, he was nevertheless quick to adopt ideas then in vogue among labor theorists. In a series of articles appearing in the Chicago *Workingman's Advocate* in 1869, he bitterly condemned the extremes of wealth and poverty that existed in the United States, warning that from such a situation revolution was a distinct possibility. A disciple of Kellogg's monetary views, Sylvis claimed that the natural increase in the nation's wealth in the past seventy years had been less than 4 per cent annually. Therefore, any rate of interest *above* 4 per cent was "direct robbery upon labor," since it took away from labor the increased product which it had been instrumental in producing.[16]

To Sylvis and other leaders of the National Labor Union monetary reform was indeed a revolutionary theory of social change, comparable in part to socialism and anarchism. Fundamentally, the labor adherents of Kellogg's philosophy were radicals who expressed their hostility to an industrial society through a plan that offered to the workers a restoration of their entrepreneurial status as well as a just share of the national income. Intended to elevate the small producer to a dominant position, currency reform also reflected labor's concern both with providing adequate money to finance co-operative undertakings and with destroying the dominance of the middleman and financier.

A second cause of labor's distress, leaders of the National Labor Union continued, was the national banking system, established by Congress in 1863. Like their Jacksonian forbears, many members of the National La-

[14] During the Civil War the federal government issued about $450,000,000 in greenbacks. After the war the debtor classes demanded not only that this money be retained as part of the national currency, but that the issue of greenbacks be enlarged.

[15] Chicago *Workingman's Advocate*, August 31, 1867.

[16] William H. Sylvis, "What is Money?," reprinted in James C. Sylvis, *Life . . . of William H. Sylvis*, pp. 351–87. These articles originally appeared in the various issues of the Chicago *Workingman's Advocate* between February 27 and June 19, 1869.

bor Union regarded all banks with great hostility. At the congress of 1868, Jonathan Fincher, the eminent labor journalist, objected to a proposed resolution dealing with the subject on the grounds that it was not within the sphere of trade unionism. Sylvis immediately arose to answer him and remarked that a "bank in any shape is a licensed swindle; and the greatest swindle ever imposed upon our people is our present national banking system." [17] Sylvis' position was quickly confirmed by the convention.

As a substitute for the national banking system, the National Labor Union urged the federal government to enter the banking field. It advocated a system whereby treasury notes would be made legal tender in the payment of all debts, public and private. These notes, in turn, would be convertible at the option of the holder into government bonds which bore a just rate of interest *below* the rate of increase in the national wealth. The creditor was to have the right to take either lawful money or the interest-bearing bonds and was to have the privilege of converting one into the other at his pleasure.[18] Under this plan the interest rate would be lowered and the machinations of bankers done away with.

Allied with currency and banking reform was tax reform. The National Labor Union demanded that all government bonds be subject to taxation and that the national debt be dispensed with as quickly as was feasible. Finally, the organization asked that the entire tax structure of the nation be overhauled. The platform pointed out that, since the rich had more at stake in the Civil War, they should pay a greater proportion of its costs.[19] Sylvis remarked that the tax system which apportioned taxes on a per capita basis was grossly unfair, for the "poor man, with a family of six, pays as much tax in the prices he pays to feed and clothe them as his neighbor worth his millions, with a family of equal numbers." [20] It seems obvious that the National Labor Union had a system of progressive taxation in mind.

A third major cause of labor's subordinate position, the leaders of the National Labor Union argued, was the land policy of the federal government. The movement for land reform in the 1860's was also an outgrowth of ante-bellum experiences, for the National Labor Union was influenced by the theories of George Henry Evans who for more than twenty years had devoted his energies to agitation for land reform. His antimonopoly and free homesteads program exerted an influence long before the single tax proposal of Henry George. The National Labor Union took over many of Evans' ideas and adapted them to its own uses. The reason for land reform was a simple one. If there were large amounts of public land

---

[17] *Proceedings of the Second Annual Session of the National Labor Union, Assembled in New York City, September 21, 1868* (Philadelphia, 1868), p. 46.

[18] Chicago *Workingman's Advocate*, August 31, 1867.

[19] *Ibid.*, September 11, 1869.

[20] Sylvis to George Babor, January 17, 1868, in James C. Sylvis, *Life . . . of William H. Sylvis*, p. 309.

available, unemployed workingmen could proceed to them. In other words, the existence of a large amount of public land would act as a safety valve.[21] Sylvis held this then-prevalent view. For example, in a speech in 1867 he observed that capital was attempting to gain possession of the public domain in order to cut off all retreat for the workingmen. "There is still hope for the toiler," proclaimed Sylvis, "though he be driven to the wilderness for sustenance, while he can stand upon a portion of God's footstool and call it his own." [22]

Congress had adopted a homestead act in 1862 granting a quarter-section of unoccupied land to homesteaders on payment of a nominal fee after five years of actual residence. Yet the National Labor Union realized that in practice the law was not living up to its expectations, and the first congress in 1866 adopted a resolution asking that public lands be distributed to actual settlers only. The following year the congress passed a more specific resolution demanding that the federal domain be sold in reasonable amounts to actual settlers only at the minimum price established by the government. In 1870 this request was modified, and the government was urged to distribute free land to actual settlers in amounts not exceeding 160 acres.[23] Fearing that further state and national grants of land to railroads and corporations would enhance their monopolistic power, the National Labor Union also sought an end to all such grants; it even asked that all uncultivated lands held by the railroads for speculative purposes be taxed at the same rate as improved lands in that locality.[24]

As another means of guaranteeing economic equality, the National Labor Union advocated the eight-hour day. Inheriting the ten-hour tradition of the Jacksonian labor movement, workingmen in the 1860's converted local efforts aimed at shortening hours into a concerted national movement. The chief prophet of this movement was Ira Steward. Although not active in the National Labor Union, he exerted influence upon its deliberations and proceedings. Steward's importance resulted from his unification of isolated efforts of workingmen to achieve the eight-hour day into a general demand for state and national legislation. His theory was that wages were dependent upon the habits, customs, and wants of workers rather than on the law of supply and demand. Since technological innovation was the only way to increase the productiveness of capital, labor could increase its surplus by encouraging the introduction of mechanization. An increase in the desires of workingmen could be brought about only if the competition of low standard labor was eliminated. Hence the eight-hour day. Steward demonstrated the stimulating effect of leisure-time consumption upon the standard of living, and its

[21] Chicago *Workingman's Advocate*, September 1, 1866.

[22] James C. Sylvis, *Life . . . of William H. Sylvis*, p. 180.

[23] Chicago *Workingman's Advocate*, September 1, 1866, August 31, 1867, August 27, 1870.

[24] *Ibid.*, August 31, 1867.

intimate connection with the increased use of labor-saving machinery. He predicted that the reduction of hours would strengthen labor's position, and that ultimately it would be possible for the workers to secure sufficient capital to set themselves up in business on a co-operative basis, thus painlessly abolishing the wage system and introducing the semisocialist co-operative commonwealth.

The first convention of the National Labor Union in 1866 decided to press for state and national legislation to secure the eight-hour day.[25] This action was a direct result of Steward's teachings, for most labor leaders of that era were well acquainted with them. Nevertheless, despite the passage of a law granting eight hours to employees of the federal government, workingmen during this period never approached the eight-hour day, and even the federal law was evaded by government officials.

Finally, the National Labor Union advocated a mild protective tariff, the purpose of which was to encourage the manufacture of articles for which this country had the raw materials. It should be noted, however, that support for this resolution came from those who wanted to use the tariff to protect American workingmen against the substandard competition of European and Chinese labor.[26] Additional demands of the National Labor Union included the establishment of a federal department of labor and mechanics' institutes, lyceums, and reading rooms.[27] This latter proposal was intended to aid in the education of workingmen, who would then be able to put their leisure time to more constructive use.

III

The National Labor Union then faced the practical problem of achieving the reforms it advocated. Here again the organization drew upon past experience. The period before the Civil War had witnessed a tremendous upsurge of humanitarianism, one aspect of which was "communitarianism"—an effort to reconstitute society along co-operative lines. Although most of the communitarian experiments failed, they left a heritage of opposition to the growth of monopolistic practices. The National Labor Union, influenced also by the British co-operative movement, revived this tradition in the 1860's in the form of efforts to establish many co-operative endeavors. The first congress, for example, adopted a resolution urging the establishment of co-operative workshops and stores.[28] By so doing, remarked a prominent labor journal, buyers would also become

[25] Chicago *Workingman's Advocate*, September 1, 8, 1866.

[26] *Ibid.*, August 27, 1870; *Address of the Executive Committee of the National Labor Union of the State of California. June 15th, 1871* (San Francisco, 1871), p. 24.

[27] Chicago *Workingman's Advocate*, September 1, 1866. The demand for a federal department of labor was placed in the platform primarily because of Sylvis' efforts. James C. Sylvis, *Life . . . of William H. Sylvis*, pp. 74, 316–17; Grossman, *William Sylvis*, pp. 255–56.

[28] Chicago *Workingman's Advocate*, September 1, 1866.

sellers and would thus eliminate the unnecessary expenses of middle-men.[29]

Sylvis, who had grown to maturity during a period of reform, was the most ardent advocate of co-operation. He regarded it as an arrangement whereby the interests of labor and capital would be united. Although Sylvis looked upon combination of laboring men as a useful device, unionization could not give workers permanent security because it did not go to the root of the problem of poverty. "The cause of all these evils," he remarked, "is the WAGES SYSTEM. So long as we continue to work for wages . . . so long will we be subjected to small pay, poverty, and all of the evils of which we complain." [30]

Unfortunately Sylvis did not fully understand the theory of co-opera-tion, for he rarely made a distinction between a producer and a consumer co-operative.[31] His union, the Iron Molders International Union, estab-lished a number of co-operatives, but most of them failed. Sufficient cap-ital could not be raised; [32] invariably, therefore, the co-operative de-generated into a joint stock company, and then the stockholders' interests as owners made them demand profit from their investments.[33] Ferdinand Lassalle in Germany recognized the basic fallacy in the co-operative move-ment—that the individual or small productive unit represented a dying economic era. He therefore advocated large factory units with the state supplying the necessary capital and credit to the productive co-operative societies.

Since the National Labor Union placed so much emphasis upon the use of co-operative techniques, it naturally minimized the use of the strike. The first congress adopted a resolution that deprecated strikes and urged their use only as a last resort.[34] This resolution was withdrawn in 1868, primarily because it might have had an adverse effect upon a strike in progress among the New York City bricklayers.[35] There was, however, no real change in principle. Workingmen in the 1860's regarded strikes

[29] *Ibid.*, May 9, 1868. Co-operation was not a peculiar monopoly of workingmen, for immediately after the Civil War many people had awakened to its inherent possibilities. See, for example, *New York Tribune*, September 22, 1869; Edwin L. Godkin, "Co-opera-tion," *North American Review*, CVI (January, 1868) , 150–75; Horace Greeley, *Recollec-tions of a Busy Life* (New York, 1868) , p. 157; Commons, *History of Labour*, II, 110–12.

[30] James C. Sylvis, *Life . . . of William H. Sylvis*, pp. 197, 266.

[31] Grossman, *William Sylvis*, p. 196.

[32] Most labor leaders realized that any attempt at establishing co-operatives would be under the severe handicap of not being able to secure sufficient capital and credit. This was an additional reason why they advocated monetary reform. With a lower interest rate it would be easier to secure the necessary funds.

[33] Jonathan Grossman, "Co-operative Foundries," *New York History*, XXIV (April, 1943) , 208–09.

[34] Chicago *Workingman's Advocate*, September 1, 1866; James C. Sylvis, *Life . . . of William H. Sylvis*, p. 68.

[35] *Proceedings of the Second Annual Session of the National Labor Union*, p. 21; Commons, *History of Labour*, II, 123, 129.

with disfavor, moreover, because few notable successes were achieved by their use during this period. Thus in adopting a hostile attitude toward strikes, the National Labor Union appears to have been in harmony with the policy of many national trade unions. For example, the Shoemakers National Union in 1868 adopted a resolution forbidding the use of the strike and maintaining that their organization was mainly co-operative in nature rather than protective.[36] The Plasterers International Union recognized that strikes were undesirable although at times necessary.[37] Similarly, the Carpenters and Joiners National Union recommended in 1869 that a system of co-operation be established, and in 1871 the International Typographical Union recommended that all disputes be settled by arbitration.[38]

The co-operative movement reached its height in 1868, but then began to decline. The practical failure of co-operation then led the National Labor Union to turn to direct political action by the workers as an alternate means of securing redress of their grievances. The tradition of using the ballot box to secure specified objectives was an established right of all Americans. It was only natural, therefore, that workingmen should attempt to use governmental machinery through the democratic process to attain their desired ends.

The problem of whether the National Labor Union should work through the two-party system or establish its own independent political party arose during the discussion over the eight-hour issue at the first congress in 1866. At this meeting the Eight-Hour Committee presented a resolution asking that all "honorable means" be used to secure the enactment of a shorter working day. It also recommended that each locality adopt those methods that were best suited to its needs. The report by the Eight-Hour Committee was rejected by the convention and referred back for further consideration. The final report recommended that a national labor party be established and put into operation "as soon as possible." [39]

The movement to establish a labor party reached fruition in 1870. The congress meeting in that year appointed a committee to call a national labor convention in order to nominate a national ticket for the election of 1872. The Labor Reform Convention, as it was called, met at Columbus, Ohio, on February 21, 1872, and adopted substantially the platform of the National Labor Union. There was, however, one minor addition. To try to attract reform votes, a resolution advocating civil service reform was adopted. Judge David Davis of Illinois and Governor Joel M. Parker of New Jersey were nominated for President and Vice-President. After the Democrats nominated Horace Greeley, Davis withdrew his candidacy.

[36] Chicago *Workingman's Advocate*, August 1, 1868.
[37] *Ibid.*, July 11, 1868.
[38] *Ibid.*, October 2, 1869; International Typographical Union, *Proceedings*, 1871, p. 49. See also the *Coopers' Journal*, I (October–November, 1870), 3.
[39] Chicago *Workingman's Advocate*, September 1, 1866.

Apparently the only reason that he had accepted the nomination in the first place was to try to strengthen his chances for the Democratic presidential nomination.[40] No candidate was chosen to replace Davis, and both the Labor Reform party and the National Labor Union disappeared as active bodies.

IV

The failure of the leaders of the National Labor Union to achieve their goal of a strong labor party, however, goes much deeper than any failure to persuade certain individuals to stand as candidates. In the end the movement failed chiefly because the mass of workers refused to become engaged in a political crusade. There were, however, other formidable problems that divided the ranks of labor and prevented the formation of a solid working-class political front.

The first was the pressing problem of Negro labor. In the South, emancipation had intensified an old rivalry between Negro and white workers by throwing the two groups into more direct competition with each other. At the first congress of the National Labor Union no mention was made of the problem. The *Address of the National Labor Congress to the Workingmen of the United States,* issued in 1867, was the first attempt to meet the problem. The committee drawing up this document recognized that the interests of labor were one and declared that discrimination on either racial or religious grounds was harmful to all workingmen.[41]

At the congress of 1867 a special committee was appointed to deal with the subject. This group reported that there was so much "mystery" involved in the question that it should be laid over until the following year. A heated discussion immediately took place. Some argued in favor of the Negro, others against. The point was raised whether the trade unions would be willing to accept the colored workers, regardless of the stand that the National Labor Union would take. It was suggested that the report be recommitted and the committee be instructed to forget about the subject. Sylvis cogently pointed out that the problem could no longer be evaded. "There is no concealing the fact," he remarked, "that the time will come when the 'negro will take possession of the shops if we have not taken possession of the negro. If the workingmen of the white race do not conciliate the blacks, the black vote will be cast against them.' "[42]

[40] *Ibid.*, August 27, 1870, February 4, 1871, February 24, 1872. See also Terence V. Powderly to S. Fish, May 13, 1880, Powderly Letter Books, Department of Archives and Manuscripts, Catholic University of America, Washington, D. C. (hereinafter cited as TVPLB).

[41] Commons, *Documentary History,* IX, 158–59. The first congress of the National Labor Union appointed a committee to prepare an address to American workingmen. The document was not completed until a few weeks before the congress of 1867 and was primarily the work of Andrew C. Cameron, editor of the Chicago *Workingman's Advocate.*

[42] Chicago *Workingman's Advocate,* August 31, 1867.

The report was finally recommitted, and the committee later reported that the constitution obviated the necessity of taking a specific stand on the subject, for it made no mention of the Negro. This position was adopted.[43] It was quite obvious that the problem was so dangerous that many labor leaders wished to avoid it if possible. Since the constitution made no mention of race, the advocates of unity could claim victory, while their opponents could claim that they had beaten down an attempt to raise the question. The problem was again evaded in 1868. By this time, however, new developments were rapidly bringing the problem to the attention of white labor. Negroes had formed their own organizations and were actively engaged in strikes, especially in the South. Negroes were also being used by many employers as strikebreakers, and white workers were being replaced by cheaper Negro labor.[44]

At the beginning of 1869 Sylvis had undertaken a trip to the South to examine conditions firsthand. His attitude toward the Negro reflected many opinions held by the great majority of whites. First of all, Sylvis ardently opposed Radical Reconstruction and attacked the Freedmen's Bureau as a gigantic fraud because it taxed the white labor of the North in order to feed the idle Negroes of the South. He sought the destruction of the Bureau and remarked that he would make "these lazy loafers work for a living, as other men do." [45] Even when his loyalty to the working class made him accept the fact that some sort of unity was absolutely necessary, he could never wholeheartedly accept the Negro. At first Sylvis advocated separate organizations, but soon he realized that this was inadequate. Even when he accepted complete unity, he was never able to rid himself of the ingrained views then so prevalent among whites. Unity to him was of a "shotgun wedding" variety.[46]

Despite the reluctance of white labor leaders to modify their views on the admission of Negroes into unions, it was becoming increasingly clear that some sort of policy was essential if working-class unity was not to be broken because of the color barrier. Negro leaders were fully aware of the danger. At the congress of 1869, for example, Isaac Myers, a Negro delegate, pointed out that white workingmen would be undermining their own objectives if they refused to admit Negroes to membership in their unions. A resolution proposed by Horace Day affirming that the National Labor Union recognized no color and inviting all Negro labor organizations to send delegates to the next convention was then adopted.[47]

The fact remains, nevertheless, that the trade unions refused to admit

[43] *Ibid.*

[44] Sumner E. Matison, "The Labor Movement and the Negro During Reconstruction," *Journal of Negro History*, XXXIII (October, 1948) , 429; John Hope Franklin, *From Slavery to Freedom* (New York, 1947) , pp. 308–09.

[45] James C. Sylvis, *Life . . . of William H. Sylvis*, pp. 226, 318, 333–34.

[46] Ibid., pp. 336–39; Chicago *Workingman's Advocate*, March 6, 27, 1869; Grossman, *William Sylvis*, pp. 229–32.

[47] Chicago *Workingman's Advocate*, September 4, 11, 1869.

Negroes into their organizations regardless of the pious pronouncements of the National Labor Union. The Cigar Makers National Union limited membership in 1868 to "white male" journeymen.[48] The International Typographical Union adopted a report that regretted that the Negro question had been raised in the first place and left the admission of Negroes to subordinate unions.[49] At the convention of the Bricklayers National Union in 1871 a heated fight took place. "I wouldn't let a nigger into our union, and if he came in I would go out," one delegate remarked. "We will not recognize a nigger bricklayer in Baltimore." [50] In the face of such opposition the convention took no position on the issue, and instead referred the problem to its locals. The Carpenters and Joiners National Union also gave its locals jurisdiction in the matter, where exclusion was often the rule rather than the exception.[51] Further proof of the failure of the unions to accept Negro members was given by two newspaper investigations in 1869 and 1871.[52]

Complicating this problem even further was the fact that there were few common objectives that whites and Negroes could agree upon. The Negro had little interest in currency reform and directed his efforts toward securing homesteads.[53] Furthermore, many Negroes were ardent supporters of the Republican party, and they looked with disfavor upon independent political action by labor. Thus, until after 1880, the Negro remained an outsider to the organized labor movement. In the meantime he acquired a reputation as a strikebreaker and one who worked for lower wages than whites.

The second problem, that of female labor, was another major obstacle to labor unity during this period. Women themselves were cognizant of the fact that employers hired them for lower wages than they paid to men, for *The Revolution*, the chief organ of the advocates of woman suffrage, remarked: "It is yet to be seen whether workingmen are wise enough to see, that so long as woman is disfranchised her labor is degraded, and capitalists will use her cheap labor to cheapen that of the man by her side." [54]

The first congress of the National Labor Union adopted a vague resolu-

---

[48] *Ibid.*, September 26, 1868.

[49] International Typographical Union, *Proceedings*, 1870, pp. 31–32.

[50] Chicago *Workingman's Advocate*, January 28, 1871.

[51] *Ibid.*, October 8, 1870.

[52] *New York Times*, March 2, 1869, and *New York Tribune*, August 23, 1871, cited in Matison, "The Labor Movement and the Negro During Reconstruction," *loc. cit.*, pp. 452–53.

[53] Memorial of the Colored National Labor Union to Congress, December 6, 1869, 41st Congress, 2d Session, *Senate Miscellaneous Document No. 3*, reprinted in Herbert Aptheker, ed., *A Documentary History of the Negro People in the United States* (New York, 1951), pp. 633–36; Washington *Daily Morning Chronicle*, January 14, 1871; Commons, *Documentary History*, IX, 254–55.

[54] *The Revolution*, II (September 24, 1868), 186.

tion affirming support of woman workers and soliciting their co-opera-tion.[55] The *Address of the National Labor Congress to the Workingmen of the United States* was more explicit, for it demanded equal rights and equal pay for women.[56] At the congress of 1868, Elizabeth Cady Stanton appeared as a delegate from the Women's Suffrage Association, accom-panied by three other women delegates, one of whom was Susan B. Anthony. After a heated debate Mrs. Stanton's credentials were accepted by a vote of forty-five to eighteen. Later, however, upon objection that ap-proval of woman suffrage would hinder the development of an independ-ent labor party, the congress adopted a motion explaining that the ac-ceptance of Mrs. Stanton as a delegate did not mean that the National Labor Union endorsed woman suffrage. In other words, Mrs. Stanton was simply being accepted as a workingwomen's representative.[57] That the convention's reservation did not disconcert Mrs. Stanton can be seen from her optimistic prediction that "The producers—the workingmen, the women, the negroes—are destined to form a triple power that shall speedily wrest the sceptre of government from the non-producers—the land monopolists, the bondholders, the politicians." [58]

The following year, however, Susan B. Anthony was expelled by the congress, primarily on the ground that she had used the Workingwomen's Protective Association as a strikebreaking agency. Admitting this charge, she claimed that women could obtain employment only as strikebreakers because unions barred them from membership and normal avenues of employment.[59] Commenting upon the affair, *The Revolution* bitterly observed "that the worst enemies of Woman's Suffrage will ever be the laboring classes of men. Their late action towards Miss Anthony is but the expression of the hostility they feel to the idea she represents." [60] But the National Labor Union never reversed its advocacy of equal rights and equal pay for women, even though it refused to endorse woman suffrage.[61] It was one of the first labor organizations to take such an advanced posi-tion. The national trade unions, however, refused to support such a

[55] Chicago *Workingman's Advocate,* September 1, 1866.
[56] Commons, *Documentary History,* IX, 156–57.
[57] *Proceedings of the Second Annual Session of the National Labor Union,* p. 23.
[58] *The Revolution,* II (October 1, 1868) , 200.
[59] Chicago *Workingman's Advocate,* September 4, 1869.
[60] *The Revolution,* IV (August 26, 1869) , 120.
[61] There was a strong minority of leaders within the National Labor Union, including William H. Sylvis and Richard Trevellick, who advocated woman suffrage. Their espousal of this cause, however, was a purely pragmatic one. They felt that it would mean more potential votes for the Labor Reform party. At first Sylvis felt that woman's place was in the home, a typical nineteenth-century attitude. He then advanced to a position where he advocated woman suffrage on "moral" issues only—intemperance, tobacco, Sunday labor, and so on. Finally Sylvis accepted social and economic equality for women. He was also influenced by humanitarian motives, for he had seen the working conditions of women and the low wages paid them. James C. Sylvis, *Life . . . of William H. Sylvis,* pp. 119–20, 399–400; Grossman, *William Sylvis,* pp. 226–29.

program, and few of them admitted women. The organization of women still remained to be accomplished.

The third development undermining labor unity was Chinese and contract labor. The use of this labor was of fairly recent origin and was becoming a favorite device of employers intent upon keeping wages at a minimum level. Under the pressure of the California delegation, a resolution was adopted in 1870 by the congress of the National Labor Union condemning the presence of coolie labor.[62] Although supporting the proponents of Chinese exclusion, the National Labor Union never objected to European immigrant labor per se, but only to the importation of contract labor specifically designed to lower wages and break strikes.

Out of the contract labor issue came the interest of the National Labor Union in the Marxian First International. Sylvis had always been a strong proponent of affiliation, and in 1870 the National Labor Union declared its adhesion to the principles of the First International and its intention to affiliate with it in the not too distant future.[63] The previous year Andrew C. Cameron had attended the meeting of the First International at Basel, Switzerland, as the unofficial representative of the National Labor Union. Cameron, however, played a minor role at the meeting.[64] The interest of the National Labor Union in the First International was clearly explained by Sylvis. He felt that the regulation of contract labor was a necessity and perhaps could be accomplished through international agreement and co-operation among workingmen of all nations.[65] This was a tacit recognition of the international competition of labor. It would be a mistake, however, to assume that the National Labor Union endorsed the radical class-conscious program of the First International. The National Labor Union was simply seeking aid in abolishing the use of contract labor, and it turned to the First International for such assistance. But when it came to actual affiliation with the First International, the National Labor Union balked at taking positive action.

V

The failure of the National Labor Union to resolve fully the problems of Negro, woman, contract, and Chinese labor was not necessarily fatal. Yet the final congress of the National Labor Union, meeting in 1872 in Cleveland, Ohio, was attended by only seven delegates. What had com-

[62] Chicago *Workingman's Advocate*, August 27, 1870. See also the *Address of the Executive Committee of the National Labor Union of the State of California*, p. 62.

[63] Grossman, *William Sylvis*, pp. 259–60, 270–71; Chicago *Workingman's Advocate*, August 27, 1870.

[64] *Report of the Fourth Annual Congress of the International Working Men's Association, Held in Basle, in Switzerland. From the 6th to the 11th September, 1869* (London, n.d.), p. 34.

[65] Letter of William H. Sylvis to the Chicago *Workingman's Advocate*, November 2, 1867 (letter dated October 26, 1867).

menced in 1866 as an enthusiastic and optimistic venture had concluded six years later in an abject and dismal failure. While labor leaders advanced numerous and varied explanations concerning the inability of the National Labor Union to unite workingmen around a common program, one vital fact stood out above all others. That fact was the steadfast opposition by the trade unionists to political action as a method of achieving the anticipated reforms. This opposition ultimately split the National Labor Union and was one of the primary causes of its failure.

The more the National Labor Union emphasized political action, the more it ceased to voice the basic needs and aspirations of the mass of workers. The trade unions, while still affirming support of the ultimate goal of reforming society, were becoming increasingly concerned over more practical matters involving their members. Slowly but surely the unions became immersed in attempts to raise wages, shorten hours, develop a set of clear work rules, establish benefit systems, and become financially solvent. The inevitable consequence of the National Labor Union's absorption in politics, however, meant a de-emphasis in trade-union goals. The result was a tension within the National Labor Union and a consequent struggle for power.

Reformers within the National Labor Union were not sympathetic toward the apparent conservatism of the trade unions. The *Address of the National Labor Congress to the Workingmen of the United States,* for example, declared that trade unions were merely the "creation of necessity, and . . . purely defensive in character." [66] Echoing this sentiment in 1870, the Chicago *Workingman's Advocate* observed that trade unions were simply a temporary expedient that could not attack the basic problems of workers.[67] The answer, these reform spokesmen asserted, lay in political action. "I have long since come to the conclusion," wrote Sylvis, "that no permanent reform can ever be established through the agency of trades-unions . . . They are purely defensive in their character." [68] His absorption in political action became even more pronounced following his election as president of the National Labor Union in 1868. "The times are big with issues of momentous import to all workingmen, the discussion of which is without the province and the settlement without the power of purely trade organizations," Sylvis informed the National Typographical Union in 1869. "Many, if not all, of the evils which affect the industrial classes are directly or indirectly traceable to glaring defects in our political system. The eradication of these defects can only be accomplished through the united and harmonious consideration and action of all workingmen." [69]

The trade unions obviously did not care for the condemnation of their

[66] Commons, *Documentary History,* IX, 153.
[67] Chicago *Workingman's Advocate,* May 14, 1870.
[68] James C. Sylvis, *Life . . . of William H. Sylvis,* p. 77.
[69] National Typographical Union, *Proceedings,* 1869, p. 28.

organizations as temporary expediencies, but there was little difficulty so long as the National Labor Union maintained a balance between reform and trade-union objectives. Trade unions during the 1860's were as yet undecided about future policy and could see no inherent conflict between a program of reform at the national level and the quest for a higher standard of living at the local level. At the formation of the National Labor Union in 1866, for example, most labor leaders greeted the experiment with enthusiasm and evinced a willingness to participate in its deliberations. Thomas W. Harris, president of the Carpenters and Joiners National Union, expressed a widely-held view when he reported that the congress of 1866 had been "characterized by ability, moderation and forecast, based upon sound principles." [70] The unions were not necessarily in complete agreement with the monetary program of the National Labor Union, but they were willing to support a national federation in the hope that it would act as an incentive to the further organization of the working class.

By 1870, however, it was obvious that the National Labor Union had become more a reform and political organization than a genuine representative of American workingmen. The trade unions found that the needs of their members were being subordinated to a utopian program that appeared to offer nothing tangible in the immediate future. Consequently there was an internal struggle for control of the National Labor Union. The reform and political element rapidly gained the upper hand, largely because the majority of workers had failed to develop a mature sense of class consciousness. The trade unions, therefore, finding themselves in the minority, began to leave the organization. In 1870, for example, the Cigar Makers National Union adopted a report that advocated severing relations with the National Labor Union "for the reason of it being an entirely political institution, and no benefits deriving therefrom." [71] The Bricklayers National Union adopted a similar resolution.[72] The delegates from the International Typographical Union to the congress of 1870 attacked the heterogeneous character of that body and remarked that they

> failed to discover any thing in the proceedings, with the exception of the report of the Committee on Obnoxious Laws, that would entitle the Congress to representation from a purely trade organization. The Congress was made up of delegates, with few exceptions, who openly avowed the object to be the formation of a political party. Played-out politicians, lobbyists, woman-suffragens, preachers without flocks, representatives of Associations in which politics are made a qualification for membership, and declaimers on the outrages per-

[70] Carpenters and Joiners National Union, *Proceedings*, 1866, p. 13. See also the Bricklayers National Union, *Proceedings*, 1867, pp. 45–46, typescript copy in the Johns Hopkins University Library, Baltimore, Maryland.

[71] Chicago *Workingman's Advocate*, February 18, 1871.

[72] *Ibid.*

petrated on poor Lo, formed the major part of the Congress. The session was one of continuous confusion, in which personalities abounded, and charges and counter-charges were made of attempts to run it in the interest of both the old political parties.[73]

William J. Jessup, president of the New York State Workingmen's Assembly and a delegate to the congress of 1870, expressed a similar view. Jessup, who had in the past spoken well of the National Labor Union,[74] charged in 1870 that the primary interest of that body was political, and for that reason he had felt out of place, representing as he did the trade union element. He could not help but compare the congress of 1866 with that of 1870. Every delegate at the opening session in 1866 represented some branch of mechanical pursuit; but at the congress of 1870 there was "a strange mixture of mechanics, workingmen, ministers, lawyers, editors, lobbyists and others of no particular occupation, some intent upon organizing a political labor party, others using their efforts to defeat that measure and benefit existing parties. With so much difference in the aims of the representatives, the Convention could be none other than it was, inharmonious." Jessup concluded by recommending that no delegates be sent to future sessions of the National Labor Union.[75]

Even the socialists adopted a hostile attitude as the National Labor Union lost its working-class character and became immersed in politics. The Central Committee of the Marxist First International refused to send a delegate to the session in 1871 because it had become a bourgeois and agrarian reform body.[76] After the congress of 1871, Friedrich A. Sorge, one of the most prominent followers of Marx in the United States, wrote that "the leaders of the N.L.U. have learned nothing and, it is to be feared, will never learn to understand the labor question." [77]

At the congress of 1871 only twenty-two delegates were present, and a majority of these were primarily agrarian reformers. There was not a single delegate from any of the national trade unions, and only two bona fide labor organizations were represented.[78] But having succeeded in transforming the National Labor Union into a political organization, reformers quickly found their victory to be a hollow and pyrrhic one, for

[73] International Typographical Union, *Proceedings*, 1871, p. 29. The previous year the convention of the International Typographical Union refused to endorse the platform of the National Labor Union because it could "find nothing to recommend in the document." *Printers' Circular*, V (July, 1870) , 184.

[74] See the New York State Workingmen's Assembly, *Proceedings*, 1869, pp. 8–9.

[75] *Ibid.*, 1871, p. 64.

[76] Hermann Schlüter, *Die Internationale in Amerika* (Chicago, 1918) , pp. 127–28.

[77] Central Committee of the North American Federation of the International Workingmen's Association, *Copy Book*, pp. 47–48, manuscript in the Wisconsin State Historical Society, Madison, Wisconsin, also reprinted in Commons, *Documentary History*, IX, 366.

[78] Chicago *Workingman's Advocate*, August 19, 1871.

the withdrawal of the trade unions had undercut the foundation upon which the National Labor Union rested.

The trade unions, although disillusioned with the National Labor Union, nevertheless reaffirmed the belief that a national federation was essential to the success of the labor movement. The president of the Machinists and Blacksmiths Union, for example, took the position that the National Labor Union could expect the support of the trade unions only if it renounced politics and confined itself to union problems.[79] Furthermore, most labor spokesmen agreed that the experiences of the National Labor Union offered ample proof that working-class leaders had to be themselves workingmen. The *Coopers' Journal* perhaps best expressed the majority opinion in an editorial written in 1872:

> A few years ago the trade unionists of the United States conceived the very brilliant and laudable idea of forming a National Labor Union. . . .
> The movement had an unusually auspicious beginning; it promised much in the future . . . and doubtless the full and complete accomplishment of these things would have resulted from the agencies and machinery set in motion by the evolving wisdom of the movement, had it not been diverted from its original purpose through the machinations of charlatans and designing tricksters, who, in an evil hour, were allowed to participate in its deliberations . . . These men succeeded in changing the National Labor Union into a Labor Reform political party. . . .
> The political Labor Reform party had a birth but its life was as ephemeral and transitory as summer dew, [and] it ended in the most ignominious failure that ever disgraced any movement; and now that it is dead, let it be buried out of sight and let us return, like sensible men, to first principles again. Let us now set to work and inaugurate a movement to be denominated the Trades Congress of North America . . . We do not propose that the proposed Congress should ignore all measures, looking towards political action. . . . What we want to avoid is separate, independent political action. The elements of the labor movement are too diverse, the interests too clashing and varied, self too predominant, and above all, knowledge and general intelligence far too limited to permit the possibility of any thinking man harboring for a moment the illusive idea of a separate political labor party for many years to come. . . . let us see to it that no wire pulling, scheming demagogues, no empirical charlatans, no visionary fire brands or other humbugs, shall be permitted within its folds; that no one shall partake in its deliberations but *bona fide* representatives of *bona fide* organizations, whose direct object is the elevation and protection of physical and intellectual labor.[80]

Trade unionists quickly made clear their steadfast opposition both to reformers and to independent political action by labor. "The fact stands out boldly," remarked a former delegate, "that the only good ever

[79] *Machinists and Blacksmiths International Journal*, IX (September, 1872), 779.
[80] *Coopers' Journal*, III (October, 1872), 598–600. See also the editorial in *ibid.*, IV (January, 1873), 21–22.

accomplished by the N. L. U. was accomplished as a *bona fide* Labor Association." [81] Echoing this view, H. J. Walls, former secretary of the National Labor Union and a prominent member of the Iron Molders International Union, defended the trade unions who had severed their connections with the National Labor Union after that body had abandoned "its original purpose of being a labor congress, where the needs and the wants of labor would be discussed, and the remedy pointed out to a labor party, which not a trade union in the country dare endorse." [82]

Even after 1872 trade unionists were wary of forming a national federation that might repeat what they considered to be the errors of the now defunct National Labor Union. For example, William J. Hammond, president of the International Typographical Union, reported to the annual convention of that body that he had received a letter from William Saffin, president of the Iron Molders International Union, stating that the latter had canvassed the trade unions upon the advisability of forming a national body. The query had resulted in an affirmative reply, but with the sole proviso that such an association had to be entirely free from political influences and composed of delegates from *"bona fide* Trade and Labor Unions." [83] Even the Chicago *Workingman's Advocate* drew a similar conclusion. In commenting upon the necessity for a new national labor federation, it also warned that *"Labor's Educators must come from Labor's* ranks. Theorists, experimentalists, and demagogues who have gained what notoriety they possess by prating about laborers' wrongs, must now take back seats." [84]

While the primary reason for the failure of the National Labor Union is to be found in the opposition of the constituent unions to a program that came to emphasize reform and political objectives to the almost total exclusion of practical ones, there were also other factors that seriously impaired the effectiveness of the National Labor Union. Composed of sovereign independent organizations and having no integral structure of its own, the National Labor Union could do little more than debate and advance recommendations. Even then the lack of funds acted as an insuperable barrier to the realization of any of its proposals. The failure to organize Negro and woman workers and thus to eliminate the menace of substandard competition was also a major source of weakness. Perhaps most important was the fact that workers were still unaware of the importance of establishing a strong labor movement having sufficient resources to render it capable of meeting employers on an equal plane.

Yet the shortcomings and weaknesses of the National Labor Union should not be permitted to obscure its pioneer character. Coming at a

[81] *Ibid.*, III (November, 1872), 683.

[82] Chicago *Workingman's Advocate*, February 1, 1873.

[83] International Typographical Union, *Proceedings*, 1873, p. 13.

[84] Chicago *Workingman's Advocate*, March 29, 1873, cited in the *Coopers' Journal*, IV (April, 1873), 162.

time when the United States was in the midst of a great economic, social, and technological revolution, the National Labor Union sought to solve or perhaps mitigate some of the problems that the working class faced. To meet some of these new developments, traditional concepts and past experiences were utilized; for problems that had no precedent, new policies were evolved.

Faith in the people was an implicit part of the philosophy of the National Labor Union. Out of this faith came the belief that the people might use the government to solve their difficulties. Precedent heavily reinforced this doctrine. The theory that the years between the American Revolution and the Civil War was a period of laissez faire is largely fiction. It was rather a period when state participation in economic life was accepted by all groups. Even those who argued against legislation regulating child labor and working hours, for example, admitted that the government had the power to pass such laws. The mature development of the antistate doctrine came only after the Civil War when the great corporation rose to a position of prominence.[85] It was only natural for the National Labor Union to accept the tradition of powerful and active government.

The National Labor Union was never a class-conscious body. It vigorously denied that the program it advocated was in the interests of a special class.[86] This was not a mere rationalization of its beliefs. The thinking of the working class was still colored by the belief that this class was the only legitimate body of the community. From this naturally proceeded the corollary that measures on behalf of the working class could not be tainted with the odium of special privilege and class legislation. This philosophy represented a genuine belief of workingmen. As the organization of business developed on a large scale and markets expanded as a result of improved transportation and communications, the factory system began to appear in a mature form. The workers, however, refused to recognize the functions that the new groups, which had arisen as a result of the industrial expansion of the nation, were performing in the new economy. Their thinking was still colored by the simple master-workman relationship in which both employee and employer performed similar functions and lines between classes were indistinct and fluid. The laboring class was prone to look upon the new groups as parasites living off the earnings of those who actually were the producers.

The program of the National Labor Union accurately reflected these

[85] Louis Hartz, *Economic Policy and Democratic Thought: Pennsylvania, 1776–1860* (Cambridge, Massachusetts, 1948), pp. 200, 202, 319–20; Oscar and Mary F. Handlin, *Commonwealth: A Study of the Role of Government in the American Economy: Massachusetts, 1774–1861* (New York, 1947), pp. 245–46.

[86] *Address of the National Labor Union to the People of the United States, on Money, Land, and Other Subjects of National Importance* (Washington, D. C., 1870), p. 3.

beliefs. Its emphasis on co-operation was designed to restore a society where the simple master-workman relationship was dominant. The analysis of many workingmen brought them inescapably to the conclusion that it was the creeping specter of monopoly which was at the root of all their troubles. When co-operation failed to achieve the anticipated relief, it was perhaps inevitable that the next weapon the National Labor Union would turn to would be political action.

In the final analysis the National Labor Union failed because of the emphasis that it placed on political action. The embryonic local trade unions were willing to support the national organization only if there were concrete benefits to be gained. As the National Labor Union came to place its primary emphasis on political action, a tension was created between the national leadership and the constituent organs that proved to be so strong that the national organization disintegrated. But the National Labor Union did play an important part in the history of American labor. It served as a guidepost for later movements, for many of the problems which it faced were similar to the problems that would be faced in the future. Its experience would prove useful in formulating a program that would succeed in meeting the challenge to the workingmen by the new industrial order.

CHAPTER THREE

The Knights of Labor

I

℘ THE DEMISE OF the National Labor Union in 1872 did not discourage further attempts to form a national federation of labor that would effectively promote the interests of the working class. Although disillusioned by their experiences with the National Labor Union, the national trade unions came together in July, 1873, in an Industrial Congress, which confined itself to trade-union problems and devoted little attention to financial reform, co-operation, and independent political action. The new organization was hailed with enthusiasm by the trade unions. "Every representative was a *bona fide* worker, as is evidenced by the unanimity with which all great questions were settled," wrote a leading union journal. "None of the clap-trap of the ward politician was vented; in fact it would not have been permitted. . . . The declaration of principles . . . can be indorsed by every *bona fide* workingman." [1]

In spite of its auspicious beginnings, the Congress was short-lived, for two months after its inception the panic of 1873 inaugurated a long depression. There was a meeting the following year, at which time the name "Industrial Brotherhood" was adopted. The platform included many trade-union demands, but the greenback panacea also played a major part at this convention. The national trade unions, however, were in no condition to implement any program, and only one national union was represented at the final meeting of the Brotherhood in 1875.

The depression, beginning with the panic of 1873 and lasting almost five years, proved to be a disaster insofar as organized labor was concerned. The embryonic labor movement was in no position to weather the stress of economic depression, highlighted by increasing unemployment, wage reductions, and the systematic repression of labor organizations by employers. Consequently, many trade unions went out of existence, and even those better able to withstand the crisis emerged from the depression with greatly decreased membership. Of the national trade unions, numbering approximately thirty prior to the panic of 1873, only eight or nine remained by 1877. The Cigar Makers International Union had slightly

[1] *Iron Molders' International Journal*, July 31, 1873, pp. 35–36. See also the *Vulcan Record . . . Containing the Proceedings of the National Forge, U. S. United Sons of Vulcan . . . 1873* (Pittsburgh, 1873), p. 23.

over a thousand members in 1877 as compared to nearly six thousand in 1869; the machinists lost two-thirds of its membership; and one of the oldest labor bodies, the International Typographical Union, saw its membership halved between 1873 and 1878.

Despite the depression, however, the ideal of a national labor federation remained as alive and vigorous as ever, and it was at this time that the Order of the Knights of Labor, a new organization destined to play a significant role in American labor history, was born. While the National Labor Union and Industrial Congresses represented attempts to form a national federation of labor from the top down, the founding of the first local assembly of the Knights in Philadelphia in December, 1869, was a movement from the ground up. Formed by nine members following the dissolution of the Garment Cutters' Association of Philadelphia, its growth during the 1870's was slow, and the second local assembly was not organized until July, 1872. By the end of 1873, however, more than eighty locals had been organized, most of them in or around Philadelphia. Following 1874 the Knights spread to other parts of the East and also gained a foothold further west. In December, 1873, the first district assembly was formed in Philadelphia.

No attempt was made to form a central governing body until 1875, and the following year a meeting was held under the auspices of District Assembly (D.A.) 1 of Philadelphia. But D.A. 3 of Pittsburgh refused to attend and held its own convention in 1877. However, the political upheaval resulting from the formation of the National Greenback Labor party, the continuing effects of the depression, and the impact of the railroad strikes of 1877, caused both sides to move closer toward each other. Under the unofficial mediation of D.A. 5 of Scranton, the first General Assembly of the Knights met in Reading, Pennsylvania, in January, 1878.[2] Subsequently the General Assembly of the Knights of Labor met at least once annually, and sometimes more often.

The basic structure of the Knights of Labor was simple. At the bottom were the local assemblies composed of the individual members. Locals, in turn, were grouped geographically into district assemblies. Each district assembly elected delegates to the annual convention or General Assembly, which elected the officers and the General Executive Board. Membership in the Knights was inclusive, and only professional gamblers, stockbrokers, lawyers, bankers, and those who lived in whole or in part by the sale or manufacture of intoxicating liquors were excluded.

Within the three organizational levels of the Knights there was much diversity. There were, for example, two forms of local assemblies, the mixed and the trade. The mixed local included men of all trades and callings, while the trade local was composed either of groups of the same craft

---

[2] The information on the early history of the Knights in the 1870's can be followed in Powderly, *Thirty Years of Labor*, pp. 131–38, 182–87, 224–39, and George E. McNeill, ed., *The Labor Movement: The Problem of To-day* (Boston, 1887), pp. 397–400.

or groups having different occupations but working at the same plant. In addition, there were mixed and trade district assemblies and also national trade assemblies.

Beginning in the early 1880's the Knights commenced a steady period of national growth, and by 1885 it had slightly over 100,000 members. Its period of greatest expansion occurred in the following twelve months, and by the middle of 1886 it boasted a total membership exceeding 700,000, making it by far the largest labor organization of the nineteenth century. The Knights, however, was not the only body to expand so spectacularly, for the trade unions also shared in this growth. In the same period the United Brotherhood of Carpenters and Joiners quadrupled and the Cigar Makers International Union doubled in size.

The phenomenal rise of the labor movement in the 1880's signified that long-term developments were reaching their climax at this time. The completion of a far-flung national transportation network after the Civil War had created a market that transcended local or regional lines. To take advantage of such a market, employers invested more and more of their capital in machinery, and the size of the productive unit increased by astronomical figures. As a result the relentlessly advancing factory system cut off a large mass of employees from any contact with their employers. Furthermore, the importance of the skills of many individuals became of less and less importance as reliance on semi-skilled and unskilled labor increased. The large accretions to the labor force, resulting from immigration and the movement from the farm to the city, also served to weaken the position of the working class. Fundamentally, therefore, the social and economic position of the working class in the 1880's was poor, and the advent of a depression in 1883 only aggravated conditions.

Under such circumstances it was not unnatural for workingmen to seek to redress their unfavorable condition through organized action, and the 1880's saw the advent of bitter struggles in American society. As one writer commented: "Our era of prosperity and of happy immunity from those social diseases which are the danger and the humiliation of Europe is passing away. Optimistic as we are, we cannot fail to know that the increasing proportion of the incapable among us is repeating here the social problems of the Old World. . . . every year brings the conditions of American labor into closer likeness to those of the Old World. An American species of socialism is inevitable. . . . We are discovering that the way to national glory is not to be a rose-strewn path." [3] Events seemed to confirm this analysis, for not only did hundreds of thousands flock to join labor organizations, but they demonstrated a militancy rarely seen before. Hundreds of strikes occurred, many of them involving large aggregations of workers and sometimes resulting in violence and bloodshed. The eight-hour movement of 1884–1886, which looked toward the establishment of a

[3] M. A. Hardaker, "A Study in Sociology," *Atlantic Monthly*, L (August, 1882), 215, 219.

universal eight-hour workday on May 1, 1886, to be achieved in part through organized economic action, attracted the allegiance of hundreds of thousands. The prevailing discontent also took the form of labor political action at both the local and national levels on a scale never before (and perhaps never since) attempted. The intensity of events reached a peak during the Haymarket Affair in 1886, when eight anarchists, unjustly accused of throwing a bomb amongst a group of policemen attempting to break up their meeting, were convicted largely because of the public hysteria brought on by fear that society was in the process of disintegration. Ultimately four of the convicted men were hung, one committed suicide, and three were later pardoned after serving jail sentences.

The feverish events of the 1880's tended to polarize the various factions of the labor movement along ideological lines. The leaders of the Knights, for example, were faced with questions not very different from their predecessors. Should the labor movement work toward the establishment of a co-operative society based on the small productive unit? Had strikes outlived their usefulness? Should the working class turn to political action to achieve its goals? What was the ideal structure for the labor movement? Above all, what was the proper function of the labor movement in American society? To such questions, as well as other ones, the leaders of the Knights generally gave clear and unequivocal answers, although they frequently shifted their means to meet changing conditions. On the whole they adopted, as we shall shortly see, the program and heritage of reform unionism, maintaining that only the basic transformation of the structure of society could solve the difficulties of the working class. To achieve this end they favored co-operation between 1880 and 1886, and at the same time demonstrated a bitter antipathy toward strikes and collective bargaining goals. After 1886, when co-operation had failed to live up to its expectations, they began to look toward political action, and in the late 1880's and early 1890's attempted to join hands with the rising Populist movement in the hope of wresting control from the dominant business interests and return it to the "producing classes."

While the Knights of Labor was attempting to implement its reformist ideology, the infant trade-union movement was reviving from the wounds it had incurred during the depression of the 1870's. Founded on an opposing set of assumptions, the trade unions began to come into conflict with the Knights over crucial ideological issues. The trade unions, for example, were opposed to broad programs of social reconstruction; they looked rather toward immediate material improvements within the framework of existing institutions, and relied primarily on economic organization and action. By 1886 the divergent roads of the Knights and the trade unions had so widened that a chasm appeared within the labor movement. Ultimately this chasm resulted in an open war between the two wings of organized labor for control of its destiny. And in the ten years following 1886, the trade unions, having founded the American Federation of Labor to act as their national spokesman, triumphed over the Knights after a bitter struggle.

This is, however, only a bare chronological outline of the momentous events in the history of the late nineteenth-century labor movement. Before proceeding to the internecine struggle that threatened the very existence of the young labor movement, let us first turn to a detailed examination of the ideological development of the Knights of Labor, studying its general aims, leadership, attitude toward strikes and collective bargaining goals, and the evolution of its political policy.

II

Although structurally dissimilar to the National Labor Union, its national predecessor during the 1860's, the Knights of Labor was nevertheless confronted with the same fundamental ideological issues that had divided the American labor movement since the middle of the nineteenth century. Although aware of the issues involved, the leaders of the Knights made no effort to resolve the cleavage, since they were committed to a basic reform of the industrial system. Their primary aim, briefly stated, was to abolish the wage system and re-establish the simple master-workman relationship of an earlier era where employer and employee performed similar functions. As Terence V. Powderly, leader of the Order during its years of national importance, succinctly stated: "The aim of the Knights of Labor—properly understood—is to make each man his own employer." [4] Efforts to assist workingmen to secure higher wages, shorter hours, and improved working conditions were mere amelioratives. "We do not believe," remarked A. W. Wright, a member of the General Executive Board of the Knights, "that the emancipation of labor will come with increased wages and a reduction in the hours of labor; we must go deeper than that, and this matter will not be settled until the wage system is abolished." [5]

The Knights of Labor, then, was the perpetuator of the reform tradition that had been carried on by the National Labor Union during the 1860's. Heir also to the democratic and equal-rights philosophy of their Jacksonian forbears, the leaders of the Knights looked to the past rather than to the future for their inspiration. Emphatically opposing the developing industrial order, they sought to re-establish the simpler and supposedly more humane society of an earlier era. In turn, thousands of workingmen, who had been hard hit by the depression of the 1870's, enthusiastically supported leaders who offered them not merely a higher standard of living, but also a position of independence and a respected status in the community.

[4] *Journal of the Knights of Labor*, XIII (May 4, 1893), 5.
[5] *The Laster*, IV (November 15, 1891), 3.

The close ideological bond linking the Jacksonian labor movement with the National Labor Union and the Knights of Labor can be found first in the similarity of aims and objectives of each. All three were professed enemies, though in varying intensity, of the financial structure of the United States, and each espoused the destruction of monopoly, to be achieved in part through currency and banking reform. There was also a direct line from the land reform theories of George Henry Evans to those of the leaders of the National Labor Union and Knights. The ten-hour movement of the 1830's and 1840's had its counterpart in the eight-hour movement of the 1860's and 1880's. In other areas as well—insistence upon the legal equality of capital and labor, the termination of foreign contract labor and convict labor, the introduction of a co-operative industrial system, the substitution of arbitration for strikes, the enactment of a weekly wage pay law, and the need for labor political action—the debt of the Knights to its reform predecessors is evident.[6]

A second important link joining the Knights of Labor to its reform progenitors was the character and background of the leaders who determined policy during its years of national importance. The Knights, on the whole, were led by men who had been born and had grown to maturity during the eventful decades preceding the Civil War. The humanitarian crusades of the 1840's and 1850's had laid the foundation for an irrevocable hostility toward industrial society and the wage system. Belonging to an America where the dev017 of an industrial economy had not yet overwhelmed a predominantly rural nation, these leaders did not think in terms of a permanent wage-earning class and its needs. Regarding the workers as the only legitimate members of the community, they sought to establish a co-operative society based upon a large number of small producers, for only under such conditions could the American democratic ideal be realized.

A look at certain leaders of the Knights will help to make this clear. Uriah S. Stephens, founder of the Knights, Master Workman of the first local, the first district, and the first General Assembly, was a typical representative of the reform character of the Order's leadership. Stephens was born in Cape May County, New Jersey, on August 3, 1821. His parents, who were Baptists, intended him for the ministry, and his education was directed to that end. But financial reverses following the panic of 1837 forced young Stephens to become indentured as an apprentice to a tailor. Becoming active in the labor movement in the 1850's and 1860's, he was one of the original founders of the Knights in 1869. At the organization of the General Assembly in 1878 Stephens was elected Grand Master Workman, holding that post for two more sessions. He resigned in September, 1879, because of the pressing nature of other commitments and

---

[6] Knights of Labor, *Proceedings of the General Assembly*, 1878, pp. 28–29; 1884, pp. 768–69 (hereinafter cited as K. of L., *GA Proc.*).

the precarious state of his health, and died of heart disease on February 13, 1882.[7]

Stephens' labor philosophy was essentially an outgrowth of the antebellum middle-class humanitarian and antimonopoly movements, which were instrumental in retarding the development of a class-conscious outlook on his part. Thus he regarded trade unions as being narrow and circumscribed, for he believed that the capitalist system was slowly destroying the foundations of unionism through the displacement of labor by the introduction of machinery and by the concentration of industry in the hands of a few individuals. The only solution, Stephens thought, lay in the abolition of a pernicious wage system and the introduction of a "Cooperative Commonwealth." [8] This objective, he explained in 1861, would be accomplished through a world-wide organization, whose purpose would be to "make labor honorable and profitable and lessen its burdens . . . make idleness a crime, render wars impossible, and obliterate national lines." [9] Unfamiliar with contemporary socialist theory, he never emphasized working-class economic action.

Stephens' successor, Terence Vincent Powderly, is another example of a reform leader. Powderly had been born in Carbondale, Pennsylvania, on January 22, 1849, the son of Irish parents who had migrated to American shores in 1827. The decade of the 1850's was an eventful one, and it left a strong imprint upon the young boy's character. His emphasis on land reform, woman's rights, and temperance all grew out of the humanitarian movements of his youth. Indeed, Powderly's ideological orientation was almost completely derived from a middle-class reformism and its periodic antimonopoly crusades.

Powderly's initial job as a railroad worker came when he was thirteen years old, and later he was apprenticed to learn the machinist trade. First entering the labor movement in 1871 by joining a local of the Machinists and Blacksmiths International Union, his ascent to national leadership was rapid, and in 1879 he was chosen to succeed the retiring Uriah S. Stephens as Master Workman of the Knights, a position he held continuously until 1893.[10]

During the 1880's Powderly was undoubtedly the most popular and renowned labor leader in the United States. His vision of a better world, his voluminous correspondence with the rank and file, and his obvious sincerity and sense of dedication and mission all contributed to his great

[7] *Journal of United Labor*, II (August 15, 1881), 137–38, (February 15, 1882), 193.

[8] *Thirteenth Annual Convention of the New York Protective Associations Affiliated With District Assembly 49, K. of L. on Labor Day . . . 1895* (n.p., 1895), not paginated.

[9] Statement reprinted in K. of L., *GA Proc.*, 1897, p. 37.

[10] Powderly to James E. Barrett, January 15, 1889, TVPLB. Powderly's autobiography, *The Path I Trod* (New York, 1940), is generally unreliable. For a discussion of Powderly as a labor leader see Gerald N. Grob, "Terence V. Powderly and the Knights of Labor," *Mid-America*, XXXIX (January, 1957), 39–55.

appeal. It was, in fact, as a publicist and educator that he made his greatest and most enduring impression on the labor movement. While developing no original organizational techniques or policies, he did focus attention on workingmen and helped to develop an awareness on their part of a growing labor movement.

The most important ingredient in Powderly's philosophy was a desire to destroy the wage system.[11] Like Stephens, his hostility toward capitalism was founded more on an emotional than a rational foundation, for he once wrote that he would banish the term "class" from the English language if he could do so.[12] Since neither Powderly nor Stephens assigned to economics an important role in the development of society, neither placed any emphasis upon the usefulness or importance of working-class economic action. Although supporting the abolition of the wage system, Powderly was apparently unacquainted with any of the major socialist theoreticians of his day. When he accepted a membership card in the Socialist Labor party from Philip van Patten in 1880, it was more a gesture of friendship than anything else, for he took no further action on it.[13] Although often identifying socialism with co-operation, Powderly was generally contemptuous of socialists because of their disruptive influence on labor organizations and their uncompromising and dogmatic tactics.[14]

[11] Powderly, "The Organization of Labor," *North American Review*, CXXXV (August, 1882), 123; Powderly, *The Path I Trod*, pp. 161, 427; K. of L., *GA Proc.*, 1880, p. 170.

[12] *Journal of United Labor*, I (June 15, 1880), 21.

[13] K. of L., *GA Proc.*, 1887, p. 1536.

[14] *The People*, April 17, 1892; Powderly to Robert D. Layton, May 1, 1882; Powderly to James McFeely, June 6, 1882; Powderly to Chester A. Arthur, November 11, 1884; Powderly to John W. Gilson, April 6, 1886, TVPLB.

The fact that the Knights had a relatively large proportion of Catholics, especially Irish Catholics, as members also raises an interesting question, namely, did the conservatism that marked Catholicism inhibit the development of an incipient radicalism within the Knights or have any direct influence on that organization? Certainly Powderly was not a radical in the full sense of the word. While always advocating the abolition of the wage system, he rarely, if ever, spoke in revolutionary or violent terms. Rather he persisted in looking to the past for his inspiration, a feature which is exemplified in the "return" aspect of American labor reformism. The program of the Knights was largely derived from the antimonopolism and utopian crusades of the ante-bellum period.

It is true that there was a considerable amount of friction between the Knights and the Catholic Church. This friction had arisen as a result of the Order's oath-bound secrecy, its Masonic aspects, its resemblance to the Molly Maguires, and its apparently socialistic or radical character. Beginning in the 1870's Powderly, who was then a faithful Catholic layman, set to work to modify the secret nature of his organization partially in response to pressure from Catholic quarters, which was keeping many workers away from the Knights. Some of the oath-bound secrecy was modified at the meeting of the General Assembly in the autumn of 1881, but the difficulties with the Church persisted, especially after Archbishop Elzear-Alexandre Taschereau of Quebec condemned the Order in his province in 1884. When it seemed as though the ban, with Papal sanction, might be extended to the United States, Powderly appealed to

In the place of economic action, Powderly proclaimed again and again the prime importance of education as the best means of abolishing the wage system. In 1888 he polled the Order on the desirability of establishing an "Educational Fund" to which contributions would be voluntary. Although the response was an affirmative one, the fund that was subsequently established never amounted to more than $20,000. In the end little was accomplished, and Powderly's one original contribution to the Knights came to naught.[15]

While Powderly and Stephens are undoubtedly the most striking examples of reform leaders, the careers of other prominent officials also illustrate the ideological link between ante-bellum humanitarianism and labor reformism in the 1880's. Eminent Knights like Charles H. Litchman, John W. Hayes, Thomas B. Barry, Albert A. Carlton, William Cook, Robert W. Keen, and Homer L. McGaw all were products of a reform environment,[16] and they retained the ideal of a society dominated by the small independent producer as an integral part of their philosophy. Both Litchman's and Hayes' careers exemplify the producer-consciousness that was so typical of the leadership of the Knights of Labor. Litchman, for example, who served as secretary of the Knights on different occasions, had been born in Massachusetts in 1849 and worked successively as a shoe salesman and shoe manufacturer. He then undertook the study of law, but lack of funds compelled him to seek employment in a shoe factory. Turning next to politics, he ran for the Massachusetts legislature first unsuccessfully as a Republican, then successfully as a Greenback Labor candidate. Litchman finally abandoned the Knights to enter

---

Cardinal James Gibbons of Baltimore. Gibbons, cognizant of the danger to the Catholic Church if workingmen should feel that the hierarchy was opposed to their hopes of improvement, was one of the clergy who interceded in Rome to prevent a ban on Catholic participation in the Knights. Though the entire affair was undoubtedly a vexing and troublesome one, it is probable that it had little to do with the formulation of policy within the Order. Cardinal Gibbons, for example, opposed a Vatican ban not only on the ground that it might alienate Catholic workers, but also because the Order was already in the process of decline. Actually the entire affair derives most of its significance from the role it played in the development of a Catholic program of moderate social reform, a goal that received Papal blessing in 1891 with the promulgation of *Rerum Novarum*. For a full and accurate treatment of the relations between the Catholic Church and the Knights see Henry J. Browne, *The Catholic Church and the Knights of Labor* (Washington, D. C., 1949) and *idem.*, "Terence V. Powderly and Church-Labor Difficulties of the Early 1880's," *Catholic Historical Review*, XXXII (April, 1946), 1–27. It is this author's belief that the difficulties between the Catholic Church and the Knights had relatively little influence over the development of the latter's ideology. For a general discussion of the relation of the Catholic Church to the American labor movement see Chapter Nine, fn. 8.

[15] *Journal of United Labor*, VIII (March 31, 1888), 2602, (May 26, 1888), 2633; K. of L., *GA Proc.*, 1888, *Report of the General Treasurer*, p. 13; 1889, *Report of the General Secretary Treasurer*, p. 13; 1890, *Report of the General Secretary Treasurer*, p. 9.

[16] McNeill, *Labor Movement*, pp. 605–06, 608–09, 611.

politics in 1888 as a Republican.[17] John W. Hayes, second only to Powderly in importance, also had an entrepreneurial background, for after the failure of the telegraphers' strike in 1883, he entered the grocery business and ultimately came to own two large stores.[18]

At the same time that the leaders of the Knights were perpetuating the reform tradition of American labor, the leaders of the trade unions were in the process of institutionalizing the collective bargaining and welfare functions of their organizations. Many of these trade-union officials were foreign-born, and were therefore little affected by ante-bellum reformism. Having been molded in a more feudal and stratified society, they had become imbued with a sense of class-consciousness. In fact, many of them at one time or another had been Marxian socialists.[19] Samuel Gompers, in his later career an ardent foe of socialists of any variety, pointed out that most successful union leaders had belonged to the Marxian First International, which had taught them the primary importance of economic organization.[20] Later divesting themselves of most of the principal tenets of socialist theory, these leaders nevertheless retained their faith in the importance of economic organization and methods to secure immediate and tangible goals.

The rank and file of the Knights and trade unions also reflected the divergent ethnic origins of their leaders. The Knights generally had a larger percentage of native-born members than the trade unions. In 1886, for example, 45 per cent of the Order's membership in Illinois had been born in the United States as compared with only 21 per cent in the trade unions.[21] Having grown to maturity during years of social ferment, most native American workers proved to be highly receptive to the reform philosophy of the Knights.

III

While the character of its leaders and members illustrates the intellectual debt that the Knights owed its forerunners, the struggle over the

[17] *Journal of United Labor,* I (June 15, 1880), 17–19, IX (September 6, 1888), 2693.

[18] McNeill, *Labor Movement,* p. 608.

[19] Samuel Gompers, Josiah B. Dyer, John Jarrett, Adolph Strasser, and Samuel Leffingwell are prime examples of the successful immigrant union leader. Even Peter J. McGuire, a native American and, excepting Gompers, the most prominent trade union leader of the 1880's and 1890's, spent his youth in the cosmopolitan atmosphere of New York City, absorbing much of his philosophy from German socialists and other Europeans who had migrated to the United States.

[20] Samuel Gompers, *Seventy Years of Life and Labor* (2 vols: New York, 1925), I, 127. See also Donald D. Egbert and Stow Persons, eds., *Socialism and American Life* (2 vols: Princeton, 1952), I, 249.

[21] Illinois Bureau of Labor Statistics, *Biennial Report,* IV (1886), 226–27, 229. See also K. of L., *GA Proc.,* 1884, p. 594. This proportion tended to vary, however, and in New Jersey in 1887 nearly half of the members of the Knights and trade unions were native Americans. New Jersey Bureau of Statistics of Labor and Industries, *Annual Report,* X (1887), 14.

formulation of co-operative and strike policies provides an even more striking example of the reformism of the Knights. This conflict, representing the traditional opposition of trade and reform unionism, was in effect a continuation of the hostilities that had resulted in the demise of the National Labor Union. Temporarily allayed by the depression of the 1870's, the conflict was resumed with the return of more prosperous times in the 1880's.

Heir to the communitarian tradition of the 1840's and the example of the National Labor Union, the leaders of the Knights turned first to co-operation as the best means of abolishing the wage system and elevating the small producer to a position of supremacy. Although co-operation was in part an outgrowth of the ante-bellum utopian tradition, it was more realistic in the sense that its supporters understood the impracticability of establishing Fourierist phalanxes or attempting experiments similar to Brook Farm. In the 1880's producer and consumer co-operation were the dominant types, and they were directed toward establishing the workers as small independent entrepreneurs. "It is intended by the Knights of Labor to supersede the wage system by a system of industrial co-operation, productive and distributive," Powderly informed the rank and file.[22] Such optimism, following closely on the heels of a paralyzing depression, appealed to workingmen, and for a brief time the vision of a new society captured the imagination of thousands of laborers. During the first half of the 1880's, therefore, a large part of the Knights' energies were channeled into co-operative activities.

Yet co-operation was not endorsed unanimously by the Order's membership. Within the Knights there existed a powerful minority of trade unions in the form of trade local, district, and national assemblies. This element, which because of ideological differences later disaffiliated from the parent body and established themselves as independent trade unions, attempted in the early 1880's to transform the Order into a collective bargaining rather than a reform body. In so doing the unionists within the Knights precipitated an internal struggle for control of the organization.

The conflict first became evident at the initial meeting of the General Assembly in 1878 in the discussions concerning a proposed resistance or strike fund. The trade proponents hoped that such a fund would be used in support of collective bargaining activities, while reformers advocated that it be applied toward co-operative undertakings. Since the delegates apparently could not reach any agreement, they finally adopted a compromise whereby the fund accumulated for two years, at the end of which period the General Assembly would make provision for its use.[23]

In the interval between the establishment of the fund and its eventual

[22] Powderly, *Thirty Years of Labor*, p. 460. See also K. of L., *GA Proc.*, 1880, pp. 170–71.

[23] K. of L., *GA Proc.*, January, 1878, pp. 9, 11–12, 14, 32.

disposition there was a tug-of-war for control. The General Assembly in 1880 finally agreed that 60 per cent of the money would be reserved for co-operation, 30 per cent for a strike fund, and 10 per cent for education. The failure of many members to pay their shares and maladroit management, however, led to the abolition of the fund the following year. In its place the General Assembly established a Co-operative Association, headed by an elective Co-operative Board. When the compulsory nature of this law aroused vigorous opposition, the Assembly in 1882 placed co-operation on a voluntary basis.[24]

Structural weaknesses inherent in the highly-centralized Knights, nevertheless, created what amount to almost insuperable obstacles, and few results were forthcoming from this venture. The Co-operative Board did not hold even a single meeting in 1883, and only four thousand dollars was paid into the co-operative fund. A new law, passed in 1883, did little to remedy matters, for while the Co-operative Board was given the authority to invest funds and establish co-operatives, it could not incur debts or liabilities. Between January and September, 1884, the Co-operative Board received only $969.55, and requests from local assemblies for funds to establish co-operatives were often ignored by the Board and the General Executive Board because the jurisdiction and powers of each had not been clearly defined by the General Assembly.[25]

By 1884 the apathy of most members of the Knights toward co-operation was obvious. A survey on the attitude of the more than one thousand local assemblies toward co-operation elicited just 212 responses, of which only 132 were favorable.[26] Even fewer members were willing to support any compulsory plan. A vote on such a proposal at the General Assembly in 1884 resulted in its defeat by the resounding margin of 73 to 14. Two years later matters had become so bad that the expenses of the Co-operative Board had to be met from the general fund. A proposal to set aside $10,000 per quarter for co-operative purposes was adopted, but the General Executive Board later decided to retain the money to defray its own expenses. In 1889 the Co-operative Board claimed that its functions and jurisdiction had not been clearly defined, and the following year asked to be dissolved. This request was approved, and although the Board was resurrected in 1893, nothing of note was ever accomplished.[27]

Despite the adoption of numerous laws and resolutions, the Knights as a national organization undertook the management of only a single co-

[24] *Ibid.*, 1880, pp. 185–87, 196, 232, 246; 1881, pp. 284–86, 312–13; 1882, pp. 354–56; *Journal of United Labor*, III (June, 1882), 247, (August, 1882), 282.

[25] K. of L., *GA Proc.*, 1883, pp. 414, 462, 490–91, 511–13, 515–17; 1884, pp. 599, 616, 679–81; Knights of Labor, *Constitution of the General Assembly* (revised September, 1883), p. 14.

[26] *Journal of United Labor*, V (September 10, 1884), 790.

[27] K. of L., *GA Proc.*, 1884, pp. 688, 700, 752, 754–55; 1886, p. 292; 1887, p. 1590; 1889, p. 60; 1890, p. 54; 1893, p. 70.

operative enterprise, and even this was a matter of pure chance. When a group of miners was locked out by their employers in Cannelburg, Indiana, in 1883, they leased some adjoining land and began mining the same vein. A lack of funds forced them to appeal to the General Executive Board for assistance. The Board then decided to purchase the property on behalf of the Knights, and the project was launched in 1884 amid great enthusiasm. The Board, however, encountered many difficulties and attempted to sell the mine the following year. When it received no satisfactory offers, it leased the property in January, 1886, to the Mutual Mining Company, which was composed of members of the Order. Eventually the mine was sold for $4,000 in 1897. After operating the mine for over thirteen years, the Knights had lost more than twenty thousand dollars![28]

Although the co-operative legislation enacted by the General Assembly produced no concrete results, much actually was undertaken on the local level by small groups of members. By the middle 1880's more than a hundred known co-operatives had been established, and the figure may have been considerably higher. In 1887, for example, co-operative enterprises begun by members of the Order included at least one bank, fifty-one grocery and eleven retail stores, eleven newspapers, and fifty-five workshops and factories.[29] The great majority of these ventures, however, were confined for the most part to rural areas, where co-operation was often regarded as the first step in the achievement of entrepreneurial status.

Nevertheless, while co-operation played a significant role in the history of the Knights between 1880 and 1887, the extravagant claims of its advocates were never realized in actual practice, and after 1887 the co-operative spirit was moribund. Members of the Order evinced a willingness to discuss and consider the merits of co-operation, but they were never attracted by the grandiose and often impractical ideas of their leaders.[30] Powderly's ideal of the abolition of the wage system through co-operation and the principles of John Samuel, the leading exponent of co-operation within the Knights, held little appeal for the mass of workers. The ordinary laborer considered co-operation in terms of what it would mean to

[28] *Ibid.*, 1884, pp. 582, 627; 1886, pp. 68–71, 76–77; 1897, p. 34. See also Ware, *The Labor Movement in the United States, 1860–1895* (New York, 1929), pp. 329–33.

[29] K. of L., *GA Proc.*, 1887, pp. 1616–23. For further evidence of co-operative activities by members of the Knights see *ibid.*, 1885, p. 36; *Journal of United Labor,* I (November 15, 1880), 68, II (July 15, 1881), 132, V (July 10, 1884), 740, (July 25, 1884), 753; *History of Coöperation in the United States* (Baltimore, 1888), pp. 69, 84, 86–88, 162–64; E. Levasseur, *The American Workman* (Baltimore, 1900), p. 200; New Jersey Bureau of Statistics of Labor and Industries, *Annual Report,* X (1887), 194–202; George B. Engberg, "The Knights of Labor in Minnesota," *Minnesota History,* XXII (December, 1941), 373; Clifton K. Yearly, Jr., *Britons in American Labor: A History of the Influence of the United Kingdom Immigrants on American Labor, 1820–1914* (Baltimore, 1957), p. 289.

[30] See the *Journal of United Labor,* V (July 25, 1884), 753.

his immediate welfare, while Powderly and other officials regarded it as a method of revolutionizing society. Ralph Beaumont, a leading Knight, complained in 1883 that workingmen were willing to join mutual benefit societies in the hope of gaining immediate advantages, but were unwilling to provide funds from their meager savings for co-operative purposes.[31] This statement accentuated a second important reason for the failure of co-operation; the fact that sufficient capital could not be raised. Often money was borrowed only at excessive or prohibitive interest rates. Powderly echoed Beaumont when he pointed out that successful co-operation required capital. Yet, as he wrote in 1884, "The workingmen who have a little capital cling to it and hold aloof from co-operation. Those who have no capital cannot embark in it."[32]

The inability to secure sufficient capital was not the sole difficulty facing co-operatives. Even when funds were available the desire for profits often became so overwhelming that many co-operatives were transformed instead into joint-stock companies. Stockholders then became intent on paying low wages in the hope of securing higher profits. Dissension within labor's ranks was also responsible for the failure of many undertakings.[33] Not unimportant were the discriminations practiced by competitors who feared the success of co-operative enterprises. Finally and perhaps most important was the fact that proponents of co-operation in the 1880's were seeking a society based on small productive units—an archaic system by modern industrial standards. The General Executive Board itself recognized that the smallness of an enterprise was not conducive to its success.[34]

While the General Assembly was passing numerous laws concerning co-operation and workers on the local level were attempting to translate theory into practice, the trade members of the Knights were vainly struggling to secure the establishment of a strike fund that would effectively aid their quest for shorter hours, higher wages, and improved working conditions. The limited financial resources of the Order, however, made simultaneous support of a co-operative and a strike fund virtually impossible. The result was an internal conflict for control of the treasury during the early 1880's. The leaders of the Knights, supported by urban and rural elements seeking to regain their lost entrepreneurial status, backed co-operation, while the trade proponents hoped to use the money as the nucleus of a central strike fund.

All efforts to turn the Knights into a collective bargaining unit, however, were bitterly resisted by the national administration. Since the leaders of the Knights were working for the establishment of a co-operative

---

[31] *Ibid.*, III (January, 1883), 383–84.
[32] Powderly to Felix Adler, January 20, 1884, TVPLB
[33] See the *Journal of United Labor*, V (February 25, 1885), 921; Engberg, "The Knights of Labor in Minnesota," *loc. cit.*, p. 373.
[34] K. of L., *GA Proc.*, 1884, p. 649.

society, they were opposed to anything that might detract from their primary objective. Furthermore, they regarded co-operation and strikes as mutually antagonistic. Stephens, while favoring the establishment of a resistance fund, confidently asserted that such a fund would prevent strikes by making the Knights so powerful that no effective opposition could be placed in its path.[35] The first issue of the *Journal of United Labor* optimistically informed its readers that when "the grand aims of the Order are fulfilled, and coöperation becomes the rule of distribution, strikes will be impossible because [they will be] unnecessary."[36] In 1882 the General Executive Board, reflecting the antistrike bias of its officials, recommended the abolition of all strike legislation and the substitution of arbitration in its place.[37]

Powderly was undoubtedly the most ardent adversary of the strike, even referring to it on one occasion as a "relic of barbarism."[38] Having witnessed few successful strikes, he came to the conclusion that all strikes were doomed to ignominious failure. His hope of reforming society also made him impatient with demands for higher wages or shorter hours. "So long as a pernicious system leaves one man at the mercy of another," he told the General Assembly in 1880, "so long will labor and capital be at war, and no strike can hit a blow sufficiently hard to break the hold with which unproductive capital to-day grasps labor by the throat."[39] Powderly's antipathy toward strikes was reflected in his unyielding opposition toward strike funds. In 1880, for example, he suggested that the name "Resistance Fund" be dropped and the money used for co-operative purposes. Eight years later he informed the rank and file that strikes would have been rendered needless had the money spent on their support been utilized for education.[40]

Nevertheless, the attitude of Powderly and the other officials did not dissuade the trade element from continuing its quest for a central strike fund. The establishment of a Resistance Fund in 1878 was inconclusive, since no decision had been made as to the use of the money. The following year an Indiana delegate to the General Assembly introduced a resolution asking that the Order renounce strikes and use the Resistance Fund for co-operation only. The General Assembly, however, defeated the resolution and instead instructed the General Executive Board to prepare a code of laws governing the use of the fund and present it to the next convention.[41]

[35] *Ibid.*, January 1879, p. 54.
[36] *Journal of United Labor*, I (May 15, 1880), 8. See also the statement of the leader of D.A. 30 of Massachusetts, in *ibid.*, VI (September 25, 1885), 1089.
[37] K. of L., *GA Proc.*, 1882, p. 332.
[38] Powderly to Robert Lucas, December 6, 1879, TVPLB.
[39] K. of L., *GA Proc.*, 1880, p. 170. See also *ibid.*, 1882, p. 278; McNeill, *Labor Movement*, pp. 415–18; *Journal of United Labor*, I (August 15, 1880), 37–38.
[40] K. of L., *GA Proc.*, 1880, p. 172; 1888, *Report of the General Master Workman*, p. 8.
[41] *Ibid.*, September, 1879, pp. 120, 130, 138.

While the General Assembly was debating the issue of co-operation versus strikes, the return of more prosperous times in the late 1870's and early 1880's led workingmen to display a more belligerent attitude in their fight for a higher standard of living. Carroll D. Wright, the first federal Commissioner of Labor, reported in 1887 that industrial disturbances had become so common in the past ten years as to characterize the period as "one of strikes and lockouts." [42] The ever-increasing restiveness of the Order's members finally forced the General Assembly in 1880 to provide for the disposition of the Resistance Fund. The plan ultimately adopted by the delegates represented a compromise between the co-oprative and strike fund advocates. The name of the fund was changed to "Defence Fund"; 10 per cent of the fund was set aside for educational purposes, 30 per cent for strikes, and the remaining 60 per cent for co-operation. [43]

Yet even while thus providing for aid to striking workers, the General Assembly also revealed its fundamental antipathy toward the use of the strike weapon. The same legislation that established the Defence Fund went on to declare that strikes ". . . (for the purpose of resisting unjust demands of employers or for securing an increase of wages) are, as a rule, productive of more injury than benefit to working people, [and] consequently all attempts to foment strikes will be discouraged." [44] Moreover, the administrative system adopted was designed to eliminate strikes by placing numerous procedural obstacles in the path of workers attempting to call them. In the first instance, an arbitration committee in the local assembly should attempt to arrange a peaceful settlement. If this effort failed, a district committee should carry on the work of the local's committee; if the district committee failed, it should be superseded by an arbitration committee composed of representatives of two adjoining districts. If no agreement had been reached by the three committees, the dispute was then to be referred to the General Executive Board. Only the Board, in consultation with the Master Workman and secretary of the Knights, had the power to initiate a walkout. [45]

This overly-complicated mechanism for calling strikes was not the sole obstacle that the trade element within the Order faced. Equally significant was the paucity of funds available to support striking workers. A year after the law of 1880 had gone into operation the Defence Fund had only eight thousand dollars, and the General Assembly ended the brief experiment by crediting each local's per capita tax amount with the money paid into the Defence Fund. The persistence of strikes, however,

[42] U. S. Commissioner of Labor, *Annual Report*, III (1887) (*Strikes and Lockouts*), 9. Between January and July, 1880, for example, there were more than forty strikes involving members of the Order. *Journal of United Labor*, I (August 15, 1880), 37.

[43] K. of L., *GA Proc.*, 1880, pp. 185–87, 189–92, 195–96, 246.

[44] *Ibid.*, p. 248.

[45] *Ibid.*

forced the Order to make some provision governing their use. In 1882 the General Assembly adopted a somewhat less complicated procedure for calling strikes, as well as a system of individual assessments intended to provide financial assistance for striking members.[46]

The system of assessments, nevertheless, like its predecessors also failed to live up to its expectations, for during 1883 only two were levied by the General Executive Board, and neither netted more than $4,500. When the Board admitted the inadequacy of the legislation providing financial assistance to striking workers, the General Assembly established an Assistance Fund. Money was to be raised through a compulsory levy of five cents per month per member. Funds could be withdrawn only upon presentation of an order signed by the chairman and secretary of the General Executive Board, which had the sole authority to authorize a strike.[47]

Yet while establishing such elaborate machinery for the regulation of strikes, the General Assembly also restated its ideological opposition to strikes. Section 8 of the law provided that "In the establishment of this fund for the purposes hereafter set forth, we declare that strikes are deplorable in their effect and contrary to the best interests of the Order, and therefore nothing in this article must be construed to give sanction to such efforts for the adjustment of any difficulty, except in strict accordance with the laws laid down in this article." [48] In every case the General Executive Board was instructed to consider the alternative of co-operation, and it was also empowered to turn over portions of the Assistance Fund to the Co-operative Board when co-operation appeared to be a practical remedy.

The struggle between the reform and trade delegates over the establishment of a central strike fund also accentuated a rural-urban conflict, which was further exacerbated as the Knights expanded into the more sparsely-populated regions of the West and South. Western delegates, representing a constituency that supported co-operation as a means of acquiring entrepreneurial status, frequently voiced dissatisfaction with any strike legislation.[49] D.A. 28 of Iowa was especially vociferous in demanding an end to strikes, and in 1882 called upon the General Assembly to take the power to strike away from local assemblies.[50] The following year the Master Workman of this district notified the General Executive Board that his district would not comply with certain assessments. "Our people in the West," he continued, "will not countenance strikes in any

[46] Ibid., 1881, pp. 284–86, 312–13; 1882, pp. 324, 352–53.
[47] Ibid., 1883, pp. 455–58, 509.
[48] Ibid., p. 510.
[49] See ibid., January, 1879, p. 85; Journal of United Labor, II (May 15, 1881), 119, IV (December, 1883), 612.
[50] K. of L., GA Proc., 1882, p. 310.

shape unless it be at the ballot box." [51] Local Assembly (L.A.) 885 of Cedar Rapids, Iowa, also protested vigorously against an assessment levied on behalf of Window Glass Workers' L.A. 300.[52]

The leaders of the Knights thus found themselves in a tacit alliance with rural elements, although not for the same reasons. The antistrike policy of the Order's leadership reflected a conviction that the condition of the working class could only be improved through the abolition of the wage system. Rural members, on the other hand, supported co-operation in place of strikes because of a middle-class hope of becoming entrepreneurs. This accord was reflected in a letter written by J. McClelland, secretary of the General Executive Board, to the Master Workman of D.A. 28:

> You nor your Western members cannot be more opposed to an assessment than I am. As a temporary measure even they are a dead failure. I judge, however, that you are under a misapprehension as to the "assistance fund." There is no such thing as "defence fund" on our books. I am looking eagerly for January 1st to come, after which a strike will be an impossibility. Read the assistance fund provisions carefully. We tried to frame them to suit all interests, but my idea—and I may say the feeling of the Board is the same—was to work carefully, and by providing that no strike will be recognized unless *sanctioned by the Board* is just as much as to say strikes are at an end. We shall use the fund only to protect our members when they are beset, and then we shall not scatter a few quarters here and there, but if our members are thrown out we shall use it in an endeavor to start them in business—lending them the money without interest and under security.[53]

Western fears, moreover, were soon further allayed by the refusal of the General Executive Board to administer the Assistance Fund aggressively. "The number of appeals for assistance now being showered on the board is frightful," Powderly complained, "and nothing but a treasury with millions in it could stand it. My advice to the board is to shut down on all appeals and stick to the original plan of the order, that of educating the members as to the folly of strikes." [54] In part because of the antipathy of the Board to the very idea of strikes, therefore, the Assistance Fund proved in operation to be of no value to the rank and file of workers.

There was also the fact that many locals refused to pay their share of the assessment to the Assistance Fund.[55] Between 1885 and 1886, the period of greatest growth of the Knights, the Assistance Fund received

---

[51] *Ibid.*, 1884, p. 621.
[52] *Ibid.*, p. 641.
[53] *Ibid.*, pp. 621–22.
[54] Powderly to William A. Varner, February 8, 1883, TVPLB.
[55] *Journal of United Labor*, III (February, 1883), 400, V (October 25, 1884), 825.

only $600.[56] As a result, the central Assistance Fund was abolished in
1887, and the local, district, trade, and state assemblies were given the
power to maintain their own funds over which they would exercise complete control.[57] Later attempts to resurrect a national fund proved abor-
tive, and thus ended the futile efforts by the Knights to exert influence
over strikes through control of the purse.

The numerous attempts of the Knights to formulate a consistent and
rational strike policy contained the seeds of failure almost from the outset. The ideological antipathy of its leaders toward strikes, the hostility
of the farm and rural element, and the general apathy of many workingmen all contributed to the Order's inability to establish a central strike
fund. Thus the efforts of the General Assembly to maintain the precarious balance between reform and trade objectives ended in failure. Consequently, many workers, finding the reform program of the Knights apparently incompatible with collective bargaining objectives, abandoned
the Order.

IV

Along with the reforming zeal of the leaders of the Knights went a
strong sense of social idealism. Thus they sought to unite all workers, irrespective of race or sex, into a single phalanx that would serve as the
instrument of social change. Like its Jacksonian predecessors, the Knights
retained the belief that the working class was the sole legitimate group in
society. Of course, this interpretation of the working class was very different from our present conceptions of that group. The Jacksonians and
their descendents thought of the laboring class as including everyone
directly engaged in the production of goods, whether worker, manufacturer, or entrepreneur, and they excluded only those engrossed in such
"parasitic" occupations as banking and finance. This broad definition of
the working class, when fused with the ante-bellum heritage of the anti-
slavery crusade and woman's rights movement, resulted in the insistance
that no worker be excluded from the Knights because of race or sex.

Yet the Knights, like the National Labor Union, was confronted by
three barriers that divided the labor movement of the 1880's—the Negro
worker, woman labor, and the large number of immigrants coming to
the United States. The way in which the Order attempted to solve the
problems posed by the exclusion of Negro and woman workers offers further evidence of its reform heritage and sense of social idealism. Its stand
on immigration, on the other hand, represented a retreat from its reform
and equalitarian outlook.

The first, the problem of Negro labor, was as pressing in the 1880's as
it had been in the 1860's. Colored workers were still being used as strike-

[56] K. of L., *GA Proc.*, 1886, p. 63.
[57] *Ibid.*, 1887, p. 1802.

breakers or else hired at substandard wages. In addition, the attitude of many white workers toward the Negro, especially in the skilled trades, had steadily grown more hostile since Reconstruction. Few trade unions in the 1880's signified their willingness to accept Negroes as members,[58] despite the fact that the lack of organization among colored workers served to undermine the objectives of white labor.

Both Stephens and Powderly, products of an abolitionist environment, advocated the admission of Negroes into the Knights of Labor either in local assemblies including white and black or all-Negro ones.[59] These views were implemented by the actions of the local and district assemblies, and the organization of the Negro became the accepted and official policy of the Knights. In areas where racial feeling was too strong to be easily surmounted, separate Negro locals were organized; in other places locals included Negro and white as members. In 1880 the *Journal of United Labor* first reported the existence of Negro locals and ones having white and colored workers. Five years later John Swinton, the prominent labor journalist, reported that "there are hundreds of colored assemblies in the South." [60] Throughout the North and South, Negroes by the thousands were initiated into the Order. "The colored people of the South are flocking to us," reported Frederick Turner to the General Assembly in 1886.[61] Colored organizers were appointed, and Negroes such as Frank Ferrell of D.A. 49 of New York City played important roles in the leadership and administration of the Knights. John W. Hayes estimated that the Knights had 60,000 colored members in 1886, and other estimates ran even higher. In the South, where the overwhelming majority of Negroes lived, the colored local was a familiar phenomenon. Richmond, Virginia, had twelve colored locals and one colored district in 1885; Atlanta, Georgia, had two colored locals; and so it went.[62] George E. McNeill, the prominent labor leader, claimed that the "color line had been broken, and black and white were found working together in the same cause." [63] The official acts of the General Assembly also reflected the widespread

[58] For a typical attitude see the *Iron Molders' Journal*, XXI (April 30, 1885), 11.

[59] See Uriah S. Stephens to R. H. Lee, June 17, 1879; Powderly to J. Stewart, October 8, 1879; Powderly to (?) Wright, September 19, 1880, TVPLB; K. of L., *GA Proc.*, 1880, p. 257.

[60] *Journal of United Labor*, I (August 15, 1880), 49; *John Swinton's Paper*, April 12, 1885.

[61] K. of L., *GA Proc.*, 1886, p. 44.

[62] Sterling D. Spero and Abram L. Harris, *The Black Worker: The Negro and the Labor Movement* (New York, 1931), p. 42; Sidney H. Kessler, "The Negro in Labor Strikes," *Midwest Journal*, VI (Summer, 1954), 17; *Journal of United Labor*, V (April 25, 1885), 969, (May 25, 1885), 992, VI (August 25, 1885), 1067; *John Swinton's Paper*, June 14, September 27, 1885, March 14, 1886; North Carolina Bureau of Labor Statistics, *Annual Report*, I (1887), 224; K. of L., *GA Proc.*, 1885, p. 31; *Journal of the Knights of Labor*, XV (July 5, 1894), 4; Ruth Allen, *Chapters in the History of Organized Labor in Texas* (Austin, Texas, 1941), p. 174.

[63] McNeill, *Labor Movement*, p. 171.

acceptance of the Negro on the local and state levels. In 1886 it recommended that D.A. 41 of Maryland admit Negroes as apprentices into the mechanical department, and the following year notified Texas locals that colored members had to be treated with respect.[64]

And yet the wall separating white and black was not so easily destroyed, for the barrier of race remained impregnable. Although Powderly was a consistent advocate of the unionization of Negro workmen, he was at the same time prevented by pressure from the rank and file from enforcing his equalitarian views with a strong hand. Thus he had to rely upon persuasion and halfway measures. "The color line cannot be rubbed out," he informed a Southern labor leader in 1887, "nor can the prejudice against the colored man be overcome in a day. I believe that for the present it would be better to organize the colored men by themselves." [65] The unionization of the colored worker, however, would not mean social equality. In 1889, for example, he told the St. Louis Farmers' Convention that the Knights did not intend to interfere with race relations in the South. "We do not ask," Powderly concluded, "that you take these people to your bosom, but we do ask that where the black man becomes a lever with which to oppress the white man . . . he shall be protected . . . So far and no further. When it comes to my home that is my concern, and none have the right to say with whom I shall associate there. No man can do otherwise." [66]

Although circumstances and fear of internal conflict within the Knights compelled Powderly to speak and act cautiously on the Negro issue, he and the Order accomplished much for the colored worker. During the 1880's it seemed at last as though a new day were dawning for the Negro. For the first time in American history a great labor organization was not merely wooing him with words but was in many instances admitting him to full membership. Although hostile feelings were still in evidence, it was clear that they were in the process of being modified.

The second group undermining labor unity in the 1880's was the working women of America, who had become an important factor in industry even before the Civil War and who constituted 16 per cent of the labor force in 1870 and 19 per cent in 1880.[67] Yet the prevailing attitude was that woman's rightful place was in the home, and that matters of politics

---

[64] K. of L., *GA Proc.*, 1886, pp. 194, 274; 1887, p. 1316.

[65] Powderly to J. M. Bannon, July 8, 1887. See also Powderly to W. H. Lynch, April 13, 1886, TVPLB.

[66] *Journal of the Knights of Labor*, X (January 16, 1890), 1–2. Many members of the Knights recognized that an overly-strong hand on the Negro issue might result in schism. The General Assembly of 1886, for example, stated that the "Knights of Labor recognizes the civil and political equality of all men and, in the broad field of labor, recognizes no distinction on account of color, but it has no purpose to interfere with or disrupt the social relations which may exist between different races in any portion of the country." K. of L., *GA Proc.*, 1886, p. 254.

[67] Edith Abbott, *Women in Industry* (New York, 1910), p. 82.

and economics were not within her rightful province. Workingmen were not immune to the popular views regarding women, and most unions refused to accept them as members. Despite the pioneering work of the National Labor Union only two of the more than thirty national trade unions enrolled females prior to 1873. Employers were quick to seize the opportunities inherent in this situation, and they hired women either for low wages or as strikebreakers.

By the 1880's, however, it was virtually impossible for organized labor to ignore women. Since prejudice against them was much less than against Negroes, these years saw the first real beginnings of progress toward the organizing of woman workers. This task was made easier by the liberating impact of the crusade for woman's rights that had originated prior to the Civil War. The Knights of Labor did not inaugurate the policy of admitting women, for the International Typographical Union had undertaken this task earlier. But the experiences of the Knights were typical of the labor movement of the 1880's, and the pattern for future developments was established during this decade.

In its early years the Knights moved slowly and cautiously. In September, 1879, Philip van Patten, an official of the Socialist Labor party, introduced a resolution at the General Assembly that would have permitted women to become members and organize assemblies under the same conditions as men. Although the committee to which the proposal had been referred submitted a favorable report, Powderly ruled that since a fundamental change was being contemplated, a two-thirds vote of approval was necessary. The initial vote was twelve to seven, just one vote short of the required two-thirds majority. A second ballot met the constitutional requirements, but the General Assembly then voted to table the entire matter and refer the question to the consideration of the rank and file.[68]

The following year the General Assembly adopted a resolution permitting women to form assemblies under the same conditions as men, but with the added proviso that a committee of five draw up regulations and rituals, with full power to put them into immediate effect, that would govern female members.[69] When the committee made no report to the succeeding Assembly, Harry J. Skeffington took matters into his own hands and, in September, 1881, organized Garfield L.A. 1684 in Philadelphia, composed exclusively of women. In turn this local elected a woman delegate to D.A. 70, which then sent her as a district representative to the General Assembly.[70] In 1882 the General Assembly, recognizing a *fait*

[68] K. of L. *GA Proc.*, September, 1879, pp. 125, 131.
[69] *Ibid.*, 1880, p. 226.
[70] Augusta E. Galster, *The Labor Movement in the Shoe Industry* (New York, 1924), p. 52; John B. Andrews and W. D. P. Bliss, *History of Women in Trade Unions*, 61st Congress 2d Session, *Senate Document 645*, vol. X (Washington, D. C., 1911), p. 115.

accompli, permitted the initiation of women over sixteen years of age into the Knights.[71]

The General Assembly's decision to accept women workers had an immediate impact. In the eighteen months preceding January, 1887, for example, 13,200 women alone were admitted to membership in Massachusetts. At the height of the Knights' growth in 1886 one out of every eight members was a female. In the single month of May, 1886, twenty-seven all-women locals were organized. Mary Stirling became the first female delegate to the General Assembly in 1883, and three years later no less than sixteen women delegates were present. In addition, women also occupied important posts at the local and district levels.[72]

The rush of female workers into the Order led the General Assembly to authorize the creation of a committee of women's work in 1885. The following year this committee was given permanent status, and Mrs. Leonora M. Barry was chosen its head with the title of "General Investigator." Left a widow with three young children to support, she had gone to work in a New York hosiery mill, earning sixty-five cents as her first week's wages. Disturbed by the difficult conditions under which women labored, she joined the Knights in the hope that the status of women in industry could be raised through unionization. During her four years in office she traveled throughout the country as an organizer and investigator, and her name became a familiar one in the labor movement. In 1889, however, after years of hard work, she sadly reported to the General Assembly that, despite her efforts, women were not organizing.[73] In 1890, following her remarriage, she resigned, and the Women's Department was discontinued.

Although the decline of the Knights in the 1890's ended its pioneering work among women workers, a significant precedent had been established for the labor movement. Working-class unity had been given further impetus by the partial elimination of the sex barrier, and increasingly the labor movement began to accept women as equal partners in the struggle for higher wages and better working conditions.

While the policy of the Knights of Labor toward the organization of Negro and women workers was in large measure an outgrowth of its reform ideology and its desire of eliminating these two sources of cheap labor, its attitude toward the immigrant, on the other hand, represented a major retreat from the democratic and equal-rights inheritance of the ante-bellum decades. In part, the Knights' actions toward the immigrant

---

[71] K. of L., *GA Proc.*, 1882, pp. 309, 347.

[72] Andrews and Bliss, *History of Women in Trade Unions,* pp. 116, 123–27.

[73] K. of L., *GA Proc.*, 1886, p. 287; 1889, *Report of the General Instructor and Director of Woman's Work,* p. 6; *Journal of United Labor,* X (July 18, 1889), 1; Andrews and Bliss, *History of Women in Trade Unions,* pp. 116–23; Leonora M. Barry to Powderly, February 27, March 1, September 4, October 4, 1888, Powderly Papers; Powderly to Barry, February 27, March 23, 29, 1888, TVPLB.

was a concession to the working-class sentiment that the large influx of foreign workers willing to work for low wages was undermining American labor's quest for a higher standard of living. Thus employers not only utilized immigrants as a ready supply of cheap labor, but they occasionally attempted to import large groups into the United States to act as strikebreakers. Although the majority of workers, regardless of nationality, had similar economic interests, cultural and language barriers made unity between different ethnic groups difficult.

The movement for immigration restriction was confined at first to action against the Chinese. The Chinese, an alien ethnic group possessing customs foreign to western civilization, were obvious targets. Opposition to Asiatics, however, was more a result of economic than racial considerations, for American workers felt that the low standard of living of the Chinese would impede their hope for material improvement. Only in later years did the movement against Asiatic immigration take on racial overtones.

The earliest signs of opposition to the Chinese had appeared during the 1850's among miners, who acted in concert to expel the newcomers. This antipathy was intensified following the Civil War. In 1870, as a result of pressure by the California delegation, the National Labor Union placed itself on record as opposing future Chinese immigration. The Burlingame Treaty, ratified the previous year, had only angered Californians by extending to China a most-favored nation status for its nationals. Throughout the 1870's the anti-Chinese agitation continued to be the mainstay of the California labor movement.

Prior to 1880 the Order was too weak to take a firm stand against Chinese labor, but with growth and national organization it soon took the lead in the movement to restrict further immigration. In 1880 the General Executive Board urged all members first to determine the attitude of their congressional representatives regarding abrogation of the Burlingame Treaty before voting for them.[74] A few weeks later the General Assembly, by a large majority, voted against a point of order that would have permitted the Chinese to become members. The Assembly then recommended that members refrain from patronizing Chinese establishments or persons employing Chinese. Members were urged to demand that their congressmen work for abrogation of the Burlingame Treaty.[75]

In the national elections of 1880 both major political parties had anti-Chinese planks in their platforms, and Powderly sent two representatives to Washington to lobby for restriction.[76] Success came in 1882 when the first Chinese Exclusion Act was passed by Congress, although a ten-year

[74] *Journal of United Labor,* I (August 15, 1880), 39.
[75] K. of L., *GA Proc.,* 1880, pp. 223, 249–50; Powderly, *Thirty Years of Labor,* pp. 426–27.
[76] Nicholas A. Somma, "The Knights of Labor and Chinese Immigration," unpublished M.A. Thesis, Catholic University of America, Washington, D. C., 1952, pp. 31–33.

limitation was imposed to meet objections raised by a presidential veto. This victory acted as a stimulant to the movement to abrogate the Burlingame Treaty, and Powderly went to Washington in the hope of influencing Congress.[77] Highly pleased with his trip, he reported that he had impressed upon Congress "that the experience of the last thirty years in California has proved conclusively that the presence of the Chinese, and their competition with free white labor is one of the greatest evils with which any country can be afflicted." [78]

The continuing agitation against the Chinese ultimately resulted in violence when a riot broke out at Rock Springs, Wyoming Territory, in the autumn of 1885. Most of the white participants were members of the Knights. The whole affair seems to have revolved around the accumulated resentment against the employment of Chinese in the area. During the uprising twenty-eight Chinese were killed, fifteen were severely wounded, and nearly $150,000 worth of property was destroyed.[79] Powderly felt that matters had gotten out of hand, and he hinted that perhaps the Knights had gone too far in its anti-Chinese agitation.[80] While there were no further incidents involving its members, the Knights never receded from its anti-Chinese attitude. Even after news of the violence had become known, the General Assembly reaffirmed its opposition to Chinese immigration.[81]

Ultimately the Knights came to support a limited form of restriction on all immigration. As early as 1884 Powderly had expressed opposition to foreigners who were "not capable of enjoying, appreciating, defending, and perpetuating the blessings of good government." The previous year the General Assembly had adopted a resolution endorsing the restriction of "pauper emigration" to the United States. "There is grave danger," Powderly told the Knights in 1892, "that in a babel of tongues we may forget that we are freemen in this country, and in losing sight of that fact allow the incoming horde to Europeanize us before we can Americanize them." In 1893 the General Assembly urged "the adoption of laws for the more effectual restriction of immigration." [82]

Thus, with the exception of its stand on immigration, much of the Knights' program was based on the experiences of workers from the age of Jackson through the National Labor Union. Refusing to accept the permanence of an industrial society, the leaders of the Knights staked their careers on the hope of re-establishing a more democratic and equali-

[77] Powderly to unidentified correspondent, November 19, 1882, TVPLB.

[78] Powderly to J. W. Adams, February 7, 1883, TVPLB.

[79] *The Chinese Question,* 49th Congress, 1st Session, *House Executive Document 102* (Washington, D. C., 1886), pp. 2, 4, 12; Isaac H. Bromley, *The Chinese Massacre at Rock Springs, Wyoming Territory* (Boston, 1886), pp. 3–17. See also Paul Crane and Alfred Larson, "The Chinese Massacre," *Annals of Wyoming,* XII (January, 1940), 47–55, (April, 1940), 153–61.

[80] Powderly to Thomas Neasham, October 31, 1885, TVPLB.

[81] K. of L., *GA Proc.,* 1885, p. 160.

[82] *Ibid.,* 1883, pp. 432, 500; 1884, p. 577; 1892, p. 5; 1893, p. 72.

tarian society based on the dominance of the small producer. Their antipathy toward strikes, their emphasis on co-operation, their hope of unifying all workers regardless of race or sex, all reflected a preoccupation with superseding existing society and elevating the individual producer to a dominant position.

CHAPTER FOUR

Widening the Gulf Between Reformers and Trade Unionists in the Knights of Labor

I

❧ THE CONFLICT WITHIN the Knights of Labor over strike and co-operative legislation reflected the fundamental differences between a leadership dedicated to reform and a powerful trade minority striving for a higher standard of living. These differences were sometimes resolved through compromise; more often they remained smoldering beneath an apparently calm exterior. Between 1880 and 1885 the task of reconstructing a labor movement shattered by the depression of the 1870's was paramount, and few members were deeply troubled by the ideological contradictions that divided their organization.

A policy of drift that evaded fundamental issues, however, could not be continued indefinitely. The rise of the Knights to national importance only emphasized the need for real direction and purpose. Such a situation was laden with opportunity. If the Knights succeeded in organizing and rallying workingmen around a common program, the working class would at last be able to bring to bear the latent power its millions of members represented. But if there was opportunity in such a situation, there was also danger. The assertion of an overly strong hand could easily cause a serious rift and alienate those members who found themselves in disagreement with official policy.

The task facing the leaders of the Knights, then, was to reconcile somehow their reform program with the ever-increasing insistence of the rank and file on immediate rather than future amelioration of their condition. Powderly and other officials, however, chose instead to continue their efforts at reforming society, thus ignoring the most pressing necessities of their constituents. In itself, such a policy would not have alienated the trade element in the Knights. But when Powderly and other officials directly attacked and undercut efforts aimed at securing higher wages and shorter hours, a conflict became inevitable. So long as differences had remained ideological in nature, it had been possible to ignore them. But when these theoretical differences were translated into practical policy, a new and radically dissimilar situation was created.

The struggle between reformers and trade unionists in the Knights revolved principally around two major issues—strikes and the eight-hour day. The leadership, on one hand, bitterly resisted any attempts to transform the Knights into a collective bargaining organization, maintaining that the question of wages and hours was subsidiary and should not be permitted to obscure the primary goal of reforming society. "The Order is opposed to strikes," Powderly informed the General Assembly in 1885, "and, no matter how just the cause, I know that there is a majority of the Order that will vote against inaugurating a strike under any circumstances." [1] Many members, on the other hand, displayed more interest in raising their standard of living than they did in the program of their leaders. During 1886, for example, no less than 538 local assemblies participated in either a strike or a boycott.[2]

The ideological opposition of the national officers to strikes sooner or later was bound to involve them in untenable situations. So long as workers concentrated on organization and agitation, there was no difficulty. But growth brought increased power, and there were many members who did not hesitate to use this power to enhance their bargaining position. These workers stood ready and willing to resort to the strike despite the antagonism that their national leaders displayed toward this weapon. It was also clear that the leaders of the Knights would become involved when local, district, and national assemblies called for help for their members during protracted strikes. Between 1883 and 1886 the ideological divisions within the Knights reached a climax. When members participated in large-scale walkouts (as they did during the Southwest and stockyards strikes in 1886), or when they lent support to the eight-hour movement of 1886, the leaders of the Knights found that their reform program was being threatened, and they fought back against those who would abandon ultimate reform for immediate gain. Thus while the labor movement was reaching hitherto unattained heights, an internal struggle within the Knights was coming to a head as its leaders adopted an attitude of open hostility toward those workers utilizing strikes.

II

One of the first national strikes involving the Knights occurred in the summer of 1883, when D.A. 45, composed of telegraphers, struck against

[1] K. of L., *GA Proc.*, 1885, p. 23.
[2] *Ibid.*, 1887, p. 1881.

Western Union, then controlled by Jay Gould. While national organizations of telegraphers had existed as early as 1863, all had proved ephemeral. In 1882 the Brotherhood of Telegraphers combined with eastern operators to form Telegraphers National District No. 45. Although conditions among the workers were not satisfactory, they contemplated no strike. Following the company's arbitrary dismissal of a New York City lineman for refusal to do carpentry work, however, the Executive Board of D.A. 45 presented a list of grievances to Western Union and requested a wage increase. The Board, moreover, pointed out that while the company was making exorbitant profits, wages had been reduced and the workload increased. The company refused to grant any of the operators' demands, and the strike began on July 19, 1883. For almost a month the men remained away from their jobs, but on August 17 the union conceded defeat and advised members to return to work. The strike had failed because of the inexperience of the leaders, the lack of adequate financial resources, the failure to order out the railroad telegraphers immediately, the lack of solidarity among the operators, and the obstinate resistance of Western Union.[3]

During the walkout there was much talk among the Knights about the possibility of raising a fund of $100,000 to assist the striking telegraphers.[4] An assessment levied on July 28 netted only $1,640.65, to which the General Executive Board added $2,000 from the funds of the General Assembly.[5] John R. Mitchell, one of the strike leaders, echoed the sentiment of most telegraphers when he expressed dissatisfaction with the action of the Knights.[6] But Powderly, who had attempted to prevent the strike, was quick to point out that the Order had made no promises to D.A. 45.[7] Other leading officials of the Knights also incurred the wrath of the defeated operators. John McClelland, a member of D.A. 45 and secretary of the General Executive Board of the Order, deserted his union when defeat appeared imminent, although his actions were probably motivated by an ideological hostility toward all strikes. S. D. Phelps, another official of the Knights, accused the telegraphers of having violated their own constitution by failing to exhaust all means of settlement before embarking on the strike. Many newspapers also quoted the antistrike attitude of the Knights' official paper, the *Journal of United Labor.*[8]

Following the end of the strike, the telegraphers withdrew from the Knights and D.A. 45 ceased to exist as a functioning organization. The *Telegraphers' Advocate,* although uncertain about the wisdom of disaffili-

[3] Vidkunn Ulriksson, *The Telegraphers: Their Craft and Their Unions* (Washington, D. C., 1953), pp. 32–48.
[4] *Ibid.,* p. 48.
[5] K. of L., *GA Proc.,* 1883, p. 456.
[6] *New York Tribune,* August 19, 1883, cited in Ulriksson, *The Telegraphers,* p. 49.
[7] K. of L., *GA Proc.,* 1883, p. 402.
[8] Ulriksson, *The Telegraphers,* p. 48.

ating from the Knights, defended this step as necessary to the welfare of the operators. "In anticipation of such questions we assert, knowing our surroundings and the obstacles with which we would contend in preserving the Brotherhood under the jurisdiction of the Knights of Labor, that our action in withdrawing is not based upon any intent to weaken, or in any way embarrass or injure the parental body, but to retain the Brotherhood in its present strength." [9] Later attempts to resurrect D.A. 45 failed, primarily because the operators never outgrew their distrust of the Knights after the strike of 1883. Although a few telegraphers rejoined D.A. 45 when that district was revived with Powderly's blessings in the mid-1880's, the majority of operators remained away.[10]

The failure of the telegraphers' strike, however, was overshadowed by a successful strike conducted by Window Glass Workers' L.A. 300 in 1883. L.A. 300, one of the first trade assemblies that transcended geographical lines, had been formed by a merger in 1880 with the approval of the General Executive Board. Its instantaneous success was due not so much to the aid of the Knights as it was to the form of organization adopted by the window glass workers. Being in effect a trade union of highly skilled workers, L.A. 300 was able to enforce its demands because of its thorough organization of the trade.[11]

In the summer of 1883 the members of L.A. 300 went out on strike in protest against a large wage reduction. In October the General Executive Board levied an assessment on behalf of the striking workers and then appointed various individuals to act as fund raisers, but the response was meager. Finally, in January, 1884, L.A. 300 emerged victorious, gaining all its demands and maintaining an unbroken control over the trade. Although the workers credited the Knights with making an important contribution to the victory, it is clear that the national body contributed little in the way of material aid, although it did share in the triumph and received the plaudits of workingmen throughout the nation.[12]

In the two years, 1885 and 1886, however, the antistrike attitude of the national leaders of the Knights of Labor was revealed in a much more decisive manner by their actions during the Wabash, Southwest, and stockyards strikes. While these walkouts were by no means the only ones conducted under the auspices of the Knights, they were undoubtedly the most famous. And when the Southwest and stockyards strikes concluded in failure, many workers held their national leaders responsible. This fact, coupled with the irreconcilable hostility of the trade unions, started

---

[9] *Telegraphers' Advocate*, cited in the *Iron Molders' Journal*, XIX (October 31, 1883), 3.

[10] *John Swinton's Paper*, April 25, June 6, July 18, 1886; *The Carpenter*, VI (June, 1886), 1: *Journal of United Labor*, IX (July 12, 1888), 2661; Powderly to Thomas H. Hughes, March 24, 1886, TVPLB.

[11] *Journal of United Labor*, I (May 15, 1880), 14, (June 15, 1880), 25.

[12] *Ibid.*, III (January, 1883), 390–91, IV (December, 1883), 608, (January, 1884), 625, (February, 1884), 644.

the Order on a spiral of decline that would result in its eventual extinction.

The first of these strikes on the Wabash Railroad in 1885, however, served only to confirm and reinforce the belief that the Knights of Labor was a successful collective bargaining organization. The background to this strike was not complex. In October, 1884, there had been a 10 per cent reduction in wages on the Missouri, Kansas and Texas Railroad. On February 26, 1885, a similar cut was put into effect on the Wabash line. As a result a strike broke out at Moberly, Missouri, and spread rapidly to the Missouri Pacific, the Missouri, Kansas and Texas, and the Wabash, all of which were controlled by Jay Gould. The Union Pacific employees then sent Joseph R. Buchanan, a leading labor journalist and prominent Knight, to the scene to organize the striking workers and with the authority to pledge $30,000 in support of the men. Buchanan quickly formed the striking workers into local assemblies. The railroads, however, withdrew the wage reductions in March, 1885.[13]

Nevertheless, the railroads continued their policy of laying off members belonging to the Knights and closed their shops on June 16, 1885. The Executive Board of D.A. 93 promptly appealed to the General Executive Board for help. The latter replied that no district had an Assistance Fund large enough to permit an assessment; that most of the locals of D.A. 93, being of recent origin, were ineligible for aid; that four other districts were simultaneously appealing for aid; and finally, that the affair was not really a lockout. It was evident that Powderly and other officials were completely opposed to any action that might lend credence to the belief that the Knights favored strikes, and that the explanation given D.A. 93 was in effect a rationalization of this policy. The striking district then sent its Board of Arbitration to visit A. A. Talmadge, the general manager of the Wabash system, but he refused even to see the committee. Another urgent appeal by the strikers for help again met with a refusal from the General Executive Board, which took the position that too many strikes were simultaneously in progress.[14]

Meanwhile, on July 25, other members of the Knights on the Southwest system, the Missouri Pacific, and the Texas Pacific, pledged themselves to stand by the Wabash strikers. Forced by quickly moving events to take some action, Powderly called for the General Executive Board to meet in St. Louis on August 14, but he himself was absent because of a convenient illness. According to Buchanan's testimony, "Turner simply kept the records of the meeting, Hayes looked on and said nothing, [and] Bailey put in most of the time at a window, trying to get on friendly terms with the elusive zephyrs that occasionally stole through Washington Avenue that hot day."[15] An attempt by Powderly to see

---

[13] Joseph R. Buchanan, *The Story of a Labor Agitator* (New York, 1903), pp. 142–45.

[14] K. of L., *GA Proc.*, 1885, pp. 84–87.

[15] Buchanan, *Story of a Labor Agitator*, p. 218.

Talmadge also concluded in failure. While the Board did nothing, the workers on the Gould line offered to leave their jobs, but only upon condition that the Union Pacific employees also be called out. Less than enthusiastic, the Board instead ordered all railroad employees to cease handling Wabash rolling stock. On August 26 a meeting between the Board and Gould finally took place in New York City. This led to another meeting between Powderly and Talmadge at which a settlement favoring the Order was negotiated. Gould's manager agreed that no members of the Knights should be discriminated against, that all employees locked out on June 16 and those who had quit in support of their fellow workers were to be "reinstated as fast as possible," and that no new men were to be hired until all old employees were back at their jobs.[16]

Thus, momentarily, the Knights of Labor stood victorious over one of the nation's most powerful financiers. But this was true because Gould had been caught unprepared when his employees on the Wabash rebelled and not because of the actions of the General Executive Board. The victorious strikers overlooked these facts, but they would have a decisive influence soon in other labor struggles.

In the months following the Wabash strike thousands of workingmen flocked to join the Order. This period, which historians call the "Great Upheaval," was one of frenzied activity. Never before had so many enlisted in the ranks of organized labor. By July 1, 1886, the Knights boasted a total membership exceeding 700,000, an increase of about 600,-000 in twelve months. Similarly, the trade unions were also undergoing a comparable expansion. Between 1885 and 1886, for example, the total membership of the United Brotherhood of Carpenters and Joiners rose from under 6,000 to over 21,000.[17] To many contemporary observers it

---

[16] K. of L., *GA Proc.*, 1885, pp. 87–91.

[17] *Ibid.*, 1886, p. 328; United Brotherhood of Carpenters and Joiners, *Proceedings*, 1900, p. 48. Ware and Perlman both agree that the major reason for the Knights' growth in 1885 and 1886 was its victory over Gould in the Wabash strike. See Ware, *Labor Movement*, p. 144, and Commons, *History of Labour*, II, 370. In a recent article, Donald L. Kemmerer and Edward D. Wickersham have taken issue with this interpretation. Kemmerer and Wickersham make much of the fact that there were few references to the Wabash strike either in the labor or the general press. They then advance the hypothesis that the great expansion of 1885–1886 was due to the impact of the eight-hour movement of 1884–1886, which had led many workers to join the Knights in the mistaken belief that it was leading the crusade. Kemmerer and Wickersham, "Reasons for the Growth of the Knights of Labor in 1885–1886," *Industrial and Labor Relations Review*, III (January, 1950), 213–20.

This interpretation, however valuable, also has certain shortcomings. To attribute ignorance to hundreds of thousands of workingmen is to assume too much. Certainly anyone who reads the labor press of these years cannot overlook the articulateness and high level of intelligence of the workers and their leaders. Kemmerer and Wickersham also neglect many intangible factors. No one can fail to be impressed, after a study of the contemporary sources, by the hyperemotionalism of the working class and the fantastic membership attributed to the Knights. Workingmen, following the depression years of the 1870's, were all too eager to improve their condition, and the feverish dec-

appeared as though the American labor movement had at last reached maturity, and henceforth would play a major role in economic and political development.

The leaders of the Knights, instead of being overjoyed at the rapid growth of their organization, became frightened and overawed by rapidly moving developments. In January, 1886, Powderly claimed that such growth was unhealthy. "It is mushroom," he continued, "too feverish to be good." [18] Neither Powderly nor the General Executive Board wanted to have striking workingmen in the Knights. "The Board should issue an order to not engage in any more strikes," Powderly suggested in March, "and if the order is disobeyed to recall the charter of the Assembly that disobeys." [19] That same month the Board ordered all organizing to cease for a period of forty days because too many newly-initiated members were embarking on strikes and boycotts.[20] Even after the lifting of this ban Powderly insisted that no striking workers be admitted to membership, for responsibility for the strikes would inevitably be attributed to the Knights.[21]

While Powderly and the General Executive Board did everything within their power to keep striking workingmen out of the Knights, they further revealed their hostility toward any militant labor action by their handling of the Southwest strike of 1886. Following his partial defeat of the previous year, Gould had begun preparations for a final showdown with the Knights. A walkout on the Texas Pacific, then in the hands of a receiver, took place on March 6, 1886, ostensibly because of the arbitrary dismissal of C. A. Hall, a member of the Order. Actually the workers had for some time expressed a growing discontent with the railroad's policies,[22] and, as Eugene Debs observed in a trip to the Southwest in April, 1886, "were struggling to improve their condition." [23] By March 10, 1886, the men on the Missouri Pacific, controlled by Gould, had also left their jobs. The leader of the strike was Martin Irons, chairman of the Executive Board of D.A. 101. Born in Scotland in 1833, Irons had migrated to the United States at the age of fourteen. Learning rapidly through observation and experience of the problems and needs of the working class, he took an active role in the labor movement. Although he later made a poor showing before a congressional committee investigating the strike, he was not necessarily unfitted, either by temperament

---

ade of the 1880's was a psychological reaction against the depression of a previous decade.

[18] Powderly to Dan F. Tomson, January 23, 1886. See also Powderly to Edward B. Irving, December 4, 1885, TVPLB.

[19] Powderly to Frederick Turner, March 25, 1886, TVPLB.

[20] *Journal of United Labor*, VI (March 10, 1886), 2019; K. of L., *GA Proc.*, 1886, pp. 80–81.

[21] Powderly to Michael Healy, December 1, 1886, TVPLB.

[22] *John Swinton's Paper*, March 14, 1886; K. of L., *GA Proc.*, 1886, pp. 81–82, 165, 170.

[23] *Locomotive Firemen's Magazine*, X (June, 1886), 331.

or experience, for the task of leading a strike of railroad workers against one of the nation's most prominent financiers.[24] Nevertheless, it is clear that his handling of the strike as well as his dealings with Powderly left something to be desired.

Following the discharge of Hall, the Executive Board of D.A. 101 sent telegrams to all locals under its jurisdiction asking for support. In response to the affirmative replies the Board ordered a walkout on March 6. Irons, however, began to suspect that the strike vote had been dishonest and called a meeting of the district Executive Board to consider this matter. The day before the scheduled meeting, Irons was forced at gunpoint to sign a statement to the effect that the strike ballot had been honest. Henceforth he was accompanied by an armed stranger for four days, with a warning not to reveal what he knew. After this time Irons probably felt that to make public his views would only undermine the strike, which by now was well under way, so he chose instead to remain silent while the strike continued.[25]

The decision to call the strike had been made without either the knowledge or consent of Powderly and the General Executive Board. Indeed, the national headquarters knew nothing of the walkout until after it had begun. Powderly, who had been blamed by a leading railroad official for the struggle, then asked for the reinstatement of Hall pending a full investigation, but to no avail. Meanwhile the governors of Missouri and Kansas, fearful of the paralyzing effects of a protracted conflict, attempted to get H. M. Hoxie, manager of the Gould system, to meet with a committee of the Knights. This effort also proved fruitless, since Hoxie was unalterably opposed to a meeting with any representatives of the Order, favoring only a meeting with actual employees.[26]

At this critical juncture, on March 13, 1886, Powderly decided to issue a secret circular to all members of the Knights. This quickly reached the hands of the newspapers and became public property. In this manifesto Powderly condemned strikes in any form.

> A stop must be called and the ship brought back to her moorings. It has always been, and is at the present time, my policy to advocate conciliation and arbitration in the settlements of disputes . . . Thousands of men who have become disgusted with the ruinous policy of the strike, as the only remedy for

[24] See Martin Irons, "My Experiences in the Labor Movement," *Lippincott's Magazine*, XXXVII (June, 1886), 618–27.

[25] This strange story was first told by Powderly in his autobiography, *The Path I Trod*, pp. 121–23. Ruth A. Allen, in her account of the affair, accepted Powderly's version as correct, although she did not have access to the Powderly manuscripts. E. T. Behrens, a close friend of Irons and also a participant in the strike, told Professor Allen substantially the same story, even though he knew comparatively little. Ruth A. Allen, *The Great Southwest Strike* (Austin, Texas, 1942), pp. 56–62. The Powderly letters fully authenticate one of the strangest affairs in the annals of American labor. See especially Powderly to Irons, March 25, 1886, TVPLB.

[26] K. of L., *GA Proc.*, 1886, pp. 81–82; Allen, *The Great Southwest Strike*, pp. 63–64.

ills we complain of were drawn to us because we proclaimed to mankind that we had discarded the strike until all else had failed. . . . No matter what advantage we gain by the strike, it is only medicating the symptoms; it does not penetrate the system, and therefore fails in effecting a cure. The only natural sequence is a relapse, and a relapse always means more medicine and a weaker patient than before. . . . You must submit to injustice at the hands of the employer in patience for a while longer. Bide well your time. Make no display of organization or strength until you have every man and woman in your department of industry organized, and then do not strike, but study, not only your own condition, but that of your employer. Find out how much you are justly entitled to, and the tribunal of arbitration will settle the rest.[27]

Powderly had expressed these sentiments many times in the past, but their repetition at this critical moment served only to place the head of the Knights in the anomalous position of publicly opposing a strike of which he was ostensibly the leader. The irony of the situation must have appealed to Gould and served only to stiffen his determination to break the power of the Knights on his railroad system.

At Iron's request, Powderly went to New York City in an effort to see Gould.[28] In a meeting on March 28 Gould adopted the position that as one of several directors he had no authority to intervene personally. He finally consented, however, to send Hoxie a telegram instructing him to give preference in rehiring to employees of the railroad, and not to discriminate against the Knights. "We see no objection," the crucial section of the message stated, "to arbitrate any differences between the employees and the company, past and future." [29] There is some circumstantial evidence that Gould sent Hoxie another message that was never made public.[30] Although Powderly had no legal power to end the strike—that authority was vested in the originating body—the Executive Board of D.A. 101 honored the settlement and ordered the workers to return to their jobs.[31]

The settlement was too vague to provide the basis for a lasting agreement. Ensuing events proved this fact, for after the strike had ended Hoxie issued a statement declaring that he was willing to meet a committee of employees "who are actually at work in the service of the company." [32] This was interpreted so as to exclude negotiators of the Knights

[27] Missouri Bureau of Labor Statistics and Inspection, *The Official History of the Great Strike of 1886 on the Southwestern Railway System* (Jefferson City, Missouri, 1887), pp. 70–71.

[28] Powderly to Irons, March 25, 1886, TVPLB.

[29] Missouri Bureau of Labor Statistics and Inspection, *Official History of the Great Strike*, p. 76; *Investigation of Labor Troubles in Missouri, Arkansas, Kansas, Texas, and Illinois*, 49th Congress, 2d Session, *House Report 4174* (Washington, D. C., 1887), Pt. I, p. 37. See also Powderly to Gould, April 11, 1886, TVPLB.

[30] *Investigation of Labor Troubles*, Pt. I, p. 22.

[31] *Ibid.*, pp. 40–41.

[32] Missouri Bureau of Labor Statistics and Inspection, *Official History of the Great Strike*, p. 78.

representing the workers. The Executive Boards of district assemblies 101, 93, and 17, after being informed by Hoxie that only 50 per cent of his former staff would be rehired and that only he would decide who would be taken back, had no choice but to order the strike to continue. Even before this occurred the Knights' General Executive Board had withdrawn its instructions ending the walkout.[33]

Throughout the entire affair Powderly insisted that the workers had erred in striking.[34] After Gould reneged on the agreement of March 28, Powderly refused to seek another conference.[35] On April 11, 1886, he asked Gould to force Hoxie to comply with the settlement. "I do not write this letter to you," Powderly remarked, "either in the spirit of anger or revenge, for you personally I have no dislike. I believe that if allowed to follow your own impulses in this matter you would have had the strike ended ere this . . . You have it in your power to make friends of these men by acting the part of the man, by taking this matter in your own hands. Will you do so and end this strife in the interest of humanity and our common country?" [36]

Powderly, however, soon became convinced that Gould did not desire an equitable settlement. "He is as untruthful as the devil," Powderly remarked, "and as full of tricks. He says in this mornings dispatches that I deceived him, well if that is true I will never go to hell for if I can deceive Gould then it will be an easy matter to get the best of the devil." [37] Powderly then issued an appeal to the Knights for financial assistance for the striking workers.[38] At the same time he wrote Litchman asking him to serve on a committee to investigate his contention that the strike was a rebellious move intended to defy the authority of the General Executive Board.[39] Finally, on May 3, the Board unconditionally called off the strike.

After the strike the Knights rapidly lost ground among the men of the Southwest,[40] many of whom resented what they considered to be a betrayal of their interests by the Order.[41] Powderly, however, always maintained that he had been thrust into an unfortunate situation not of his own making.[42] Failing to see that employers in the 1880's would rarely

[33] *Ibid.*, pp. 78–80, 87–88; *Investigation of Labor Troubles*, Pt. I, p. 27.
[34] Powderly to James Ward, April 8, 1886, TVPLB.
[35] Powderly to William O. McDowell, April 8, 1886. See also Powderly to McDowell, April 10, 11, 1886, TVPLB.
[36] Powderly to Jay Gould, April 11, 1886, TVPLB.
[37] Powderly to McDowell, April 13, 1886. See also Powderly to John W. Hayes, April 14, 1886, TVPLB.
[38] Powderly to Frederick Turner, April 12, 1886; Powderly "To the Order Wherever Found," April (?) 1886, TVPLB; Missouri Bureau of Labor Statistics and Inspection, *Official History of the Great Strike*, p. 101.
[39] Powderly to Litchman, April 17, 1886, TVPLB.
[40] See the *Journal of United Labor*, VII (November 10, 1886), 2200.
[41] See the New Haven *Workmen's Advocate*, March 5, 1887.
[42] K. of L., *GA Proc.*, 1886, p. 39.

concede anything to the workers voluntarily, Powderly had dealt with Gould on the apparent assumption that the financier would deal fairly with his employees without the compulsion of an effective strike.[43]

At the hearings before a congressional committee that investigated the strike, Powderly and the General Executive Board made a determined effort to blame Martin Irons for the entire debacle. For example, they accused Irons of placing barriers in the way of a settlement in April following Powderly's meeting with Gould. Such an indictment, however, was refuted by the fact that the General Executive Board had countermanded its return-to-work order even before the Executive Board of D.A. 101 did so. Litchman admitted to the General Assembly that it was a relatively simple matter to make Irons the scapegoat for the defeat.[44] Probably the purpose in placing the blame upon Irons' shoulder was to divorce the Knights from the implications of such a momentous setback. Powderly, who could have silenced all the malicious rumors concerning Irons, chose instead to maintain his silence. Perhaps he feared a potential competitor for his position as Master Workman. In any event, the entire affair reflected little credit upon the Order's leadership.[45]

A few months later, following quickly upon the heels of the disastrous defeat inflicted by Gould, came the strike in the Chicago stockyards. Its origins lay in the eight-hour movement of 1884–1886. On May 1, 1886, the stockyard workers had successfully struck for eight hours. During the following summer the packers attempted to reduce wages by offering their employees nine hours' pay instead of ten for an eight-hour day. When the workers refused to accept the cut, the employers reinstituted the ten-hour day. The General Assembly, then in session, decided to send T. B. Barry, a member of the General Executive Board, to Chicago with instructions not to involve the Knights.[46] This order was given in spite of the fact that three-quarters of the workers were members of the Knights.

Barry, upon his arrival in Chicago, concluded an agreement with two companies for a return to the eight-hour day and an end to the strike. At a later date the two companies would break away from the packers' organization and institute an eight-hour day with nine hours' pay. Barry consented to this settlement because he felt the workers were "fighting a losing fight." [47] The workers returned to their jobs but resumed the strike two weeks later. Barry immediately returned to Chicago. The General Executive Board then decided to send Albert A. Carlton to assist him, again with orders that he should not involve the Knights.[48]

[43] See Powderly to Gould, April 11, 1886, TVPLB; *Investigation of Labor Troubles*, Pt. I, p. 17.

[44] K. of L., *GA Proc.*, 1886, pp. 171–72.

[45] See Allen, *The Great Southwest Strike*, pp. 124–26.

[46] K. of L., *GA Proc.*, 1886, pp. 174–75; 1887, p. 1419.

[47] Barry to Powderly, October 19, 1886, Barry to Powderly and the General Executive Board, November 7, 1886, reprinted in K. of L., *GA Proc.*, 1887, pp. 1480–81.

[48] *Ibid.*, pp. 1420–21.

Before Carlton's arrival in Chicago, Powderly, in consultation with the General Executive Board, sent the following communication to Barry:

In a circular issued March 13, 1886, I stated the policy of the Knights of Labor on the eight-hour question. That circular was read to and approved by the General Executive Board before it went out. It was afterward approved by the entire Order. In opposition to that circular the men at stock yards struck for eight hours. The Order of Knights of Labor was not brought into controversy, hence no action was necessary during the session of the General Assembly. Men at stock yards struck again. You were sent to try and settle, but, in case of failure, the Order was not to be involved or asked for assistance. You settled by ordering the men back at the old hours. They have, in violation of law and your order, and without notifying us, again struck for eight hours. The Board instructs you and Carlton, who will be with you to-day, to settle by putting the men back at the old hours until the Order of Knights of Labor takes definite action on the eight-hour plan. If the men refuse, take their charters. We must have obedience and discipline.[49]

This dispatch, immediately becoming public property, strengthened the determination of the packers not to concede. While Powderly was uninformed of Barry's previous agreement, the time was not propitious for such instructions. Barry and Carlton immediately informed Powderly of their opposition to his orders, but by now it was too late to affect the outcome.[50] "I felt then that the issuing of the Order at that particular moment was an error," Carlton reported, "and had the effect of creating just what it probably was intended to prevent, viz., a crisis. Two or three days, at the outside, would have ended the whole affair one way or the other." [51] As a consequence, the embittered workers blamed Powderly for their defeat,[52] and the Knights immediately entered a period of decline in Chicago.

Powderly so resented what he regarded as the unjustified attacks upon his actions during the Southwest and stockyards strikes that he decided not to interfere in any way during the walkout on the Reading Railroad system in the winter of 1887–1888. After writing a conciliatory letter to the president of the railroad, Powderly changed his mind and refrained from sending it.[53] "From the information at hand and from the experience of the past," he wrote in explanation, "I am led to the opinion that my interference will do no good and inasmuch as I have been blamed for the failure of the Southwest strike, the Stock yards strike and other strikes in which I was forced to interfere after they had been started without any

[49] *Ibid.*, p. 1421.
[50] *Ibid.*, p. 1482.
[51] *Ibid.*, p. 1422.
[52] See the resolution adopted by L.A. 1597 of Chicago attacking Powderly's interference. *Ibid.*, pp. 1484–85.
[53] Powderly to Austin Corbin, January 12, 1888 (letter never sent), TVPLB.

advice from me, I feel that I am justified in doing as the men requested in 'keeping hands off' and giving them a show." [54]

Powderly's hostility toward strikes was frequently the determining factor in his official acts and attitude as leader of the Knights. At times there appeared to be no limits to which he would not go to prevent men from leaving their jobs in disputes with employers. For example, before the strike on the New York Central Railroad in 1890 he first counseled caution. Later he warned against a strike under any circumstances and even advised workers to quit their positions to demonstrate to the railroad that efficient employees could not be retained for low wages. Finally he suggested that the men migrate to the West.[55] Such advice was based on the assumption that workers shared his reform labor ideology, which in many cases they did not. "It is not necessary to tell you," the leader of the Knights on the New York Central wrote to Powderly, "that accessions to our ranks are recruited from the ranks of dissatisfied, poorly-paid men, who come into the Order for the sole purpose of bettering their condition financially, for you know that success is the god that they worship." [56] Powderly, however, paid scant attention to the growing demand by workers for a higher standard of living. He did not understand what the trade unions of the 1880's were beginning to realize, namely, that often only the potential or actual use of coercion would compel employers to negotiate with their employees.

In addition to the nation-wide strikes involving members of the Knights, there were also hundreds of smaller and less-publicized walkouts on the local and district level.[57] Yet workingmen paid scant attention to the small victories or defeats. Instead, they pointed to the national strikes as evidence of the duplicity of Powderly and the General Executive Board. A committee of the American Federation of Labor (A.F. of L.) charged in 1887 that "the great strikes which have taken place within the past few years in connection with the Knights of Labor have made the members of that body discontented with the management of their affairs, as it has been customary to allow strikes involving tens of thousands of men to take place, and after their local funds were exhausted, order them back

[54] Powderly to John W. Hayes, January 13, 1888. See also Powderly to Hayes, February 7, 1888; Powderly to Litchman, February 13, 1888, TVPLB. In his autobiography Powderly stated that during the strike he had been ill and had known absolutely nothing about the walkout. Powderly, *The Path I Trod*, p. 165. His personal papers, however, contradict this statement.

[55] Powderly to Edward J. Lee, February 3, April 17, August 2, 1890, in K. of L., *GA Proc.*, 1890, *Report of the General Master Workman*, pp. 5–9.

[56] Edward J. Lee to Powderly, February 10, 1890, *ibid.*, p. 6.

[57] I have not attempted to recount a complete history of all strikes undertaken under the auspices of the Knights. Such a topic would itself require a single volume. Instead I have chosen those strikes having a decisive influence upon the attitude of the rank and file toward the national organization.

to work at the employer's terms." [58] Following the Southwest and stockyards defeats in 1886, a vast exodus commenced from the Knights. The membership of the Order, which had stood at a peak of 700,000 in 1886, dropped to 511,351 by the following year, and by 1888 had plummeted to 259,518.[59] The trade unions, which had become involved in an intense struggle with the Order after 1885, encouraged workers to leave the Knights and join or establish unions of their own trade.

Numerous factors were responsible for the unsuccessful strike policy of the Knights. In the first place, the hostile attitude of Powderly and the General Executive Board, conditioned by a hope of abolishing the wage system and reforming society, often made it difficult for workers to embark on a strike united in their determination to achieve victory. The national leaders of the Order often acted in such a manner as to stiffen employer resistance while at the same time weakening labor's hand. Secondly, the structure of the Knights was not conducive to the conduct of strikes. With the exception of the national trade assemblies, the large majority of local and district assemblies were organized along geographical lines. In a market that was becoming increasingly national in its orientation, geographical units found it difficult to function efficiently. In addition, mixed and regional assemblies did not and could not possess the organization and discipline characteristic of many of the successful unions, and their heterogeneous character often resulted in strikes led by men who had little or no knowledge of existing trade conditions. Consequently, strikes by mixed assemblies rarely achieved any degree of success. Finally, the failure to provide sufficient funds for a strike reserve made it difficult, if not impossible, to maintain a united front for any protracted length of time.[60]

III

On a second major issue of the 1880's—the eight-hour day—the leaders of the Knights executed policies that served again to thwart a basic objective of the rank and file and thereby widened the gulf between themselves and the trade unionists both within and without the Knights. The hope of the eight-hour day, first stimulated by Ira Steward and the National Labor Union during the 1860's, was one of the most powerful

[58] A.F. of L., *Proceedings*, 1887, p. 26. All citations from the *Proceedings* of the A.F. of L. are from the 1905–1906 reprinting of the originals. The reprints differ only in pagination and not in content.

[59] K. of L., *GA Proc.*, 1887, p. 1850; 1888, *Report of the General Secretary*, p. 2.

[60] Perlman claims that the large proportion of hitherto unorganized and unskilled workers in the Knights—"an element which had no previous experience in the management of strikes and could easily be replaced by strike-breakers"—was a prime factor in the failure of many strikes. Commons, *History of Labour*, II, 349. As we will see later, however, Perlman greatly exaggerates the strength of the unskilled in the Knights.

forces behind the success of the labor movement's organizational campaigns in the 1880's. Labor leaders, recognizing the wide appeal that a
reduction of hours held for the overwhelming majority of workingmen,
sought to turn its popularity to good use and thereby to induce laborers
to join the ranks of organized labor. "Eight hours," wrote Gompers, "is
the cry which can unite all forces at least for the present and will check
the indifference and want of confidence too prevalent to-day." [61] Consequently, all labor organizations in the 1880's included an eight-hour
plank in their platforms.

Bowing to the inevitable, the Knights early in its history proposed that
eight hours should constitute a normal working day.[62] Nothing further
came of this proposal because of the failure of the General Assembly to
provide a definite plan for its implementation. In 1881 a delegate introduced another resolution at the General Assembly suggesting that the first
Monday in September, 1882, be set aside as the day on which all workingmen would make a concerted demand for eight hours. The delegates
present, however, refused to sanction its passage on the grounds that the
only result would be a demonstration of the weakness of the Knights. In
1884 the Constitution of the Order was amended to include the following
objective: "To shorten the hours of labor by a general refusal to work for
more than eight hours." But again no means of implementing this plank
was provided.[63]

Meanwhile, in 1884 the Federation of Organized Trades and Labor
Unions of the United States and Canada, predecessor of the A.F. of L.,
adopted a resolution stating that "eight hours shall constitute a legal day's
labor from and after May 1, 1886." Labor organizations were left free to
choose the methods they would use in winning the goal.[64] The following
two years saw feverish preparations for the great campaign. Unwittingly,
perhaps, the Federation had seized upon an issue that best coincided with
the aspirations of American workers. Eight hours was a slogan that had
a widespread appeal, and one that seemed possible of achievement within
a relatively short span of time. An important result of the ensuing agitation was a vast increase in the membership of trade unions, as craft leaders quickly took advantage of the popularity of the movement.

When May 1, 1886, arrived, thousands of workingmen throughout the
nation participated in what by that time had become a short-hour rather
than an eight-hour movement. *Bradstreet's* estimated that perhaps 340,000
workers, most of them members of trade unions, took part in the day's

[61] Gompers to John S. Kirchner, February 28, 1889, Samuel Gompers Letter Books,
A.F. of L.—C.I.O. Building, Washington, D. C. (hereinafter cited as SGLB).

[62] K. of L., *GA Proc.*, January, 1879, p. 74.

[63] *Ibid.*, 1881, pp. 269, 309; 1884, p. 769.

[64] Federation of Organized Trades and Labor Unions of the United States and Canada, *Proceedings*, 1884, p. 14. All citations are from the 1905 reprinting of these *Proceedings*, which differ from the original only in pagination.

demonstration. Of this number 42,000 were successful in their attempt to shorten the working day. An additional 150,000 reduced their working hours without striking.[65] The victories won, however, soon proved ephemeral, as few workers long retained the fruits of their endeavors.

While the trade unions and the Knights of Labor both supported the eight-hour day, there was a wide gulf between the two over appropriate means of winning the goal. Unions, if necessary, stood ready to strike for shorter hours. The leaders of the Knights, on the other hand, violently opposed such a policy. Powderly, although advocating eight hours in theory, claimed that the abolition of the wage system would automatically resolve the question. He felt that workers were ignorant of the significance of the movement, and emphasized that eight hours was more a political than an economic problem.[66]

In making preparations for the demonstrations on May 1, 1886, the Federation of Organized Trades and Labor Unions had asked the Knights for help. Gabriel Edmonston, secretary of the Federation, wrote to the secretary of the Knights asking for support, but received no answer.[67] At the General Assembly of the Knights in 1885, however, a resolution was introduced advocating compliance with the Federation's request. But the Assembly refused to take any action and instead referred both the request and the resolution to the General Executive Board.[68] Powderly informed the convention that no support should be given to the movement. "The date fixed is not a suitable one," he gave as his reason, and "the plan suggested to establish the system is not the proper one." [69]

During the succeeding months Powderly continued to reiterate his opposition to the means adopted by those active in the eight-hour movement.[70] In a secret circular of March 13, 1886, he ordered all assemblies to refrain from striking for eight hours. "Let us learn why our hours of labor should be reduced," continued Powderly, "then teach others." [71] Even after May 1, 1886, had passed, he persisted in expressing his opposition. At the special session of the General Assembly a month later he supported the plan of a Chicago manufacturer, Edwin Norton, for a gradual reduction of hours to be achieved through a series of mutual agreements between employer and employee.[72] At the regular meeting of

[65] *Bradstreet's*, May 15, 1886, cited in Commons, *History of Labour*, II, 384.

[66] K. of L., *GA Proc.*, 1885, p. 15.

[67] Gabriel Edmonston to Frederick Turner, June 8, July 26, 1885, SGLB; Federation of Organized Trades and Labor Unions of the United States and Canada, *Proceedings*, 1884, p. 17; 1885, p. 9.

[68] K. of L., *GA Proc.*, 1885, pp. 125, 128, 135.

[69] *Ibid.*, 1885, p. 15. See also Powderly's article, "The Army of the Discontented," *North American Review*, CXL (April, 1885), 369–77.

[70] Powderly to John Franey, December 4, 1885, TVPLB.

[71] Missouri Bureau of Labor Statistics and Inspection, *Official History of the Great Strike*, pp. 72–73.

[72] K. of L., *GA Proc.*, 1886 special session, pp. 5–11; Powderly, *Thirty Years of Labor*, p. 505.

the General Assembly in the autumn of 1886 Powderly told the delegates that his course toward the eight-hour movement had been correct, and the convention endorsed his actions.[73]

Despite the General Assembly's approval, Powderly's policy stirred the wrath of many trade unionists both within and outside the Knights. Thousands of workingmen, to whom the eight-hour movement had become almost a religious crusade, bitterly condemned the leaders of the Order. The legislative committee of the Federation of Organized Trades and Labor Unions, for example, while conceding that the opposition of employers was perhaps the major obstacle to the success of the movement, also laid part of the blame at the door of the Knights. "The Trades Unions," the committee reported, "as a rule, responded most zealously to the appeals of this Federation, and had their efforts been met with that co-operation by the Knights of Labor . . . there would have been no room for reproach, and the loss is therefore chargeable to the expressions of hostility coming from leading members of the Knights of Labor." [74] In the end the actions of Powderly and his associates had served only to widen the gulf between themselves and the rank and file.

The appeal that eight hours held for workingmen was not forgotten by the trade union leaders, and in 1888 the A.F. of L. decided to embark on another eight-hour crusade and fixed May 1, 1890, as the date to inaugurate the eight-hour day. The realization that a general movement would probably conclude in failure led to the decision by the A.F. of L. the following year that better results could be achieved by concentrating on a few trades having at least a fair chance of success.[75]

Gompers again asked the Knights to co-operate with the Federation, and he met with Powderly and other officials in August and October, 1889, in the hope of concluding a working agreement between the two organizations. At the conference Gompers agreed to furnish the General Assembly with a written statement of his views, but the letter he sent was vague as to proposed means of implementation.[76]

Meanwhile, at the General Assembly of the Knights in 1889, Powderly again came out in support of Norton's plan for the reduction of hours, expressing the hope that a "gradual" plan of action would be adopted, so as "not to disarrange business, or in any way work hardship to either side in the controversy." [77] Similarly, the Committee on the State of the Order found nothing in Gompers' communication "in the nature of a proposi-

---

[73] K. of L., *GA Proc.*, 1886, pp. 39, 273, 278. See also Powderly to (?) Bennet, July 27, 1886, TVPLB.

[74] Federation of Organized Trades and Labor Unions of the United States and Canada, *Proceedings*, 1886, p. 6. See also Gompers to N. E. Mathewson, October 10, 1890, SGLB.

[75] A.F. of L., *Proceedings*, 1888, pp. 24–26; 1889, pp. 29–30.

[76] K. of L., *GA Proc.*, 1889, *Report of the General Executive Board*, pp. 35–36; Gompers to the General Assembly of the Knights of Labor, November 9, 1889, SGLB.

[77] K. of L., *GA Proc.*, 1889, *Report of the General Master Workman*, p. 8.

tion or plan upon which we might legislate, or in which we might be expected to co-operate with the Federation," and instead recommended a version of the Norton plan.[78] Powderly, therefore, introduced a vague resolution stating that the Knights agreed with Gompers on the undesirability of a general strike for eight hours on May 1, 1890, and promising to give "moral support" to those trades pressing for shorter hours.[79]

Actually, however, the Knights gave no assistance to the organizations active in the struggle for a reduced working day. The *Journal of United Labor* expressed its hostility to the Federation through its support of the Norton plan. "Let the agitation go steadily on," it declared. "The light is spreading; and if the spring of 1890 finds the people prepared to receive the eight-hour day without seriously upsetting the business of the country, we shall exclaim 'Amen.' But we fear the stride is too long a one to be taken at once. We have no desire to see re-enacted the scenes of 1886. Lasting reforms are never secured in a hurry." [80] Privately Powderly lambasted the leaders of the Federation. "Shout 8 hours until April 30, 1890 and whisper it on May 1st. 1890," he wrote to Hayes. "Boycott the Base Ball League and save labor. Thus run the declarations of the Federation now. Great is the intellect of McGompers, powerful is (the smell) of McFoster. We are saved and the country will prosper henceforth and forever more Amen." [81]

Powderly's views on the establishment of the eight-hour day were perhaps best expressed in a letter to an employer in December, 1889:

> We do not believe in disrupting business by sudden changes, do not believe in forcing one manufacturer, or employer, to reduce the hours of labor while his competitors are working long hours. Do not believe that when the hours of labor are reduced to eight that the wages should continue at the ten hour rate, for we are satisfied that the regulations of business will gradually raise the wages. If the system of gradually reducing the hours of labor were mutually agreed upon by your association and ours, and a compact entered into of a character that would guarantee that both sides would live up to the terms of the agreement, I feel certain that in three or four years the eight hour workday would be working to the complete satisfaction of employer and employed, and no such thing as an untimely or foolish strike would throw the workman and employer into a wrangle that would mean loss of business and money to both.[82]

Basically Powderly was hostile to the Federation's plan because of his ideological antipathy toward strikes. He and other reformers in the Knights felt that the short-hour slogan was treating the symptom rather

[78] K. of L., *GA Proc.*, 1889, p. 51.

[79] *Ibid.*, p. 52.

[80] *Journal of United Labor*, IX (May 9, 1889) , 2834.

[81] Powderly to Hayes, December 16, 1889. See also Powderly to Hayes, December 15, 1889; Powderly to A. R. Lake, December 21, 1889, TVPLB.

[82] Powderly to M. J. Byrne, December 21, 1889, TVPLB.

than the disease. Although favoring eight hours—at least in theory—Powderly's opposition to concrete means made him in effect an opponent of the movement. Instead, he relied on a vague belief that education and the abolition of the wage system would ultimately result in a reduction of hours.[83]

The unwillingness of the leaders of the Knights of Labor to provide effective support for the eight-hour movements of 1886 and 1890 led the trade unions to condemn them in bitter terms. Gompers regarded Powderly's resolution of 1889 as a meaningless platitude.[84] "I would add that it is ambiguous," Gompers wrote to an English labor leader concerning the attitude of the Knights toward the movement. "They have it as one of the demands in their platform yet never take action to secure it and have really antagonized our movement." [85] Similarly, the convention of the A.F. of L. accused the Knights of "insincerity." [86]

Aside from antagonizing the trade unions, the leaders of the Knights also succeeded in further widening the gulf between themselves and their constituents by opposing the eight-hour movements. Their promises of a new and more humane society, which had stimulated thousands of workingmen to join the Knights between 1883 and 1886, now appeared void of substance. By ignoring and even opposing their constituents' insistence upon immediate benefits, the leaders of the Knights had destroyed the strongest centripetal force sustaining their organization. The chasm between leaders and members widened imperceptibly at first, then with ever-increasing speed. When the process was completed the trade unions had displaced the Knights as the dominant force in the labor movement.

Yet before being toppled from its pinnacle of importance, the Knights of Labor attempted to revive its sinking fortunes by uniting workingmen and farmers behind a common program. The failure of co-operation and the persistence of strikes led the leaders of the Order to seek new and different methods of abolishing the wage system and reforming society. Ultimately they conceived the idea of uniting the producing classes—the workers and the farmers—into an irresistible coalition that would regain all that the monopolists and nonproducers had stolen. Consequently, the history of the Knights of Labor following 1886 was to be quite different from its previous history.

[83] See *John Swinton's Paper*, December 27, 1885; Powderly, "The ˙ ˙ for Eight Hours," *North American Review*, CL (April, 1890) , 464–69; Powderly to ˙ ᴵ. M. Cullen, May 21, 1888; Powderly to Tom O'Reilly, December 19, 1889; Powderly to J. T. Lavery, July 15, 1890, TVPLB; *The People*, April 17, 1892.

[84] Gompers to N. E. Mathewson, October 10, 1890, SGLB.

[85] Gompers to Tom Mann, September 2, 1891, SGLB.

[86] A.F. of L., *Proceedings*, 1889, p. 30. P. J. McGuire, head of the Carpenters Union, felt that the Knights should have kept quiet rather than expressing hostility toward the eight-hour movement. *The Carpenter*, X (August 23, 1890) , 3.

CHAPTER FIVE

Reform Labor Unionism
and Politics

I

 THE TRADITION of labor participation in politics in the United States has long been an underlying *motif* in the history of the working class. The relatively early adoption of universal manhood suffrage made it natural for labor to regard political action with a favored eye, especially because more direct weapons like the strike did not produce many notable victories. In the ante-bellum period the right of government —state and national—to regulate the economy was accepted by many. The limitations placed by the Manchester School of liberals upon governmental intervention in economic life during the nineteenth century had never been fully accepted by even its most ardent advocates. Even after the Civil War, when laissez faire became the dominant keynote in economic theory, there were many who dissented from the majority view.[1] With government playing an important role in economic affairs, labor continued its efforts to influence policy through political activity.

Most native-American labor leaders, therefore, had grown to maturity at a time when powerful and active government, especially on the state level, was the rule rather than the exception, and the tradition of strong government left a visible imprint upon their labor philosophy. This was as true for the leaders of the 1860's, like Sylvis, as for later ones, like Powderly and Litchman. The ballot, then, came to be accepted   a legitimate means of securing favorable legislation.

More often than not, however, attempts to forge a working class united in politics concluded in failure. An important cause for this failure was the fact that many workers refused to accept the permanency of their wage status and instead identified themselves with the middle class and its periodic antimonopoly campaigns. Thus it happened that the labor movement of the 1880's was afflicted with a peculiar duality of character. Traditionally the workers had regarded themselves as the producers and

---

[1] Sidney Fine, *Laissez Faire and the General-Welfare State: A Study of Conflict in American Thought 1865–1901* (Ann Arbor, Michigan, 1956) , pp. 18–23, 29–31, *et passim.*

the only legitimate group in society. The rapid advance of industrial society, however, had reduced them to a position of dependence upon the owners of the means of production. Yet their thinking was still predicated upon the assumption that their independent position could somehow be restored, and hence they refused to accept the permanency of the capitalistic system. At the same time, they struggled for increased benefits within the framework of capitalistic society, thus implicitly acknowledging the permanency of their wage status. This duality made unanimity on specific issues difficult to achieve, especially since the workers persisted in retaining a middle-class viewpoint. While all labor leaders might agree upon the necessity of political action, they could not come to terms on aims and objectives.

There were also other forces responsible for the ineffectiveness of labor political action. For one thing, there was the impelling force of party loyalty, which played an important role because of the absence of an authentic class consciousness. For another, the rising tide of immigration placed additional barriers in the way of successful political action. Many immigrants, because of their nonpolitical background, were unable to participate in politics independent of the major parties, while intellectuals migrating to the United States rarely understood American traditions and had an outlook derived from experiences in feudal and stratified societies. In the third place, since the industrial working class alone never constituted a majority of the population, it had to seek alliances with other groups, especially the farmers. But differing economic interests often made a farmer-labor coalition a relatively ephemeral one. Fourthly, the grandiose plans of labor reformers frightened many nonworkers who were willing to support legislative reforms on behalf of the working class but who were decidedly unwilling to endorse programs looking toward the abolition of private property. Finally, a relative scarcity of labor and a rapidly expanding economy provided the workers with opportunity for advancement. The favorable economic environment acted, at least in part, as a safety valve.

All of these factors contributed to labor's inability to participate successfully in politics between 1828 and 1873. Yet the negative experiences of these years merely gave added force to labor's determination to use the machinery of government to serve its ends. Thus the Knights of Labor, like its predecessors, also found it necessary to take into account the political aspirations of its constituents, a task that was complicated by a lack of agreement on basic ideals and objectives. Despite the paradoxes and pitfalls involved in labor political action, the leaders of the Order never claimed that their organization had no political interests or goals. Because of their reform ideology and lack of a mature sense of class consciousness, however, they looked upon political action as a means of implementing their hope of abolishing the wage system and thereby restoring the small individual producer to a dominant position.

II

With the revival of the labor movement after the depression of the 1870's had run its course, workers once again turned to the political arena. The Knights was not excluded, and after its organization on a national level in 1878, the advocates of political action gained in strength, for this was the time during which the agitation that culminated in the formation of the National Greenback-Labor party in February, 1878, was at its height. Rising to importance after the panic of 1873, the Greenback movement involved not merely western agrarian inflationist agitation, but also urban working-class elements who looked upon monetary reform as a means of retarding industrial capitalism and introducing a co-operative society based on small productive units. It was not surprising, therefore, that many labor leaders who had grown to maturity during the equal-rights and antimonopoly ferment of the ante-bellum period should have looked with sympathy upon the movement. By 1878 many of them were participating in politics under the aegis of the Greenback-Labor party, and Ralph Beaumont and Uriah S. Stephens represented the Knights of Labor at the National Greenback-Labor convention in February, 1878.

Despite such promising beginnings, the connection between the Knights and the Greenbackers never grew into an effective working alliance. Indeed, the Knights never even formally affiliated with the Greenback-Labor party. The failure to do so was largely a result of the disillusioning political experiences of the leaders of the Order. Men like Stephens, Powderly, Litchman, and others, had entered the political arena in the middle and late 1870's, but had achieved few results either for themselves or their constituents. Stephens, to cite one instance, received the Greenback nomination for Congress in Philadelphia in 1878 but failed to be elected in the ensuing campaign. After the election he announced that the Knights was not a political organization. "At the same time," he remarked, "I should hope as all the evils that labor rests under are matters of law and to be removed by legislation our members would govern themselves accordingly." [2] Therefore the Knights, Stephens concluded, "ought to be the teacher of political economy in its true sense, and thus give birth to political parties and issues." [3]

While Stephens was partly responsible for the failure of the Knights to affiliate with the Greenback-Labor party, Powderly was instrumental in laying the foundation for the future political policy of the Order. As General Master Workman for more than fifteen years, he exerted great influence over the formulation and adoption of policy. Between 1878 and

[2] Stephens to Joseph Cowell, November 25, 1878, TVPLB.

[3] Stephens to Richard Griffiths, November 15, 1878, reprinted in the *Journal of the Knights of Labor*, XI (February 12, 1891), 2.

1882 Powderly was active in Pennsylvania politics under the banner of the Greenback-Labor party, being elected mayor of Scranton three times. Yet his commitment was not without reservations. Cognizant of the dangers of introducing partisan politics into labor organizations, he maintained that no man could be forced to vote for a particular candidate or party, for the objective of the Knights was to educate both men and parties. At the same time, he recommended support of candidates who were members of the Order.[4]

The official position of the General Assembly, the highest governing body of the Knights, reflected the cautious approach of the national leadership. In 1879, for example, the Assembly approved a resolution authorizing local assemblies to take political action that would enhance the interests of the membership. But only a few months later it imposed certain limitations on political activities in order to minimize the danger of internal dissension. Assemblies were permitted to enter politics and endorse that party willing to support its demands. But the matter could be taken under consideration only when the regular meeting had been formally closed. Moreover, assemblies could engage in politics only if three-quarters of the members present approved; even then, no members could be compelled to vote as the majority dictated.[5]

In the years following 1880, however, the attitude of the Knights toward politics began to change, and the close but unofficial relationship with the Greenback-Labor party was dissolved. This transformation was largely a result of the actions of the Greenback-Labor movement in Pennsylvania and their disenchanting impact upon Powderly and other leaders, and not because of any fundamental doctrinal differences. Throughout his career in the labor movement Powderly evinced interest in political office and often attempted to use his position to further personal ambition. His refusal to accept the nomination for the post of Secretary of Internal Affairs of Pennsylvania in 1882 merely reflected his belief in the insignificance of the office.[6] Powderly's reluctance to participate in politics at this time grew out of his conviction that the Greenback-Labor party had cheated him out of a seat in Congress.[7] With Powderly and other leaders so disillusioned, it was natural that the policy of the Knights should undergo a change. Consequently, all attempts to force the General Assembly to adopt a more vigorous political policy were defeated.[8]

[4] K. of L., *GA Proc.*, 1880, p. 258; McNeill, *Labor Movement*, pp. 417–18.

[5] K. of L., *GA Proc.*, January, 1879, pp. 57, 67; September, 1879, pp. 120, 130.

[6] See the *Journal of United Labor*, III (June, 1882), 241–42.

[7] Powderly to Joseph Labadie, November 13, 1882, TVPLB; Edward T. James, "American Labor and Political Action, 1865–1896: The Knights of Labor and Its Predecessors," unpublished Ph.D. dissertation, Harvard University, Cambridge, Massachusetts, 1954, pp. 189, 199–200.

[8] K. of L., *GA Proc.*, 1880, pp. 192, 194, 229, 232; 1881, pp. 287, 295, 307, 309; 1883, pp. 445, 508.

Between 1882 and 1885 the complexities of expansion and the persistence of strikes overshadowed the Order's political activities. Its leaders found themselves immersed in administrative details and problems arising from rapid growth. The rank and file, however, was still working through normal party channels and electing members to legislative bodies, especially on the local and state levels. Throughout the more populous urban areas of the industrial Northeast, labor attempted to use its influence and insure the election of candidates favorable to its interests.[9] Often labor worked through one of the major parties; in other cases it put forth its own candidates.[10] In isolated cases, working-class political activity was highly successful. In Massachusetts, for example, one Knight was elected to the House of Representatives in Washington, D. C., several more were sent to the state legislature, and the mayors of Lynn and Lawrence were Knights.[11] Similar situations existed in other areas. In 1884 the Order claimed nineteen representatives and senators in the Michigan legislature, five of whom came from Detroit.[12]

Despite these relatively minor and isolated victories, the political activities of local and district assemblies were not notably successful. Purely labor candidates could rarely attract a significant percentage of the vote, and when individual members were elected with major party support, it was often more a victory for the party than the Knights. In New York City in 1883, for example, labor elected two out of eight assemblymen, and even these two victories were achieved only with major party backing. Similarly, in a Philadelphia local election in 1885, fourteen Knights were presented as candidates as magistrates, but the ticket received the support of only five hundred workingmen.[13] It was becoming evident that discussions concerning fair and and equitable laws was one thing; to elect men favorably disposed toward their passage was another. "How many wage-workers were elected to congress or State legislatures?," complained a leading trade union journal. "In the large cities *nobody else* ought to have been elected. Labor can stand by its trade unions, but when it comes into a political fight it throws away its arms and surrenders to the fiction of a 'party.' It is our parties that divide us, and gives us to the common enemy. There seems to be no hope through political action." [14]

In legislature after legislature labor found its voice unheeded, its bills defeated or else pigeon-holed in committee. "It is the hardest of all jobs," reported John Swinton, "to get through any of our State Legislatures even

[9] See, for example, *John Swinton's Paper*, October 21, November 4, 1883.
[10] *Ibid.*, November 11, 1883.
[11] *Journal of United Labor*, III (December, 1882) , 369.
[12] *Iron Molders' Journal*, XX (November 30, 1884) , 13. For further evidence of local political activity by labor in Michigan see the Michigan Bureau of Labor and Industrial Statistics, *Annual Report*, I (1884) , 71; *John Swinton's Paper*, April 6, 1884; *Journal of United Labor*, VI (May 10, 1885) , 982.
[13] *John Swinton's Paper*, November 11, 1883, March 1, 1885.
[14] *The Carpenter*, III (April, 1883) , 3.

the pettiest bill to lighten the shackles of labor." [15] In the legislatures of
Maine, Pennsylvania, Rhode Island, Connecticut, Missouri, and Michigan, bills regulating the hours of women and children were either defeated or pigeon-holed in committee.[16] At every turn the working class
found its political efforts frustrated and its voice ignored.

III

The unparalleled growth of the Knights of Labor in the 1880's, however,
soon placed an important and perhaps more effective technique in the
hands of its leaders—to use the potential political strength of a numerically powerful organization as a lever with which to compel the passage
of favorable legislation. The enactment of the first Chinese Exclusion Act
in 1882, in which the Knights had taken a prominent though not a decisive hand, stimulated the belief that labor's interests could be served best
through a process of bargaining with the established political parties.

The first real lobbying effort by the Knights came in 1884 over a bill to
prohibit legally the importation of contract labor. During the previous
year the window glass manufacturers had begun to import foreign workmen in an attempt to break the power of Window Glass Workers L.A.
300, the most highly-developed national trade assembly within the Order.
This organization, in turn, decided to lobby for congressional action to
halt what it regarded as a dangerous practice, and one of its members
prepared a bill that would supposedly meet the exigencies of the situation.
The General Assembly of the Knights and many trade unions lent their
support to the proposed legislation.[17]

A bill making illegal the importation of contract labor was introduced
into the House of Representatives in January, 1884, by Martin A. Foran,
former president of the Coopers International Union. At the hearings before the House Committee on Labor, Powderly, Turner, and Barry
argued for its passage. In addition, Turner presented a petition bearing
35,000 signatures, and both L.A. 300 and various miners' organizations
sent representatives. Further support came from the trade unions.[18] Several public meetings called by the Knights to urge passage of the bill were
held in various parts of the country, and Powderly issued a circular
designed to stimulate workingmen to bring to bear their influence on the
national legislature.[19] Congress, however, adjourned while the bill was still
pending in the Senate, the House having approved its passage.

[15] *John Swinton's Paper*, April 26, 1885.
[16] *Ibid.*
[17] Amalgamated Association of Iron and Steel Workers, *Proceedings*, 1884, p. 1390;
K. of L., *GA Proc.*, 1884, pp. 623–24, 726, 787; Powderly, *Thirty Years of Labor*, pp. 442–
43.
[18] House Committee on Labor, 48th Congress, 1st Session, *House Report 444* (Washington, D. C., 1884), pp. 8–12.
[19] *John Swinton's Paper*, January 13, April 6, 1884.

During the remainder of the year the Knights continued to agitate for congressional action. When Congress reconvened, Powderly wrote the President of the Senate in an attempt to force action.[20] The bill was finally reported out of committee and became law in February, 1885. Its passage, however, cannot be attributed to the lobbying activities of the Knights, for the bill received support from other labor organizations, as well as protectionists, merchants, manufacturers, and state boards of charity. Furthermore, the spokesmen for American industry were not opposed to the legislation because industry was not deeply involved in importing European labor, and also because it wanted to retain labor support for a high tariff. Finally, both major political parties had condemned contract labor in their election platforms in 1884, a concession that hurt no important business interest.[21]

Although the Order had in reality done little to influence the bill's passage, victory in this lobbying effort caused it to examine more closely the possibilities inherent in pressure-group tactics. Following the success of the contract labor law, Powderly suggested that the Knights establish lobbies in all state capitals and in Washington, but the General Assembly did not adopt his proposal.[22] The following spring, however, the Assembly authorized the creation of a special three-member National Legislative Committee to visit Congress and attempt to influence legislation, especially those measures dealing with land reform.[23]

On June 11, 1886, Ralph Beaumont arrived in Washington to take his place as chairman of the National Legislative Committee of the Knights of Labor. But the high hopes of the Committee members were quickly and rudely shattered. The failure of the Southwest strike, the public statements by Jay Gould claiming that the backbone of the Knights had been broken, and press reports of internal dissension, all had given rise to rumors that the organization would disintegrate before the fall elections. Thus from the beginning the Committee found itself operating under a severe handicap. To counteract these unfavorable impressions, it decided to flood Congress with a succession of petitions, some of them containing more than 300,000 signatures. The Committee, on the whole, directed its major energies toward securing congressional approval of a series of land reform measures, an objective quite consistent with the reform ideology of the Knights.[24]

While continuing his lobbying activities in Washington, Beaumont began at the same time a campaign to influence the congressional elections of 1886. The establishment of a congressional labor bloc, in his opinion,

[20] Powderly to George Edmunds, January 14, 1885, TVPLB.
[21] Charlotte Erickson, *American Industry and the European Immigrant 1860–1885* (Cambridge, Massachusetts, 1957), pp. 158–65.
[22] K. of L., *GA Proc.*, 1885, pp. 15–16, 103, 134–35.
[23] *Ibid.*, 1886 special session, pp. 40–42.
[24] *Ibid.*, 1886, pp. 139–48.

would strengthen his hand as a lobbyist. Powderly lent his approval and suggested concentrating on a few districts where the Order was strong. Maine was chosen for the test, but the results proved unfortunate, as the individual marked for defeat won by an even larger than usual majority.[25]

Beaumont's plan of rewarding friends and punishing enemies, therefore, did not win widespread acceptance. Instead, local units of the Knights together with other labor organizations launched independent political tickets throughout the country. These activities were all a heritage of the emotional fervor of the "Great Upheaval" of 1886, during which time the membership of the Knights reached the unprecedented figure of nearly 703,000, while other labor groups were undergoing a similar growth. This expansion, which seemed to awaken a slumbering working class from a long sleep and endow it with an ardor and spirit never before matched in American history, had an important influence in the political sphere.[26] Despite their previous disillusioning and disappointing experiences, workingmen enthusiastically re-entered politics in the hope of achieving their objectives. At least twenty-six states were affected by independent political movements, and for a time it appeared as though labor was intent upon revolutionizing the structure of American politics. "We have a vast mass of material which we cannot print, showing the drift of the workers toward politics," John Swinton reported. "From California and Oregon to Maine and Massachusetts,—from Illinois and Michigan to Texas and Virginia, we have the news of this drift. All the various organizations appear to be moving under the same impulse." [27]

What were the results of the intense political activities of the working class during the campaign of 1886? Undoubtedly the outcome of the New York City mayoralty campaign between Henry George, Abram Hewitt, and Theodore Roosevelt, was most impressive. George, with labor backing, succeeded in polling nearly 68,000 votes, as opposed to 90,000 for Hewitt and 60,000 for Roosevelt. While the New York contest attracted the most publicity, labor's showing in other areas surpassed even the most sanguine predictions. In Chicago the vote of the United Labor party reached nearly 25,000, and it elected seven members to the Assembly and one to the Senate in Springfield, five judges, and fell short of electing a congressman by only 64 votes. In Milwaukee the People's party polled more votes than the Democrats and Republicans combined, carrying the whole county ticket and electing the labor candidate for Congress. Although failing to elect the governor, the labor slate in Wisconsin polled between 25,000 and 30,000 votes. Municipal labor tickets won out in Lynn, Massachusetts, Rutland, Vermont, Naugatuck and South Norwalk, Connecticut, Key West, Florida, and Richmond, Virginia. In localities in

[25] Powderly to Beaumont, July 27, 1886, TVPLB; James, "American Labor and Political Action," pp. 278–87.

[26] For a discussion of the reasons for this expansion see above, Chapter Three, fn. 17.

[27] *John Swinton's Paper*, August 8, 1886.

Colorado, Illinois, New Jersey, Kentucky, and Missouri, the workers made their presence felt. Labor made its poorest showing in the South and, with the single exception of the sixth congressional district of Virginia where the Order's candidate was elected, could claim few victories in this section. Aside from the independent labor candidates, many workers also ran as Democrats or Republicans. Martin A. Foran in Ohio and B. F. Shively in Indiana, for example, were sent to Congress as Democrats, and in Massachusetts Robert Howard, the acting Master Workman of D.A. 30, was re-elected to the State Senate.[28]

Labor's spectacular showing during the campaign of 1886 led to a concerted effort to transform the temporary labor parties into permanent organizations. On February 22, 1887, the National Industrial Union Conference, an outgrowth of a convention held in the summer of 1886 to organize a national party of farmers and laborers, met in Cincinnati and organized the National Union Labor party. Although Trevellick and other members of the Knights attended, few of the 458 delegates were workingmen, and all the members elected to the national executive committee were farmers. The platform, however, did endorse most of the labor demands of the preamble of the constitution of the Knights. In the Middle West, labor organizations readily united with the new party, but in the East similar efforts were bitterly resisted by working-class leaders.[29]

The organization of the National Union Labor party, however, did not decrease working-class absorption in independent political action. In the spring of 1887, for example, no less than seventy-three labor tickets, two-thirds of which were in the Middle West, were in the field. In Milwaukee and at least nineteen other localities labor tickets swept to victory.[30] Within the ranks of organized labor hopes ran high. While Powderly adhered to his nonpartisan policy of refusing to permit the Order to become involved with the National Union Labor party,[31] Litchman wrote an enthusiastic editorial about the potentialities of labor political action.[32]

Despite the high hopes of many labor leaders, the fall elections of 1887 demonstrated that the political fervor aroused by the "Great Upheaval" had passed its peak and was subsiding. The lack of unity and internal dissension further contributed to the decline in labor's political activities. Indeed, the presidential campaign the following year merely accentuated the decline of the efforts of the Knights of Labor in the political arena, for many members were openly taking sides. On August 25, 1888, Litch-

---

[28] Edward B. Mittelman, "Chicago Labor in Politics 1877–96," *Journal of Political Economy*, XXVIII (May, 1920), 421; *John Swinton's Paper*, November 7, 1886; Commons, *History of Labour*, II, 463.

[29] *John Swinton's Paper*, February 27, 1887; Commons, *History of Labour*, II, 464–65.

[30] James, "American Labor and Political Action," pp. 336–37; Commons, *History of Labour*, II, 466.

[31] *Journal of United Labor*, VII (February 5, 1887), 2276.

[32] *Ibid.*, VII (April 16, 1887), 2356.

man, then secretary of the Knights, resigned his post to campaign for Harrison and a high tariff.[33] Circumstantial evidence warrants the conclusion that the Republicans made a deal with Litchman, who received a berth in the Treasury Department after the election. L.A. 300 made substantial contributions to the campaign fund of the Republican party, and Indiana assemblies of the Knights openly supported Harrison. Many members, on the other hand, either backed Cleveland or else worked through one of the independent labor parties in their area.

While numerous assemblies of the Knights were supporting either Harrison or Cleveland, Powderly outwardly maintained his nonpartisan attitude. He still hoped that the political activities of the Knights would be confined to legislative lobbying and not third-party action. "I do not favor the turning of the Knights of Labor into a party, and will not have anything to do with parties," Powderly wrote in May, 1888. "My vote will be cast for that party or man who will do the most good."[34] Powderly also rebuffed Republican attempts to utilize a speech he made in 1883 favoring a high tariff, explaining that although he believed in tariff protection, he also believed it was not a proper issue for the Knights to act upon.[35] Yet, while denying that he was a candidate for political office, Powderly apparently engaged in secret political negotiations with both major parties in the summer and autumn of 1888. That he did not support either presidential candidate did not so much attest to adherence to principle as it did to the fact that no offer was sufficiently tempting to make him renounce his nonpartisanship.[36]

The results of the presidential campaign of 1888 proved discouraging. On the state level the Knights were victorious in isolated contests. In St. Louis, for example, eleven members were elected to the lgislature, and in Pennsylvania, Illinois, New York, and West Virginia local assemblies made systematic attempts to pledge candidates.[37] On the national level, however, there was only disaster. Almost every pro-labor member of Con-

[33] *Ibid.,* IX (September 6, 1888), 2693; Powderly to Hayes, September 7, 1888, Powderly-Hayes Correspondence, Catholic University of America, Washington, D. C.

[34] *Journal of United Labor,* VIII (May 5, 1888), 2622. See also *ibid.,* IX (August 16, 1888), 2681.

[35] *Ibid.,* IX (August 16, 1888), 2681, (September 13, 1888), 2697. For Powderly's attitude toward the tariff see Powderly to E. H. Ammidown, July 24, 1886; Powderly to E. W. Pierce, November 22, 1886; Powderly to W. A. Karr, December 12, 1886, TVPLB.

[36] Litchman indirectly attacked Powderly's course. "I hold it more honorable to lay down official duties that would hamper private action than to retain such position and at the same time be engaged in political scheming in secret with the party agents whom it is necessary ostensibly to publicly denounce." Litchman to Powderly, August 29, 1888, *Journal of United Labor,* IX (September 6, 1888), 2693. The *National Labor Tribune* echoed Litchman's charge. *National Labor Tribune,* September 8, 1888; *Journal of United Labor,* IX (September 13, 1888), 2698. See also James, "American Labor and Political Action," p. 433.

[37] James, "American Labor and Political Action," p. 461.

gress was defeated.[38] "Never in the history of American civilization did the wageworker have a better opportunity to display his intelligence in the use of the elective franchise than was presented on Tuesday of last week," the official journal of the Knights remarked, "and never did he make a poorer use of it than on that occasion. . . . Labor's friends have been defeated on every side by Labor's foes." [39] Aside from a major political defeat, many assemblies were disrupted because of internal political rivalries, and the General Executive Board later claimed that the partisan political activities of several of its officers during the presidential campaign cost the Order no less than 100,000 members.[40] Thus ended the political agitation inspired by the "Great Upheaval."

Why, then, did all of this political enthusiasm produce so few results? In the first place, conditions between 1886 and 1888 did not support the optimistic hopes held by many labor leaders. American workingmen obviously were not hostile toward political action, provided that such action would yield concrete and immediate benefits. Yet after two years of intense political strife workingmen found that their efforts had resulted in more harm than good. When labor's votes had been uncommitted, the major parties evinced more readiness to consider its grievances. Hence the anticontract labor bill was able to receive a more favorable reception in Congress in 1885. When labor committed its forces to a particular party or individual, however, it could no longer threaten to use its influence against its enemies. The commitment of its forces thus had eroded the foundation upon which its bargaining position depended.

Secondly, independent political action was predicated upon the conviction that the working class could be united behind a common political program and party. Yet the facts did not warrant such an optimistic assumption. The experiences of the National Legislative Committee of the Knights of Labor, for example, were not unique. Launched at the height of the "Great Upheaval," the Committee members soon found that they did not command the allegiance of the men they purported to represent in Washington. "[We are] of the opinion that the rank and file of the Order do not take as much interest in the question of legislation as they ought to," the Committee reported to the General Assembly in the autumn of 1889. "We feel that the efforts of a committee at the capital are powerless if they do not have the active support of the Order by petition and also by votes at election times." [41]

In the third place, the process of building a cohesive and powerful labor party was slow and arduous. The years between 1828 and 1873 had witnessed many working-class political crusades, but all had failed to live

[38] K. of L., *GA Proc.*, 1889, *Report of the National Legislative Committee*, p. 2.
[39] *Journal of United Labor*, IX (November 15, 1888) , 2734.
[40] Commons, *History of Labour*, II, 469.
[41] K. of L., *GA Proc.*, 1889, *Report of the National Legislative Committee*, pp. 3–4.

up to their expectations. Workingmen, on the other hand, supported independent political movements to the degree that they coincided with their interests, and when these movements failed to bring the anticipated relief, the workers quickly abandoned their stillborn progeny.

Finally, the political background of the working class militated against the success of independent political action, for individuals, conditioned by strong party ties that were the habit of years, could not so easily abandon their traditional allegiance. Many members of the Knights recognized this omnipresent danger and warned against partisan action. Even before the Order embarked upon a political crusade, the Master Workman of D.A. 55 of Michigan sounded a note of caution. "Wherever we have allowed political action as a body," he warned, "it has worked us an injury, and put the growth of the Order at a stand-still, and breeds dissension and hard feelings in the Assemblies when peace and harmony should prevail." [42] This sober observation was supported by many other members, one of whom perhaps expressed most eloquently the dangers of independent political action:

> I find no fault with political action when it goes no farther than demanding what we want—if we have decided on what we want, and it is just and right and can be gained by legislation—or crushing out of political existence known enemies who always oppose what we want and favor what we don't want— when it goes no farther than we can go united, which is thus far, then I say never lose an opportunity; but when it goes as far as *"elect your own men!"* then we divide, for on that as on religion we cannot agree, because to harmonize we all should have to take the same view of human nature, which is impossible. Hence we must steer clear of this danger under all circumstances.[43]

IV

The failure of independent political action, however, did not remove the Knights from politics. Instead, the political activities of the Knights were channeled into a different direction. Beginning in the mid-1880's, the Order moved slowly but steadily toward forging an alliance with the farmer. Circumstances appeared propitious for such a coalition. The mechanization of agriculture had forced the farmer into a difficult position. Caught between decreasing farm prices, an ever-increasing surplus, and relatively high costs of transportation, the nation's farmers were in revolt against their depressed condition by the 1880's. With the continued existence of grievances in farm and labor groups, it was only natural that attempts would be made for union on a program of mutual relief.

Conditions augured well for the success of the movement. To begin with, the rural element had always been numerically strong in the

[42] *Journal of United Labor,* V (July 10, 1884), 740.
[43] *Ibid.,* VII (June 11, 1887), 2422.

Knights, and after 1886 they gained proportionately in strength and provided a strong impetus for a farmer-labor coalition.[44] In the second place, the Order's leaders were wedded to the concept of a fluid society lacking in class distinctions, and they thought in terms of a community of interests between farmers and workers. The fact that both were producers lent credence to this belief. Thirdly, its growing preoccupation with land reform led the Knights to gravitate toward the farmer as a possible source of additional strength. In the fourth place, Powderly himself gave strong support to the proposal for such an alliance. Although maintaining his nonpartisan political attitude, he assumed that workers and farmers could unite behind a common program, using their combined strength as an irresistible lobby.[45] Finally, there was the fact that Populism and labor reformism had emerged from the same traditions. Both were descended from the equal-rights and antimonopoly movements of the 1830's; both had been nourished upon the monetary schemes in vogue between 1840 and 1880; and both had supported various co-operative undertakings.

There had been sporadic attempts at union between farm and labor groups,[46] but the campaign that would succeed began in 1885 when the General Assembly of the Knights referred a resolution to the General Executive Board advocating the establishment of closer relations with the farmer so as to enhance the political bargaining position of both groups. In the spring of 1886 the Assembly went further and sent a hopeful communication to the National Grange. The following year it appointed a committee on fraternal relations with the Grange. The immediate outcome of the ensuing negotiations was agreement that each organization should maintain a lobbying committee in Washington, which would "consult and confer together, with the view of securing such legislation as will conduce to the interest and welfare of both organizations." [47]

By 1889 relations between the Knights and the farmers had passed beyond exchanges of greetings and promises to work together in harmony. The General Assembly meeting in that year appointed a Committee on

---

[44] *The Laborer*, cited in *John Swinton's Paper*, September 27, 1885. See also *ibid.*, August 30, 1885.

[45] *Journal of the Knights of Labor*, X (April 24, 1890), 1, (May 1, 1890), 1. Powderly's faith in land reform made him receptive to the vision of a farmer-labor coalition, which he believed would function best as a lobby and not as a political party. Powderly, as we will see, was not an ardent supporter of the Populist party and continued to proclaim his steadfast nonpartisanship between 1889 and 1892. For his views on land reform see Powderly to J. G. Malcolm, December 3, 1882; Powderly to Thomas H. Dever, September 22, 1883, TVPLB; K. of L., *GA Proc.*, 1882, pp. 282–83; 1885, pp. 13–15; Powderly, *Thirty Years of Labor*, pp. 369–73.

[46] For evidences of farmer-labor collaboration on the state and regional level see Eugene Staley, *History of the Illinois State Federation of Labor* (Chicago, 1930), p. 28; *John Swinton's Paper*, February 24, April 6, 1884, August 30, November 29, 1885; *The Craftsman*, II (September 5, 1885), 2, (September 19, 1885), 2.

[47] K. of L., *GA Proc.*, 1885, pp. 100, 106, 135; 1886 special session, p. 70; 1887, pp. 1637, 1792.

Mortgage Debtors as a concession to the agrarians. The committee, in turn, pledged the Order to work for revision in the foreclosure laws of the various states. Although it did not specifically single out the farmer, the committee's report obviously was a concession to the farm element. Following the adoption of this report by the General Assembly, the delegates listened to addresses by a delegation from the Farmers' Alliance of Georgia. Expressing optimistic hopes for farmer-labor co-operation, the delegation bade the Knights send representatives to the December meeting of the Farmers' Alliance in St. Louis.[48]

The growing *rapprochement* between the Farmers' Alliance and the Knights reflected developments on the local and state levels. The loss of thousands of members in the more industrialized regions of the East and Midwest strengthened proportionately the rural elements in the Knights. In many states members of the Order began to meet with agrarian representatives to draw up a common platform. At the South Dakota Farmers' Alliance convention, for example, the leader of the Knights in that state informed the delegates that "the labor organizations in the towns would stand shoulder to shoulder with the Alliance organizations of the country in righting the wrongs of legislation and raising the standard of politics." [49] In New York, Kansas, Alabama, Illinois, Indiana, Nebraska, Minnesota, Texas, and North Carolina, local and district assemblies of the Knights worked in harmony and co-operated with farm organizations.[50]

Action on the national level came at the St. Louis Farmers' convention in December, 1889, where Powderly, Beaumont, and Wright spoke for the Knights and helped to prepare a platform for union, under which each group pledged itself to support only those candidates supporting farmer-labor demands. The platform included such diverse planks as the abolition of national banks and the substitution of legal-tender notes in the place of national bank currency, outlawing dealings in the future sale of commodities, the free and unlimited coinage of silver, prohibition of alien land ownership, recovery of all land grants not actually used by the railroads, an end to class legislation, governmental control and operation of the means of communication and transportation, and mutual recognition of all seals and labels.[51] "Never before was the future so full of hope," sang the official journal of the Knights. "With fidelity to conviction, all we ever hoped for is now within our reach." [52]

---

[48] *Ibid.*, 1889, pp. 73–76, 87–93.

[49] *Journal of United Labor*, X (July 11, 1889), 1.

[50] *Ibid.*, X (October 31, 1889), 1; *Journal of the Knights of Labor*, X (March 27, 1890), 2, (June 12, 1890), 1, 4, XI (July 10, 1890), 4, (August 21, 1890), 1, (November 27, 1890), 2, (April 2, 1891), 1, XII (July 16, 1891), 1, (October 8, 1891), 1, (May 5, 1892), 1; Ruth A. Allen, *Chapters in the History of Organized Labor in Texas* (Austin, Texas, 1941), pp. 23–24.

[51] *Journal of the Knights of Labor*, X (December 12, 1889), 1, (January 16, 1890), 1–3.

[52] *Ibid.*, X (December 12, 1889), 2.

Although the St. Louis platform was heavily weighted in favor of the farmer, the General Assembly of the Knights approved it in November, 1890. Moreover, the Assembly decided to send delegates to the meeting of the Farmers' Alliance at Ocala, Florida, to arrange for the convening of a National Reform Industrial Convention to "formulate an independent political platform upon the principles of the preamble of the Knights of Labor, so that this order shall give its endorsement and support to that at the ballot box." [53]

Meanwhile, the results of the congressional and state elections in the autumn of 1890 strengthened the proponents of an independent farmer-labor party. In Kansas, for example, the reform forces swept the state offices and elected a congressman and a senator. Similarly, in the third congressional district of Nebraska an Alliance candidate defeated his Republican and Democratic opponents. Benjamin R. Tillman was elected governor of South Carolina on a coalition ticket, and in North Carolina and Georgia the reform forces also fared well.[54] Trevellick claimed that the farmer-labor bloc could count on the support of fifty-two congressmen, twenty-three of whom had been elected on independent tickets.[55]

A few weeks after the election, the Farmers' Alliance met at Ocala, Florida, and Powderly, Beaumont, and Wright again represented the Knights. The gratifying results of the election of 1890 had spurred the political enthusiasts to new efforts, and after the adoption of a platform similar to the one adopted at St. Louis, the delegates called for another convention to meet in Cincinnati on February 23, 1891, to form a new national political party. Powderly, however, had also issued a call for a National Reform Industrial Convention to meet on that date, and he and several Ocala delegates therefore agreed to have the farmers postpone the Cincinnati meeting until May.[56]

In the interim between the Ocala convention and the meeting scheduled for Cincinnati in May, 1891, Powderly, Hayes, and Wright met with representatives from the various farm organizations in Washington on January 21, 1891. Unwilling to abandon his nonpartisanship and unhappy at the idea of turning the Knights into a political party, Powderly tried desperately to hold back the political enthusiasts in the Order. "The proposition to elect Congressmen and Legislators through the new party

---

[53] Perlman interprets this statement to mean that the Knights supported the formation of an independent political party. Commons, *History of Labour*, II, 493. Actually the General Assembly was simply endorsing a *platform*, and it indicated its willingness to support any party that endorsed this platform. K. of L., *GA Proc.*, 1890, pp. 63–64, 70–71.

[54] *Journal of the Knights of Labor*, XI (November 13, 1890), 1, (November 20, 1890), 1, XI (February 5, 1891), 3; Commons, *History of Labour*, II, 492–93. For a full discussion of the election of 1890 see John D. Hicks, *The Populist Revolt* (Minneapolis, Minnesota, 1931), pp. 153–85.

[55] *Journal of the Knights of Labor*, XI (November 20, 1890), 1.

[56] *Ibid.*, XI (December 11, 1890), 1, (January 8, 1891), 1.

is good, but to elect them independent of party is better," he had written earlier. "It is not a new party we want so badly as new measures, new men." [57] Nothing of importance, therefore, came out of the conference, except the indication that the Knights would not officially join any political party.[58] While Powderly had succeeded in temporarily postponing any proposal to amalgamate the Knights with the Farmers' Alliance, his plan of calling a National Reform Industrial Convention to formulate a nonpartisan program also met with defeat. When only local assemblies of the Knights responded to Powderly's call, he was forced to cancel the meeting scheduled for February 23.[59]

By the spring of 1891, therefore, a definite pattern had emerged. The farmers were still seeking to secure labor support for the People's party, but only on their own terms. The Cincinnati convention meeting in May, for example, laid the groundwork for the formal organization of the People's party. Although over fourteen hundred delegates attended, few were bona fide working-class representatives, and the convention was completely dominated by agrarian reformers. The delegates unanimously supported the formation of a new party, and again reaffirmed the St. Louis and Ocala platforms.[60]

Powderly, nevertheless, still fought off all attempts to commit the Knights to outright support of the Populists. Despite the increasing pressure on him by western members of the Knights, he insisted on pursuing a nonpartisan policy and continued to warn against the dangers of partisan politics:

> Properly understood and intelligently worked our organization could be made the propelling power in reform politics, and it has always been a puzzle to me why our members can not see it as I do. . . .
>
> Now as to the [subject] of the Knights and organized labor generally organizing in districts and clubs for political action, that must be determined in the locality where such action is necessary. In the Eastern States, just at present, it would be folly to do such a thing in the hope of winning reforms through a third party, and the effort is to capture the old parties or enough of one of them to drive those who are opposed to labor into one or the other of the old parties.
>
> In the west and south-west labor is active in independent politics, and there is no reason why our members should not co-operate with other reformers in that work. . . . to my mind nothing seems easier than for a Knight of Labor, a trade Unionist, a Single Taxer and a Farmers' Alliance man to sit down and agree to work together for certain reforms on which they can agree, and at the same time agree to build up their separate organizations so that those who would not vote for reform measures this year, and who would not under any

[57] *Ibid.*, X (May 22, 1890) , 1.

[58] *Ibid.*, XI (January 29, 1891) , 1.

[59] *Ibid.*, XI (February 12, 1891) , 1. Powderly also canceled a later convention that he had scheduled. *Ibid.*, XII (July 9, 1891) , 1.

[60] *Ibid.*, XI (May 28, 1891) , 1.

circumstances join a new party, will be educated through the medium of these organizations to see the necessity for reform and eventually the taking of independent political action.

The formula . . . must differ in different places, and I could not for the life of me lay down a rule that will work the same in different localities.[61]

Powderly's suggestions, however, did not find widespread support, and the movement to establish the People's party on a firm foundation with labor support continued unabated. In February, 1892, another convention met in St. Louis to unite the various reform organizations solidly behind the new party. Of the 860 delegates present, only eighty-two were from the Knights. Altogether, including delegations from the International Association of Machinists, the United Mine Workers of Ohio, the International Wire Workers, plus some local unions, labor accounted for approximately 25 per cent of the delegates, the remainder coming from the various farm organizations. Eastern labor was entirely unrepresented. The convention made a show of unity by electing Hayes temporary secretary and Hugh Cavanaugh, General Worthy Foreman of the Knights, chairman of the platform committee. In addition, A. W. Wright also headed the subcommittee on land reform.[62]

Despite the concessions apparently granted to organized labor, the platform adopted by the delegates was primarily an agrarian rather than a labor document. After proclaiming the unity of farmers and workers, the platform went on to attack existing conditions. "The fruits of the toil of millions are boldly stolen to build up colossal fortunes unprecedented in the history of mankind, and the possessors of these in turn despise the Republic and endanger liberty. From the same prolific womb of governmental injustice we breed the two great classes—paupers and millionaires." [63] As a remedy, the platform demanded a flexible national currency issued by the federal government, the establishment of the subtreasury plan as recommended by the Farmers' Alliance, the free and unlimited coinage of silver, a graduated income tax, postal savings banks, land reform, and governmental ownership of the railroads, telegraph, and telephone. The only concessions granted organized labor were embodied in the form of two supplemental resolutions endorsing the label of the Knights and also National Trade Assembly 231 in its struggle against the clothing manufacturers of Rochester, New York.[64]

The St. Louis meeting then made provision for a nominating convention, and the structure of the new political edifice was completed in July, 1892, in Omaha, when the People's party nominated General James B. Weaver of Iowa and General James G. Field of Virginia for

[61] Powderly to A. H. Shank, January 15, 1892, TVPLB.
[62] *Journal of the Knights of Labor,* XII (March 3, 1892) , 1–2.
[63] *Ibid.,* XII (March 31, 1892) , 1.
[64] *Ibid.,* XII (March 3, 1892) , 4.

President and Vice-President. Although Hayes was elected permanent secretary, control of the convention remained in agrarian hands and the delegates reaffirmed the platform adopted at St. Louis the previous February. To court working-class support, however, the convention adopted a supplementary platform. These additions supported the restriction of contract labor and undesirable immigration, offered sympathy to labor's efforts to shorten working hours, denounced the use of Pinkerton detectives in industrial disputes, and endorsed the Order's boycott of the Rochester clothing manufacturers.[65]

In the ensuing campaign the Knights played a minor role. Although assemblies were active in Weaver's behalf throughout the West and South, they were more appendages of farm groups than bona fide labor organizations. While the Knights made isolated efforts to rally eastern workingmen behind the Populist banner,[66] its endeavors met with little success. Although the *Journal of the Knights of Labor* strongly backed Weaver's candidacy,[67] Powderly's activities on behalf of the People's party were anything but enthusiastic. In June, 1892, he refused to accept credentials as a delegate-at-large from Pennsylvania to the Omaha convention. "While I intend to support the People's Party right along, and help in every way to make it successful," Powderly explained, "I will do so as a citizen and not as a member of the party." [68] During the campaign he did little except make occasional speeches and write a few letters. "I can make no speeches in the campaign owing to the instructions of my doctor," Powderly wrote at the end of September. "I shall use my pen from now until the campaign closes in behalf of the People's Party, but only where candidates stand squarely upon that platform and no other." [69] His support of Weaver, however, did not prevent him from expressing his preference for Harrison rather than Cleveland.[70]

While the results of the campaign of 1892 were enthusiastically hailed by the People's party, it was also clear that the attempt to weld a farmer-labor coalition had completely failed. Although Weaver polled over a million popular votes and won twenty-two electoral votes, the results of the election showed that the main strength of the Populists lay in the rural areas of the West. East of the Mississippi River the People's party received only a sprinkling of votes. In the urban areas of Illinois the Populist vote was less than half of 1 per cent of the total, and out of 249,000 ballots cast in Cook County, the Populist candidate received only 1,214.

[65] *Ibid.*, XIII (July 7, 1892) , 1.
[66] See *ibid.*, XII (May 5, 1892) , 1, XIII (November 3, 1892) , 1.
[67] *Ibid.*, XIII (July 14, 1892) , 2.
[68] Powderly to F. Reed Agnew, June 14, 1892, TVPLB. See also the *Journal of the Knights of Labor*, XII (June 2, 1892) , 1, (June 30, 1892) , 1.
[69] Powderly to J. A. Fox, September 30, 1892, TVPLB.
[70] Powderly to G. F. Washburn, October 13, 1892, TVPLB.

In the industrialized states of New York, New Jersey, Pennsylvania, and Massachusetts the total Populist vote was under 30,000.[71]

Undoubtedly, the fact that the farmers and workers had interests that were not identical contributed to the failure to forge an effective alliance between the two. *The People,* organ of Daniel DeLeon and the Socialist Labor party, for example, pointed out that the Omaha platform contemplated "the promotion of the interests of the small farmer . . . by relieving him at the expense of the worker." [72] The underlying antagonisms of both groups, accentuated by differing economic interests, were never fully resolved. The farmers wanted high agricultural and low industrial prices—exactly opposite from what the workers demanded. In turn, the workers ardently supported eight hours, while the farmers looked askance upon such a demand.[73]

Yet, as one historian has pointed out, "both small farmers and urban craftsmen might well have profited from a limited program of state action that was restricted to cheap credit, cheap transportation, cheap communication and utility rates, and a minimum program of protective labor legislation, together with the destruction of monopolies and the reduction of great fortunes through taxation shifted somewhat from the shoulders of the masses." [74] The failure of the People's party to recruit a following from the ranks of organized labor between 1889 and 1892, then, was not merely a result of antagonistic economic interests, for both also had common interests. The events that transpired during these three momentous years had a deeper significance, for they were symptomatic of the changes taking place in the labor movement itself. It is important to note, for example, that the farmers chose Powderly as the man to negotiate with instead of Gompers, the representative of the trade unions. The Populists could succeed in their effort to attain labor support only if workingmen still adhered to an older form of reformism whose roots lay embedded in the equal-rights and antimonopoly tradition of American radicalism. To the agrarians the Knights of Labor seemed to represent that heritage best. They could not turn to Gompers because he regarded the Farmers' Alliance as composed partially of employers with interests that differed with those of the workers.[75] So the Populists turned instead to the Knights. By

[71] Chester M. Destler, *American Radicalism 1865–1901* (New London, Connecticut, 1946), p. 168; Mittelman, "Chicago Labor in Politics 1877–96," *loc. cit.,* p. 423; U. S. Bureau of Statistics, *Statistical Abstract of the United States,* XXXIII (1910) (Washington, D. C., 1911), p. 662.

[72] *The People,* July 1, 1894.

[73] See the statement of a Colorado farmer in regard to eight hours in *John Swinton's Paper,* July 11, 1886.

[74] Destler, *American Radicalism,* p. 223.

[75] Gompers to Tom Mann, September 2, 1891; Gompers to J. F. Tillman, September 12, 1891; Gompers to O. P. Smith, February 10, 1892; Gompers to John McBride, February 6, 1893, SGLB; Gompers, "Organized Labor in the Campaign," *North American Review,* CLV (July, 1892), 93.

pinning their hopes on the chance that American workingmen would still support a domestic species of reform, the Populists hoped to realize their dream of an irresistible farmer-labor alliance. Their choice of partners, however, turned out to be an unfortunate one, for the Knights of Labor no longer represented the aspirations of the American worker. From a peak of 700,000 in 1886, the membership of the Order had plummeted to less than 100,000 by 1890. Instead of wooing organized labor, the Populists were merely negotiating with a band of individual reformers whose influence on the labor movement was fast disappearing.[76] Thus the failure of the Populists to win labor support through an alliance with the once-powerful Knights demonstrated that workers for the most part had finally abandoned their absorption in reform and the older equal-rights and antimonopoly heritage. Herein lay the real significance of the failure of farmer and worker to come to terms between 1889 and 1892.

[76] The political activities of the Knights of Labor after 1892 deserve but passing mention. Powderly was deposed in 1893 by an alliance of eastern socialists led by Daniel DeLeon and western agrarians led by James R. Sovereign. This alliance proved to be ephemeral, and the already emaciated Order was further fragmented. These events not only removed the Knights from any important position it might have held in the labor movement, but also destroyed any political influence it might have conceivably exerted. After 1893 the western agrarians led by Sovereign joined in all-out support of the People's party, ardently seconding Bryan's candidacy in 1896, while the eastern socialists seceded and formed a rival organization in New York City.

CHAPTER SIX

Conflict: Reform vs. Trade Unionism, 1878–1886

I

❦ THE YEAR 1886 was destined to be a crucial one in the history of the American labor movement. The eight-hour crusade, the numerous strikes, the Haymarket bomb, the entrance of workingmen into the political arena at the state and national levels, and the mushroom growth of labor organizations all contributed to the agitation and excitement of the year. Yet the importance of these events was overshadowed by a development that was to have such far-reaching implications that it would determine the future of the labor movement for the succeeding half century. That development was the declaration of war by the trade unions against the reform unionism of the Knights of Labor.

The rift between the unions and the Knights was not an unexpected nor a precipitous episode. The earlier experiences of the National Labor Union had demonstrated that ante-bellum reformism and trade unionism could not always work together toward a common goal in peace and harmony. The destructive impact of the depression of the 1870's upon labor organizations momentarily allayed the mutual antipathy of trade unionists and labor reformers. The rise of the Knights of Labor and the rebirth of the trade unions after 1878, however, marked the resumption of the conflict for control of the labor movement.

The struggle between the Knights and the other unions represented a clash of two fundamentally opposing ideologies. The Knights of Labor, on the one hand, grew out of the reform and humanitarian movements of ante-bellum America, and was the direct descendent, through the National Labor Union, of the labor reform tradition of the Jacksonian era. Banking on the leveling influence of technological change, its leaders sought to organize the entire producing class into a single irresistible coalition that would work toward the abolition of the wage system and the establishment of a new society. "It is necessary that we recognize the vast and essential difference between our Order and Trades' Unions," the General Executive Board told the General Assembly in 1884. "This essential difference is that our Order contemplates a radical change in the existing industrial system, and labors to bring about that change, while Trades' Unions and other orders accept the industrial system as it is, and endeavor to adapt themselves to it. The attitude of our Order to the existing industrial system is antagonistic, and is necessarily one of war." [1]

The reform ideology of the Knights, in turn, had an important impact upon the development of its structure, which followed a heterogeneous rather than a homogeneous pattern. Minimizing the utility of organization along trade lines, the Order emphasized instead the grouping of all workers, regardless of craft, into a single body.[2] Highest priority therefore was given to the mixed local assembly, which included all workers irrespective of their trade or degree of skill. Neither a trade, plant, nor industrial union, the mixed assembly could never be more than a study or debating group. Including many diverse elements (even employers), it could not adapt itself to meet the problems of a specific industry or trade. The mixed assembly might agitate for reform or participate in politics, but it could never become the collective bargaining representative of its members.

Given the predominance of the mixed over the trade local, the structure of the Knights inevitably developed along geographical rather than jurisdictional lines, and the district assembly, which included mixed as well as trade locals, became the most characteristic form of organization. The highest governmental body of the Knights—the General Assembly—was not intended as a medium for collective bargaining. Indeed, its very inclusiveness precluded such a possibility.

The trade unions, on the other hand, rejected the broad reform goals of the Knights, emphasizing instead higher wages, shorter hours, and job control. Such objectives were clearly incompatible with an organizational structure such as that developed by the Knights. Eschewing the multitrade local that had been so prevalent during the 1860's and was being perpetuated by the Order, the trade unions began to stress the craft-industrial form of organization both at the local and national levels. A relative scarcity of labor, together with a rapidly expanding economy, had created a favorable environment for the trade unions. Gambling on the hope that the rise of a national market made organization along trade rather than geographical lines more effective, union leaders chose to concentrate upon the task of organizing the workers along trade lines into unions designed for collective bargaining rather than social reform.[3]

Therefore, given the inherent differences in ideology and structure, the conflict between the Knights and the trade unions was, if not inevitable,

[1] K. of L., *GA Proc.*, 1884, pp. 716–17.

[2] For the antitrade unionism of the national leadership of the Knights see the *Journal of United Labor*, I (June 15, 1880), 21; K. of L., *GA Proc.*, 1880, p. 169; 1897, p. 37; Powderly, *Thirty Years of Labor*, pp. 155–56; Powderly to James Rogers, December 19, 1892, TVPLB; Grob, "Terence V. Powderly and the Knights of Labor," *loc. cit.*, pp. 41–42.

[3] See Lloyd Ulman, *The Rise of the National Trade Union* (Cambridge, Massachusetts, 1955), pp. 348–77.

certainly not an unexpected or surprising development.[4] Undoubtedly the antagonistic personalities of partisans on both sides hastened an open rift.[5] Yet the hostilities between the Knights and the trade unions cannot be explained solely in terms of personalities, for the conflict was not simply a struggle for power between two rivals. It was a clash between two fundamentally different ideologies—with the future of the labor movement at stake.

I I

The contest between trade unionists and reformers for control of the labor movement developed on two planes. Commencing first as an internal struggle within the Knights, it eventually expanded and soon involved the national unions. Within the Knights the struggle revolved around the unresolved question as to which form of organization best met working-class necessities. On the surface the issue of mixed versus trade locals was simply a structural problem. In reality, however, the differences between the two forms indicated the existence of a fundamental cleavage in ultimate objectives, for the mixed assembly could be utilized only for reform or political purposes, while the trade assembly was generally a collective bargaining organization.

Although the national leadership of the Knights regarded the mixed assembly as the ideal type of unit, a large proportion of its local assemblies were trade rather than mixed. The first local, composed of garment cutters, was strictly craft, and remained so to the end. Most of the other locals that followed were also trade assemblies.[6] On January 1, 1882, according to the *Journal of United Labor*, there were 27 working districts and over 400 local assemblies. Of the latter, 318 were trade and only 116 were mixed. Thirteen additional districts, not functioning, had 53 trade and 87 mixed locals, attesting to the relative instability of the mixed form of organization. Of the 135 locals attached directly to the General Assembly, 67 were trade and 68 were mixed.[7]

Despite the wide latitude given them to organize trade local assemblies, the trade element within the Knights nevertheless found it difficult to function efficiently. Local trade assemblies, no matter how inclusive in their particular area, were often ineffective when operating in a market that was regional or national rather than local in character. So long as employers could find a ready supply of nonunion labor elsewhere, efforts

[4] See Carroll D. Wright, "An Historical Sketch of the Knights of Labor," *Quarterly Journal of Economics*, I (January, 1887) , 155; *Cigar Makers' Official Journal*, XI (June 1886) , 6; *The Carpenter*, VI (February, 1886) , 4, (April, 1886) , 4.

[5] Norman J. Ware emphasized the importance of conflicting personalities. See Ware, *Labor Movement*, pp. 162–63, *et passim*.

[6] See Wright, "An Historical Sketch of the Knights of Labor," *loc. cit.*, p. 146.

[7] Ware, *Labor Movement*, p. 158. The statistics on trade locals in the Knights are unsatisfactory and misleading, since many of them admitted workers belonging to different trades.

at collective bargaining by locals would be ineffective. The only solution lay in national organization, and the trade exponents within the Knights pressed for national and regional trade districts that would transcend the limited geographical area normally encompassed by the local or district assembly.

The General Assembly, therefore, meeting in January, 1879, authorized the establishment of autonomous national trade districts within the framework of the Knights. But only nine months later the Assembly completely reversed itself by declaring that trade locals were "contrary to the spirit and genius of the Order," and it returned exclusive jurisdiction over all locals to the district assembly of their area.[8]

In December, 1881, however, the Federation of Organized Trades and Labor Unions, predecessor of the A.F. of L., held its first convention. Of the 107 delegates present, no less than 50 came from the Knights.[9] The following September the General Assembly also heard the secretary of the Knights warn that trade sentiment was growing rapidly. "Many Trades Unions have also written me," he remarked, "stating that they were seriously meditating the propriety of coming over to us in a body, freely expressing the opinion that their proper place was in our Order." [10] To prevent any mass exodus from the Order to the rival Federation, and also to recruit members from the trade unions, the General Assembly enacted legislation authorizing and encouraging the formation of national and regional trade districts. This move was reaffirmed and even extended at the meetings of the General Assembly in 1884 and 1886.[11]

While permissible, at least in theory, the establishment of trade districts was not a simple matter. The basic philosophy of the Knights militated against organization along craft lines, and the establishment of autonomous trade units within the framework of the Order aroused strong opposition. "I do not favor the establishment of any more National Trade Districts," Powderly told the General Assembly in 1885, "they are a step backward." [12] Other reform unionists, echoing Powderly's sentiments, charged that trade districts violated the fundamental principles of the Knights.[13] Holding tenaciously to their reform concepts, the leaders of the Knights were insistent in their demands that organization should not proceed along trade lines.

[8] K. of L., *GA Proc.*, January, 1879, pp. 69–70, 72; September, 1879, pp. 98, 129.

[9] Federation of Organized Trades and Labor Unions of the United States and Canada, *Proceedings*, 1881, pp. 7–9. Powderly was suspicious of the new organization, and he expressed the hope of capturing it. See Powderly to A. M. Owens, October 22, 1881, TVPLB.

[10] K. of L., *GA Proc.*, 1882, pp. 296–98. See also the statement of the General Executive Board in *ibid.*, p. 334.

[11] *Ibid.*, pp. 364, 368; 1884, pp. 705–07, 776; 1886, pp. 265–66.

[12] *Ibid.*, 1885, p. 25.

[13] See the *Journal of United Labor*, VII (June 25, 1886) , 2100; *John Swinton's Paper*, September 6, 1885; K. of L., *GA Proc.*, 1884, pp. 716–17.

Applicants for trade districts therefore could not always be certain that charters would be granted them, even though they had met all the formal requirements. In some cases charters were granted without any questions. Window Glass Workers' L.A. 300 was chartered as a national trade district at a time when such districts were contrary to the laws of the Knights, and the telegraphers were organized nationally in 1882 as D.A. 45. For a while these two were the only national districts, although before 1886 there were two district assemblies composed of miners, five of shoemakers, three of railroad employees, and one each of printers, plumbers, leather workers, government employees, and streetcar employees. Between 1883 and 1885 the General Assembly went on record as favoring the establishment of trade districts of shoemakers, plate-glass workers, and plumbers.[14] On the other hand, after sanctioning the formation of builders' districts in 1882, it refused the following year to permit these districts to be represented on the General Executive Board.[15] Even while passing legislation authorizing trade districts, the General Assembly refused to allow woodworkers, cigarmakers, and carpenters to organize trade districts. Furthermore, it passed a resolution stating that no charter for a trade district would be granted unless the applicants could demonstrate to the satisfaction of the General Executive Board that the craft could not be effectively organized under the system of mixed or territorial districts.[16] The attitude of the Board, however, was often conditioned by the anti-trade unionism of its officers. In 1886, for example, it refused to sanction the request of five building trade locals that they be permitted to withdraw from D.A. 66 and organize their own district. At the same time it empowered a New Hampshire local to change from a trade to a mixed assembly.[17]

Trade units, generally speaking, were authorized usually in efforts to attract workers to join the Knights. Thus the International Trunkmakers Union came into the Order as a trade district.[18] Once inside, however, workers found it considerably more difficult to secure trade charters. After affiliating in 1882, to cite one case, the plumbers later left the Knights when they encountered difficulty in obtaining a charter for a national trade district, and they established the International Association of Journeymen Plumbers, Steam Fitters and Gas Fitters.[19]

The hostility of the national leadership of the Knights was not the sole

[14] K. of L., *GA Proc.*, 1883, pp. 438, 443, 502; 1884, p. 787; 1885, pp. 127, 133; *Journal of United Labor*, V (December 10, 1884) , 856.

[15] K. of L., *GA Proc.*, 1882, pp. 325, 347; 1883, pp. 445, 498.

[16] *Ibid.*, 1882, pp. 311, 351; 1883, pp. 439–40, 498, 502.

[17] *Ibid.*, 1886, pp. 126–27.

[18] *Ibid.*, 1883, p. 506; 1884, p. 619. This was also the case in the affiliation of the harness workers. *Journal of United Labor*, IV (June, 1883) , 511, (July, 1883) , 520–21. The Knights also aided the barbers, horse railway men, miners, railway men, and ax makers in attempts to get them to join.

[19] New York Bureau of Labor Statistics, *Annual Report*, V (1887) , 202–03.

obstacle to the formation of trade units. Mixed and territorial districts, which were first in the field and were already established as functioning organizations, were also antagonistic toward trade districts. If the latter were formed, not only would a mixed district suffer a loss of membership to a trade district, but it would also surrender its absolute jurisdiction over a given territorial area, since the autonomous trade district would exercise control over the entire craft in that area.

The General Assembly and the General Executive Board often supported the mixed and territorial districts in disputes with trade districts. Frequently the district's consent was a prerequisite to secession and the establishment of a trade district. This consent was not easily obtained. In 1886, D.A. 30 of Massachusetts turned down an application by four of its locals for permission to withdraw and form a national trade assembly of rubber workers.[20] D.A. 49 of New York City tried to force the plumbers of Local Association 35, International Association of Journeymen Plumbers, Steam Fitters and Gas Fitters, back into L.A. 1992 after they seceded from the Knights because of difficulty in obtaining a charter for a national trade district and fear that the interests of their craft were being disregarded.[21] While the General Assembly supported a district court decision that members of trade locals could not be compelled to join mixed locals, the General Executive Board refused to force trade members of mixed locals to transfer to trade assemblies.[22]

Even after obtaining a charter, trade districts encountered difficulties with the mixed district in their areas. Dual jurisdiction often led to friction, though in theory the system of mixed and trade districts appeared perfectly harmonious and compatible. For example, D.A. 64 of New York City, composed of workers in the printing and publishing business, became embroiled in a rivalry with D.A. 49 (mixed). In 1883, D.A. 64 failed to get exclusive jurisdiction over all workers in the trade. Soon afterward D.A. 49 charged that the printers were accepting locals not of their trade, and that these locals had also withdrawn from D.A. 49 without permission. An investigation by the secretary of the General Executive Board disclosed that D.A. 64 had been initiating lithographers, typefounders, pressmen, and feeders in order to strengthen itself as a bargaining unit, and that it had not engaged in raiding forays against D.A. 49. Although the Board upheld D.A. 64, the decision did not resolve the rivalry, and the two districts continued their feud.[23]

With the single exception of L.A. 300, trade districts did not enjoy any appreciable measure of success between 1878 and 1885.[24] The far-reaching

[20] *Quarterly Report of District Assembly No. 30 . . . July . . . 1886* (Boston, 1886), p. 69.
[21] New York Bureau of Labor Statistics, *Annual Report,* V (1887), 202–04.
[22] K. of L., *GA Proc.,* 1885, pp. 102–03, 140; 1886, p. 130.
[23] *Ibid.,* 1883, pp. 467, 508; 1884, p. 617; 1885, pp. 125, 135; 1887, pp. 1714, 1757.
[24] Even the successful career of L.A. 300 cannot be attributed to the Knights. It was due primarily to the skilled nature of the trade which permitted the window glass

reform goals of the Knights and its structural inclusiveness left the advocates of trade organization in the position of a perpetual minority. The expansion of the Knights into the more sparsely populated regions of the South and West, moreover, further diminished trade influence, since the mixed assembly was dominant in rural areas. Lacking a majority, the trade members were unable to establish a central strike fund or concentrate on collective bargaining, and they found that their immediate goals were being subordinated to and sacrificed for more utopian objectives.

III

The struggle between trade unionists and reformers within the Knights, however, was completely overshadowed by the rupture of relations in 1886 between the Knights and the national unions. The latter, stronger and more cohesive than the trade districts of the Order, were better able to take the lead in the conflict between reform and trade unionism. Disillusioned with labor reformism, the trade unions acted upon the premise that the traditional programs of the past were no longer suitable to the changing environment, and they led the assault against the Knights of Labor in 1886.

During the early 1880's, however, it was by no means evident that the Knights and the national unions were predestined to clash. The Federation of Organized Trades and Labor Unions permitted district assemblies of the Knights to be represented at its annual conventions,[25] and many trade-union leaders also belonged to the Order.[26] Local unions and assemblies often co-operated in joint boycotts, and expressions of friendliness by the national unions toward Powderly and other officials of the Knights were not uncommon.[27] The International Typographical Union expressed appreciation in 1882 for the aid given it by the Knights in a number of cities, and then went on to adopt resolutions recommending co-operation with other labor organizations and permitting its members to join any body that would further the interests of the craft in their particular locality.[28] In other words, the national unions regarded the Knights as a valuable economic ally.

In turn, the Knights vehemently denied having any hostile designs upon

---

workers to organize thoroughly, restrict output, and regulate apprenticeship requirements. See Pearce David, *The Development of the American Glass Industry* (Cambridge, Massachusetts, 1949), pp. 126–30.

[25] Federation of Organized Trades and Labor Unions of the United States and Canada, *Proceedings*, 1882, pp. 5, 16, 20, 23.

[26] For a partial list of trade union leaders belonging to the Knights see *The Painter*, II (February, 1888), 3.

[27] See the *Iron Molders' Journal*, XIX (June 30, 1883), 9, XX (June 30, 1884), 10, XXI (November 30, 1885), 14; Amalgamated Association of Iron and Steel Workers, *Proceedings*, 1882, p. 955; *The Craftsman*, II (January 17, 1885), 2, (August 15, 1885), 2.

[28] International Typographical Union, *Proceedings*, 1882, pp. 43, 58, 62, 78, 83, 87.

the trade unions, and the General Assembly in 1885 adopted a resolution affirming that "unfair craftsmen" were not desirable members. When a group of malcontents attempted to force the Amalgamated Association of Iron and Steel Workers into the Order in 1882, they were promptly repudiated by the General Assembly.[29] The General Executive Board also refused to stop subordinate units from sending representatives to the meeting of the Federation of Organized Trades and Labor Unions.[30] Undoubtedly the Knights' claims that it had no desire to harm the trade unions were made in good faith.[31] Nevertheless, with its structural inclusiveness and reform ideology, it was perhaps inevitable that the Order, in its efforts to bring all workingmen into a single organization, would undercut trade-union organizational efforts. Thus the General Assembly authorized a committee in 1883 to confer with union representatives in the hope of incorporating all the trade unions within the Knights.[32]

In the absence of any national or international union, the absorption of local unions by the Knights in the form of trade assemblies created no friction. Indeed, isolated local unions were eager to affiliate with such a powerful national organization.[33] By 1886, therefore, the Knights claimed nearly eleven hundred local assemblies, many of which undoubtedly represented local trade unions having no parent national union.

When, however, the Knights began to organize workingmen in trades already having national organizations, friction was quick to arise. The trouble that followed the Order's expansion into the realm of the trade unions was not simply a jurisdictional rivalry between similar organizations. As we have seen, the Order and the national unions had opposing conceptions of the legitimate functions of the labor movement, which in turn had led to different structural forms. The expansion of the Order's mixed units thus served to undermine the economic functions of the trade unions, since the heterogeneous character of the former prevented them from exercising any appreciable degree of economic power. Furthermore, the structural diversity of the Knights caused trouble when its trade assemblies sought to perform tasks that logically fell within the purview of the trade unions.[34] The national unions, moreover, took the position that geographical trade assemblies were inadequate to meet the challenge of a nationalized economy, and in fact were little better than mixed district assemblies. In defense, union officials generally refused to consent to a

[29] K. of L., *GA Proc.*, 1885, p. 138; 1882, p. 270.

[30] *Ibid.*, 1885, p. 73.

[31] See Powderly to J. P. McDonnell, September 24, 1882, TVPLB.

[32] K. of L., *GA Proc.*, 1883, pp. 460, 467, 505–06.

[33] Ohio Bureau of Labor Statistics, *Annual Report*, IX (1885), 28; Grace H. Stimson, *Rise of the Labor Movement in Los Angeles* (Berkeley, California, 1955), p. 45.

[34] Differences over wages, hours, and working conditions frequently ensued between trade assemblies and local and national unions, especially since no formal co-ordinating bodies existed. For an example of such a disagreement see K. of L., *GA Proc.*, 1884, pp. 703, 764, 768.

mutual recognition of working cards,[35] and they demanded that the Knights cease interfering in trade affairs. As a leading trade union publication remarked:

> It is well known that the Knights of Labor was not instituted with the view to action in the matter of regulating wages. The objects included education, the bettering of the material condition of the members by means of such schemes as co-operation, etc., and the elevation of labor by legislation through political action, but not taken, however, in a partisan way. The plan of the organization did not include the management of strikes or aught else pertaining to wages and terms of labor, and it is not surprising, therefore, that the machinery has not proven equal to those occasions, when the Knights went outside of their original objects. It would be a blessing to all concerned if the Knights of Labor shall resolve to return to first principles and devote undivided attention thereto.[36]

The Knights, however, did not heed the warnings of the national unions, and its organizers continued their sporadic work in trades having national unions. "Every week," John Swinton reported in 1885, "Trades Unions are turned into Local Assemblies, or Assemblies are organized out of Trade Unions." [37] As early as 1881 a district leader attempted to capture a typographical union local, and by 1884 there were over forty local assemblies of printers in the Knights.[38] The overzealous activities of the Order's organizers also led to trouble with the Bricklayers and Masons International Union.[39]

The trade unions continuously charged that the Order had accepted scabs and unfair workers.[40] It is probable that the unions greatly exaggerated this grievance, but there is little doubt that the existence of two labor organizations, each purporting to accomplish different ends, created a disciplinary problem. Intraunion disagreements frequently concluded with one party seceding and joining the Order as a local assembly. Thus the trade unions found that the Knights were attracting dissidents who normally might have remained in the union. In Washington, D. C., some members of local union 1 of the United Brotherhood of Carpenters and

---

[35] Iron Molders International Union, *Proceedings*, 1882, pp. 15, 54–55.

[36] *National Labor Tribune*, July 7, 1883, cited in Commons, *History of Labour*, II, 353. "With other trade unionists," Gompers recalled, "I joined the Knights of Labor for the purpose of confining that organization to theoretical educational work and to see that the Trade Unions were protected from being undermined or disrupted." Gompers to N. E. Mathewson, October 10, 1890, SGLB.

[37] *John Swinton's Paper*, April 12, 1885.

[38] *Journal of United Labor*, II (September–October, 1881), 158; *John Swinton's Paper*, March 2, 1884.

[39] Bricklayers and Masons International Union, *Proceedings*, 1884, p. 9; Henry O. Cole to Powderly, March 9, April 28, 1883, Powderly Papers.

[40] *The Carpenter*, III (February, 1883), 3; International Typographical Union, *Proceedings*, 1884, p. 12.

Joiners engaged in a dispute with the national office over the payment of assessments for a new benefit system. At the end of 1883 they seceded to form L.A. 1748, and were later active in the movement to establish a national trade district of carpenters in opposition to the national union.[41] A similar situation also involving the Carpenters occurred in Philadelphia, where some members of local union 8 seceded in 1882 to form Carpenters L.A. 18.[42] The Granite Cutters National Union was also faced with a similar problem.[43]

Despite the proselytizing activities of the Knights, there was no general conflict with the other unions before July, 1885. At this time the membership of the Order was slightly over 100,000, and examples of clashes with the trade unions were generally the exception rather than the rule. When differences did arise, the trade unions often made conciliatory efforts at peaceful adjustment. Thus the convention of the International Typographical Union agreed in 1884 to its president's suggestion that he confer with Powderly in order to iron out existing grievances, although it refused to sanction a proposed amalgamation with the Order.[44]

In only one major case—that involving the Cigar Makers International Union—did the differences between a national union and the Knights erupt in open hostilities before 1886. Historians, placing much emphasis upon this particular conflict, have credited Adolph Strasser and Samuel Gompers, the leaders of the Cigar Makers, with the dual responsibility of helping to precipitate the internecine war between the national unions and the Knights, and then founding the A.F. of L. as a rival national federation.[45]

While the national unions generally supported the Cigar Makers in its struggle with the Knights,[46] it is improbable that sympathy for the Cigar Makers would have led to a fight with the Order. Undoubtedly Strasser and Gompers exerted great efforts to induce the unions to lend them support. The fact is also incontrovertible that both were determined, forceful, and sometimes ruthless men. Nevertheless, their efforts would have been useless unless a solid basis of discontent had already existed. In other words, for the unions to break with the Knights, there must have been more compelling reasons than simply the activities of two individuals, neither of whom had an official mandate to speak for the trade unions.

[41] *The Carpenter*, III (October, 1883), 2, VI (March, 1886), 4, VIII (February 15, 1888), 1; Robert A. Christie, *Empire in Wood: A History of the Carpenters' Union* (Ithaca, New York, 1956), pp. 50–51.

[42] *John Swinton's Paper*, February 1, 8, 1885.

[43] K. of L., *GA Proc.*, 1885, pp. 106, 109, 140.

[44] International Typographical Union, *Proceedings*, 1884, pp. 12, 65–66, 70, 72, 102.

[45] See especially Ware, *Labor Movement*, pp. 258–79, 285, *et passim*, and Commons, *History of Labour*, II, 401–02.

[46] *Iron Molders' Journal*, XXII (March 31, 1886), 14; *The Craftsman*, III (August 7, 1886), 2.

IV

To understand the conflict that split the labor movement, the rapid growth of the Knights after 1885 must be examined. In the twelve months between July, 1885, and June, 1886, the Order's membership increased from 100,000 to over 700,000. This growth, at least in part, came about at the expense of the trade unions. In many cases workers abandoned their trade unions to join the Knights. The Journeymen Tailors National Union found that many of its locals had transferred to the Knights, resulting in a considerable loss of membership. A vice-president of the Amalgamated Association of Iron and Steel Workers complained in 1886 that some sublodges in his area had been disbanded because of inroads by the Order.[47] Further difficulty was caused by overzealous organizers who made determined efforts to transform trade unions into local assemblies. In February, 1886, the secretary of the Journeymen Bakers National Union protested against such activities. "We never knew," responded the secretary-treasurer of the Knights, "that the K. of L. was proscribed from bringing into its folds all branches of honorable toil." [48]

The Knights, in other words, had adopted an organizational policy diametrically different from that of the trade unions. The traditional concept of organization held by the A.F. of L. (the representative of the trade unions) required that federal labor unions (local units including workers of all trades having no separate unions of their own) be splintered into separate homogeneous craft units as soon as there were enough workers in that locality to form such bodies. The aim of such a policy was to develop the collective bargaining potentialities of the various trades. The Knights, on the other hand, sought to reverse this strategy and proceed in the opposite direction, and it encouraged the combining of trade units into mixed assemblies, which at most were reform or political units. Beneath the structural and organizational differences of the two groups therefore, lay opposing goals.

To what extent did the Knights encroach upon the domain of the trade unions? Peter J. McGuire of the Carpenters claimed that between 150 and 160 trade unions, including the Molders, Boiler-Makers, Bakers, Miners, Typographical, and Granite Cutters, had grievances against the Order.[49] Only in the case of the Bricklayers and Masons International Union, however, is the evidence fairly complete. In response to a survey conducted in

[47] John B. Lennon, "Journeymen Tailors," *American Federationist*, IX (September, 1902), 599; Amalgamated Association of Iron and Steel Workers, *Proceedings*, 1886, p. 1793.

[48] New Haven *Workmen's Advocate*, December 10, 1887.

[49] K. of L., *GA Proc.*, 1886 special session, pp. 50–51.

the summer of 1886, the union's secretary received eighty-seven replies. Eight locals reported the existence of bricklayers and masons assemblies within their jurisdiction, four claimed the Knights were working for sub-union wages, and three asserted the Knights were working longer hours. "But there are a large number of such men scattered throughout the country who belong to mixed assemblies," the secretary reported—and herein lay the union's major grievance.[50] The complaints of the Brick-layers and Masons were echoed by most of the other major national unions.[51]

In general, the national unions were fearful of the Knights for two closely related reasons. The mixed assembly, in the first place, was incompatible with trade-union goals. In theory both structural forms could exist side by side, each pursuing its own ends. Thus the mixed assembly could concentrate on reform and politics, while the trade unions could develop their collective bargaining functions. This *modus vivendi*, however, presupposed that workers could belong simultaneously to both trade unions and mixed assemblies. At a time when the labor movement's primary problem was to organize and stay organized, such an assumption was unwarranted, and trade-union leaders recognized the mutual hostility of the mixed assembly and trade union.

In the second place, trade-union officials opposed the chartering of trade assemblies within the Knights for the reason that these units had proved incapable of developing collective bargaining and other union institutions. Furthermore, the geographical and regional organization of the Knights meant that there was little hope for the mature evolution of the national trade assembly. Since local trade assemblies were often ineffective when operating in an environment marked by a nationalized economy and the geographical mobility of labor, trade-union leaders argued that these units were attempting to perform functions that logically belonged to the national unions, and in the long run tended to undermine the standards of membership and employment that the unions had struggled so fiercely to establish.[52]

By the spring of 1886 relations between the trade unions and the Knights had so deteriorated that a collision appeared imminent.[53] The

[50] Bricklayers and Masons International Union, *Proceedings*, 1887, pp. 70–75.

[51] *Iron Molders' Journal*, XXII (February 28, 1886), 10, 14, (April 30, 1886), 8, (August 31, 1886), 6, XXIII (December 31, 1886), 7; *The Craftsman*, III (May 15, 1886), 3; *Granite Cutters' Journal*, X (April, 1886), 3; *The Carpenter*, VI (May, 1886), 2; *Cigar Makers' Official Journal*, XI (April, 1886), 6; *Printers' Circular*, XXI (June, 1886), 66; International Typographical Union, *Proceedings*, 1886, pp. 90, 93–94; Iron Molders International Union, *Proceedings*, 1886, pp. 16, 25, 31.

[52] For typical examples involving the Knights in difficulties with the Typographical and Carpenters unions, see *The Craftsman*, III (February 6, 1886), 2, (March 20, 1886), 1; W. J. Shields, "The Early History of the United Brotherhood of Carpenters and Joiners of America," *The Carpenter*, XXIV (December, 1904), 5.

[53] *John Swinton's Paper*, March 21, 1886; Illinois Bureau of Labor Statistics, *Biennial Report*, IV (1886), 160–61.

actions of the Knights, observed the secretary of the Bricklayers, "to seduce subordinate Unions of trades craft [*sic*] and their members individually to renounce allegiance to their parent order created disturbance and dissension to such a degree that decided and united action was necessary to prevent such encroachments." [54] On April 26, 1886, therefore, a circular written by McGuire of the Carpenters and endorsed by Strasser of the Cigar Makers, Fitzpatrick of the Molders, Dyer of the Granite Cutters, and Foster of the Federation of Organized Trades and Labor Unions, was sent to all national and international unions. Charging that an element within the Knights was bent on destroying the trade unions, it called for a conference of union officials on May 18 in Philadelphia to devise a plan that would be submitted to the Order.[55] That same day Powderly issued a summons for a special session of the General Assembly in Cleveland on May 25 to consider, among other things, the troubles with the trade unions. Powderly then invited union officials to meet with him in Cleveland and arrange an amicable settlement.[56]

At the meeting in Philadelphia on May 18, twenty-two delegates representing twenty national and international unions were present, and twelve other organizations sent pledges of support. After detailing the grievances of the trade unions against the Knights, the conference appointed a committee composed of Strasser, McGuire, Fitzpatrick, Weihe, and Evans to draw up a treaty with the Knights.[57] McGuire was undoubtedly the leading figure among this coterie of union officials. Completely dedicated to the interests of the working class, he had helped to give the young labor movement a sense of direction and an articulate philosophy. Although a devoted trade unionist, McGuire, like many of his contemporaries, never regarded craft organizations solely as a medium for the skilled workers. Trade unions, he argued, "are organized on the autonomic basis of trades lines, for trade objects; they have a historic basis that insures their permanency." [58] Nevertheless, he did not accept the inevitability of a conflict between the Knights and the unions. "The Knights of Labor," he commented, "is an organization with which our Brotherhood [the Carpenters] has no antagonism. We are not at war with it. On the contrary, many of our members belong to mixed assemblies of the Knights of Labor. Against that we have naught to say. We believe the K. of L. as an organization has a legitimate work to perform—and that is to organize all branches of unorganized labor that have no trade head of their own. But where there is a National or International Union of a trade, the men of that trade should

---

[54] Bricklayers and Masons International Union, *Proceedings*, 1887, p. 62.

[55] *Ibid.*, p. 63; *The Carpenter*, VI (May, 1886) , 2.

[56] K. of L., *GA Proc.*, 1886 special session, pp. 1–2; Powderly to P. J. McGuire, May 11, 1886; Powderly to Adolph Strasser, May 11, 1886, TVPLB.

[57] *The Carpenter*, VI (June, 1886) , 3; *Cigar Makers' Official Journal*, XI (June, 1886) , 7; Bricklayers and Masons International Union, *Proceedings*, 1887, pp. 64–66.

[58] *The Carpenter*, VI (April, 1886) , 4.

organize under it. And in such cases the K. of L. should not interfere." [59]

Under McGuire's moderating influence the committee drew up a
"treaty," which it presented to the General Executive Board of the
Knights on May 25. By the terms of this treaty the Knights would refrain
from organizing any trade having a national organization, and also would
revoke the charter of any existing trade assembly having a parent union.
In the second place, any workers guilty of ignoring trade union wage
scales, scabbing, or any other offense against a union, would be ineligible
for membership in the Order. Third, any organizer who tampered with or
interfered in the internal affairs of trade unions would have his commission revoked. Finally, local and district assemblies were not to interfere
while trade unions engaged in strikes or lockouts, and the Knights would
not be permitted to issue any label or trade-mark where a national union
had already done so. [60]

On the surface it appears surprising that the trade unions, which
claimed to represent about 350,000 workers (although their actual membership was about 160,000), would present such a document to an organization having 700,000 members. Yet the treaty was neither a bargaining
offer nor a declaration of war. [61] It was rather the logical outcome of the
duality that had pervaded the labor movement since the Civil War. Under
its terms the labor movement would be divided into two separate and distinct compartments. The Knights of Labor, on the one hand, would continue its efforts to abolish the wage system, reform society, and educate
the working class. The national union, on the other hand, would be left
paramount in the economic field, and the Order would no longer be permitted to exercise any control over wages, hours, working conditions, or
the process of collective bargaining. In other words, trade unionism and
reform unionism had come to a parting of the ways.

In one sense the treaty was an expression of the fear of the skilled
workers that they were being subordinated to the interests of the unskilled. [62] Yet the polarization implied in such an interpretation should
not be exaggerated, for it cannot be said that the Knights themselves represented the unskilled workers. The Order was not an industrial union,

[59] *Ibid.*, VI (February, 1886), 4.
[60] A.F. of L., *Proceedings*, 1886, p. 16.
[61] Cf. Ware, *Labor Movement*, p. 284.
[62] See, for example, the Bricklayers and Masons International Union, *Proceedings*,
1887, pp. 67–68, and the K. of L., *GA Proc.*, 1886 special session, p. 38. Professor Perlman
has interpreted the conflict between the Knights and the trade unions as one between
skilled and unskilled workers. Commons, *History of Labour*, II, 396–97. Undoubtedly
the skilled workers feared the Knights. The Knights, however, was not necessarily an
organization of unskilled workers, as the large number of trade assemblies would
indicate. While the unions jealously guarded their autonomy and independence, the
conflict that developed in 1886 was more than simply a struggle between the skilled
and unskilled elements in the labor movement, although this aspect of the struggle
should not be neglected.

nor did it emphasize collective bargaining. It was rather a heterogeneous mass that subordinated the economic functions of labor organizations to its primary goal of reforming society. The mixed assembly, while including workers of all trades and callings, was in no sense an industrial union, since it was not organized either by industry or factory. Moreover, the trade unions had never excluded the unskilled from the labor movement; they simply maintained that organization along craft lines was historically correct. "In truth," remarked Gompers, "the trade union is nothing more or less than the organization of wage earners engaged in a given employment, whether skilled or unskilled, for the purpose of attaining the best possible reward, [and] the best attainable conditions for the workers in that trade or calling." [63]

On May 25, the same day that the trade-union committee presented a copy of its treaty to the General Executive Board of the Knights, the special session of the General Assembly opened its deliberations in Cleveland. Leaders on both sides realized the crucial nature of the convention. While the trade unions had stated their position in no uncertain terms, the Knights had as yet to take a stand.[64] It was obvious to partisans on both sides that failure to reach an agreement might be tantamount to a mutual declaration of war.

The problem facing the delegates to the special session of the General Assembly was whether or not to conduct negotiations using the treaty as a basis for discussion. The trade element within the Knights evinced willingness to do so, but the antiunionists, led largely by the "Home Club" of D.A. 49 of New York City,[65] succeeded in sidetracking a resolution authorizing the appointment of a committee to confer with the trade-union representatives.[66] The Home Club then went on to seize complete control of an enlarged General Executive Board.[67] Nevertheless, the trade advocates within the Knights proved a moderating influence and, after four days of wrangling, succeeded in inducing the General Assembly to approve a somewhat conciliatory circular addressed to the unions.[68] The terms of agreement offered to the unions included protection against unfair workers, a mutual exchange of working cards, and the holding of a joint conference before either organization presented wages and hours

[63] Gompers to George H. Daggett, January 4, 1896. See also Gompers to Albert C. Stevens, November 1, 1889; Gompers to Frank D. Hamlin, May 6, 1890; Gompers to Charles W. Nelson, April 29, 1892, SGLB.

[64] Powderly, while publicly maintaining that there was no serious or irreconcilable conflict with the unions, had privately expressed the view that the unions were trying to destroy the Order. See Powderly to Charles H. Litchman, April 17, 1886; Powderly to John W. Hayes, April 30, 1886; Powderly to [?] Bannan, July 29, 1886, TVPLB.

[65] The Home Club was composed of Lassallean socialists committed to an anti-trade union policy. For the origins and activities of the Club see Ware, *Labor Movement*, pp. 103–12, 181, *et passim*, and Foner, *History of the Labor Movement*, II, 78–79.

[66] K. of L., *GA Proc.*, 1886 special session, pp. 11–13.

[67] *John Swinton's Paper*, June 6, 1886.

[68] Buchanan, *Story of a Labor Agitator*, pp. 301–02.

demands to employers. The Assembly also authorized the appointment of a committee of five to negotiate with the unions.[69]

The position taken by the General Assembly was clearly in fundamental disagreement with that of the trade unions. The latter had demanded unitary control over the economic field, while the Knights had demanded equal jurisdiction over membership and working standards. Thus neither side evinced willingness to compromise over basic issues. Furthermore, the Assembly also adopted a resolution instructing members to support labels and trade-marks issued by the Knights in preference to any other.[70] This action was hardly designed to placate the unions, many of which already had their own labels.

Although failing to conclude a settlement with the trade unions, the special session of the General Assembly did not close the door to further negotiations. For the time being, therefore, the conflict remained in abeyance. While matters were pending, however, the Knights made a determined effort to end friction by intensifying its campaign to bring the national unions under its control. The national unions, however, recognized that the structure of the Knights was incompatible with trade-union objectives, and the policy of the Order was only partially successful. Some of the smaller unions, including the Seamen's Benevolent Union, the Eastern Glass Bottle Blowers' Association, and the Western Green Bottle Blowers' League, joined the Knights.[71] The American Flint Glass Workers Union, on the other hand, refused to go along with the other glassworkers because of an earlier dispute with the Order.[72] In New York City the Knights made a determined but unsuccessful attempt to capture the German shoemakers and the Associated Jewelers.[73] Most of the larger and more important unions emphatically rejected the Order's overtures. The members of the Amalgamated Association of Iron and Steel Workers overwhelmingly defeated a referendum on the subject, while a similar poll conducted by the secretary of the Bricklayers and Masons resulted in the same conclusion. The Iron Molders' convention turned down the merger proposal by a vote of 114 to 27.[74] Furthermore, the Typographical

[69] K. of L., *GA Proc.*, 1886 special session, pp. 53, 55, 67.

[70] *Ibid.*, p. 73.

[71] *Journal of United Labor*, VIII (August 20, 1887), 2476; *John Swinton's Paper*, July 25, 1886; David A. McCabe, *The Standard Rate in American Trade Unions* (Baltimore, 1912), pp. 155–56; K. of L., *GA Proc.*, 1887, p. 1334. The glassworkers probably joined the Order in the hope of emulating the success of L.A. 300.

[72] *Iron Molders' Journal*, XXII (February 28, 1886), 10; *Cigar Makers' Official Journal*, XI (August, 1886), 6; William J. Smith and John Ehmann, "The Flint Glass Workers," Secretary of Internal Affairs of the Commonwealth of Pennsylvania, *Annual Report*, XVI (1888), Pt. III, *Industrial Statistics*, Section F, pp. 18–19.

[73] *The Carpenter*, VI (October, 1886), 1.

[74] Amalgamated Association of Iron and Steel Workers, *Proceedings*, 1886, pp. 1807–08, 1818–19, 1846; 1887, pp. 1959–62; Bricklayers and Masons International Union, *Proceedings*, 1887, pp. 71, 76; Iron Molders International Union, *Proceedings*, 1886, pp. 17–20.

Union, the Carpenters, the Plumbers and Gas Fitters, the Coal Miners, and the Stationary Engineers all rejected the invitation to join the Knights.[75]

The proselytizing activities of the Knights, moreover, simply had the effect of forcing the unions to adopt an even more inflexible position. The Carpenters, for example, adopted a resolution in August, 1886, "emphatically discourag[ing] Carpenters and Joiners from organizing as Carpenters under the Knights of Labor, as we believe each trade should be organized under its own trade head in a trade union." [76] The attitude of many other trade unions toward the Knights also began to harden.

Meanwhile, McGuire, following the adjournment of the special session of the General Assembly, had written to Powderly on June 12, inquiring about the appointment of the committee authorized by the Assembly to negotiate with the unions. "In view of the fact that it would be a difficult thing to call five men away from their homes and occupations on a moment's warning or notice," Powderly responded, "and, inasmuch as the General Executive Board . . . are to be at headquarters, 500 Locust Street, Philadelphia, it will greatly facilitate business to have the General Executive Board act with similar committees from other labor organizations when appointed. I feel confident that much better results will follow the action at the hands of the Board than at the hands of a new and inexperienced committee." [77] By appointing the Board as the negotiating committee for the Knights, Powderly virtually ensured a conflict, since the antiunionists of the Home Club dominated the group.

On September 28 the trade-union committee went to Philadelphia and met with Powderly, Turner, Hayes, and Barry. Since the General Assembly was to open its regular convention in Richmond the following week, the unionists proposed that the treaty be given "due consideration," that officials on both sides attempt to settle outstanding issues, and that the special committee authorized by the Cleveland Assembly investigate union grievances and recommend remedial legislation. Powderly apparently agreed to lend his support to these propositions at the General Assembly.[78]

On October 4 the General Assembly opened its deliberations in Richmond, Virginia. Over 800 delegates, representing more than 700,000 members, were present. The 61 delegates of D.A. 49, however, easily controlled the convention through their alliance with the 75 delegates of D.A. 30. Furthermore, whether willingly or unwillingly, Powderly had

[75] *John Swinton's Paper*, June 20, 1886; *The Carpenter*, VI (October, 1886), 1. As early as March, 1886, the Brotherhood of Locomotive Firemen had vigorously expressed its firm opposition to any consolidation with the Knights. *Locomotive Firemen's Magazine*, X (March, 1886), 141.
[76] *The Carpenter*, VII (February, 1887), 2.
[77] *Ibid.*, VI (November, 1886), 3.
[78] *Ibid.*

joined the ranks of the antiunionists.[79] Moreover, the great majority of delegates, attending the convention for the first time, were not schooled in the intricacies and subtleties of parliamentary maneuvering. Their inexperience, coupled with an unbounded admiration for Powderly, virtually assured D.A. 49 of a free hand.

At the outset Powderly reneged on the promises he had given the previous week to the trade-union committee. Instead of presenting some definite proposals, he issued an optimistic statement maintaining that a settlement was still possible despite the fact that both sides had committed mistakes.[80] The General Assembly, moreover, did not categorically state its terms. On the contrary, it adopted a resolution introduced by D.A. 49 ordering all workers holding cards in both the Knights and the Cigar Makers International Union to leave the latter under pain of expulsion.[81] This resolution was tantamount to a declaration of war. "It was at Richmond," Buchanan later recalled, "that the seal of approval was placed upon the acts of those members who had been bending every energy since the Cleveland special session to bring on open warfare between the order and the trades-unions." [82]

Alarmed by this turn of events, the trade-union committee issued a call on November 10, 1886, for all trade unions to send representatives to a convention in Columbus, Ohio, on December 8, to form an "American Federation or Alliance of all National and International Trades Unions." [83] Out of this meeting came the American Federation of Labor, an organization destined to control the labor movement for the succeeding half-century. Completely dominated by the national trade unions, the December convention excluded assemblies of the Knights from membership, and then proceeded to establish the new organization on a firm foundation.[84]

Soon after the trade-union convention began its deliberations, a committee from the Knights made an appearance. The ensuing negotiations simply showed that the Order was unalterably opposed to any settlement on the basis of the union treaty. Indeed, it is dubious that the Knights even desired an agreement, for its committee refused to consider any of the "substitutes" that had been advanced at the Cleveland special session of the General Assembly. It quickly became clear that the Knights' committee had neither authority nor instructions. About all it would agree to do was to listen to the unions. One of its members, in fact, suggested

[79] Buchanan, *Story of a Labor Agitator*, pp. 316–17. Powderly was definitely hostile to the Home Club, but might have joined it in order to maintain his position. See Powderly to J. T. McKechnie, July 5, 1886; Powderly "To whom it may concern," July 24, 1886, TVPLB.

[80] K. of L., *GA Proc.*, 1886, p. 42.

[81] *Ibid.*, pp. 200, 282.

[82] Buchanan, *Story of a Labor Agitator*, p. 314.

[83] Bricklayers and Masons International Union, *Proceedings*, 1887, pp. 79–80.

[84] A.F. of L., *Proceedings*, 1886, pp. 13–15.

that consolidation with the Knights was the only realistic solution.[85] "Much is said by the leaders of trade organizations about the destruction of their unions by absorption into the Knights of Labor of their members, and the necessity on their part to oppose any tendency in that direction that the autonomy of their distinctive trade may be preserved," the committee later reported to the General Assembly. "Such arguments are but an evidence of the ignorance, of those who advance them, of the principles and workings of our Order, which has given opportunity to any trade to organize within the Order and perform its functions as a trade organization when the conditions involved would justify." [86]

The belligerent tone of the Knights was matched by the new Federation. "The K. of L. have persistently attempted to undermine and disrupt well-established Trades' Unions, organized and encouraged men who have proven themselves untrue to their trade, false to the obligations of their union, embezzlers of moneys, and expelled by many of the unions, and conspiring to pull down the Trades' Unions, which it has cost years of work and sacrifice to build," the trade unionists charged. Therefore, "we condemn the acts above recited, and call upon all workingmen to join the unions of their respective trades, and urge the formation of National and International Unions and the centralization of all under one head, The American Federation of Labor." [87]

Thus by the end of 1886 the die had been cast, and the Knights and national unions prepared for war. Why had all negotiations failed? Undoubtedly the intractability of leaders on both sides contributed to the difficulties, but there were also those who had made sincere efforts to head off the impending conflict. The trade unions, furthermore, had encountered jurisdictional rivalries with the Knights, but this has been an endemic problem of the labor movement, and one which has not always had an unhappy ending.

The conflict between the Knights and the trade unions, then, had a much broader significance than the negotiations between them indicated, and represented the culmination of decades of historical development. The Knights, growing out of the humanitarian and reform crusades of ante-bellum America, emphasized the abolition of the wage system and the reorganization of society. To achieve this purpose it insisted on the prime importance of the mixed assembly, which would serve as the nucleus of an organization dedicated to reform. The trade unions, on the other hand, accepted their environment, and sought to take advantage of the relative scarcity of labor and the rising scale of production. Hence they emphasized the collective bargaining functions of labor organizations, thus tacitly accepting the workers' wage status.

Perhaps grounds for compromise did exist, but neither side was prone

85 *Ibid.,* pp. 17–18; K. of L., *GA Proc.,* 1887, pp. 1445–47.
86 K. of L., *GA Proc.,* 1887, p. 1447.
87 A.F. of L., *Proceedings,* 1886, p. 19.

to make any concessions. The national unions, by insisting upon strict trade autonomy as a *sine qua non* of settlement, were in effect demanding that the Knights should virtually abandon any pretense at being a bona fide labor organization. It is true that the unions could have organized as national autonomous trade districts if the Knights had been ready to grant permission. The leaders of the Knights, however, were unwilling to permit their organization to be transformed into what the A.F. of L. ultimately became. Indeed, after 1886 many national trade districts left the Order because of their inability to function within the framework of that body. The national unions, moreover, were not encouraged by the experiences of trade districts within the Knights before 1886. Finally, there was the simple element of power, and both the trade unions and the Knights, as established organizations, were adamant in their refusal to surrender any part of it.

Between reform and trade unionism, therefore, existed a gulf that the leaders of the 1880's were unable to bridge. By 1886 this chasm had widened to such a degree that co-operation between the two seemed virtually impossible and war appeared to be the only solution. Reform and trade unionism had at last come to a parting of the ways, and upon the outcome of the ensuing struggle hinged the destiny of the American labor movement.

CHAPTER SEVEN

The Defeat of Reformism, 1887–1896

I

℘ THE KNIGHTS OF LABOR, Gompers remarked in the spring of 1887, "are just [as] great enemies of Trades Unions as any employers can be, only much more vindictive. I tell you that they will give us no quarter and I would give them their own medicine in return. It is no use trying to placate them or even to be friendly." [1] At first glance Gompers' belligerent and uncompromising attitude seemed to be based largely on wishful thinking rather than facts, for the Knights, with a membership more than triple that of the trade unions, appeared to be in firm control of the field. With its roots firmly embedded in the American past, the Order's apparent superiority over the unions seemed self-evident to many observers.

Yet beneath an imposing façade lay certain elements of weakness that in the final analysis were to prove fatal to the Knights in its struggle with the unions. Numerically the Order was paramount, but mere numbers is not always a reliable criterion of relative strength. The instability of the Knights' membership was notorious. Organized for reform rather than collective bargaining, mixed local and district assemblies often found the turnover of members a highly disruptive factor. The lack of institutional ties binding the worker to his assembly further contributed to this instability. Thus under the emotional enthusiasm aroused by the "Great Upheaval," the Knights' membership increased sevenfold between 1885 and 1886; but the subsidence of this fervor produced a consequent decline. A heterogeneous organization, the Knights did not possess a high degree of discipline, and its trade element, sympathizing with the union cause, proved to be a source of weakness instead of strength. Troubled by internal rivalries and petty jealousies, the Order was unable to use its vast resources in an efficient manner.

The trade unions, on the other hand, though numerically weaker, constituted a much more cohesive and homogeneous group. Composed

[1] Gompers to P. J. McGuire, April 22, 1887, SGLB.

119

largely of skilled mechanics bound together by economic and social ties, they proved to be more stable than their opponents and were therefore able to enforce a much greater degree of discipline. Functioning in a rapidly-expanding and acquisitive society, the unions proved better adapted to their environment than the Order. Perhaps one of the unions' greatest advantages lay in the quality of their leaders. Gompers, president of the newly-formed A.F. of L., was both a devoted unionist and an implacable foe of the Knights. Exceeding Powderly in both resourcefulness and determination, he tailored his techniques to the necessities of each individual situation.[2] No less important were the leaders of the national unions, who also proved themselves formidable protagonists.

II

Soon after the formation of the A.F. of L., the Knights opened an offensive designed to resolve the conflict. Having failed previously to induce the unions to affiliate with it, the Knights did the next best thing; it commenced to organize a large number of national trade assemblies, some of which directly challenged existing national and international unions. At the General Assembly of 1887 no less than twenty-two trade districts, with 654 local assemblies having an aggregate membership of nearly 54,000, were represented.[3] Despite its antipathy toward trade organization, the Assembly approved the General Executive Board's actions granting national trade charters in a number of cases.[4] Throughout the remainder of 1887 and 1888 the Knights continued to organize trade districts.[5]

The Knights, moreover, did not limit its organizational activities to those trades lacking national unions. On the contrary, it organized a number of rival national trade assemblies, probably with the intention of weakening the unions and thereby forcing them to surrender their autonomy and affiliate with the Order. At the end of 1887 a national assembly of molders and one of bakers and confectioners was organized despite the existence of the Iron Molders International Union and the Journeymen Bakers and Confectioners International Union.[6] Early in 1888 a national assembly of carpenters and joiners was established under

[2] For Gompers' generalship in the conflict with the Knights see Gompers to William Weihe, February 25, 1887; Gompers to H. J. Skeffington, September 14, 1887; Gompers to P. J. McGuire, May 10, 1888; Gompers to William Martin, October 16, 1888, SGLB.

[3] Figures compiled from K. of L., *GA Proc.*, 1887, pp. 1847-50. See also the New Jersey Bureau of Statistics of Labor and Industries, *Annual Report*, X (1887), 8-10.

[4] See, for example, K. of L., *GA Proc.*, 1887, pp. 1381, 1387-88, 1410, 1418-19, 1428.

[5] For evidence of such activities see the *Journal of United Labor*, VIII (September 24, 1887), 2494, (October 29, 1887), 2514, (December 17, 1887), 2543, (January 7, 1888), 2555, (June 16, 1888), 2646, IX (August 23, 1888), 2686, (March 21, 1889), 2806.

[6] *Ibid.*, VIII (September 3, 1887), 2483, (September 17, 1887), 2490.

the leadership of Ira B. Aylesworth, a suspended member of the United Brotherhood of Carpenters and Joiners.[7] The Knights also organized rival organizations in direct defiance of the Amalgamated Association of Iron and Steel Workers and the Furniture Workers Union.[8]

The unions were granted one apparent concession when the General Assembly in 1887 agreed to reinstate the members of the Cigar Makers International Union expelled from the Knights pursuant to the resolution adopted in 1886.[9] This decision, however, was not prompted by any conciliatory motives but was a response to the widespread opposition by members of the Order to the resolution.[10] Powderly had never favored its passage, and afterwards he worked quietly for its repeal and was generous in granting dispensations suspending its application in individual cases.[11] At the General Assembly in 1887 he declared that the resolution was in conflict with the constitution, and was therefore illegal.[12] Nevertheless, immediately after the General Assembly adjourned Powderly vested Litchman with the authority to organize a national trade assembly of cigar makers. Soon afterwards a rival cigar makers assembly came into being, completely neutralizing the conciliatory effect of the repeal of the disputed resolution.[13]

The Knights' sudden shift in encouraging the formation of national trade assemblies, however, also served to intensify internal structural problems. If it were to sanction trade organization on a wide scale, the dominance of the mixed assembly would be seriously challenged. The Order's commitment to a policy of social reform consequently would be forced to undergo considerable modification, for the existence of trade assemblies, especially at the national level, implied that primary emphasis would be placed upon collective bargaining.

Nevertheless, while the leaders of the Knights were willing to use national trade assemblies as a weapon against the unions, they were unwilling to modify or abandon any of their own plans for social regeneration. Trade assemblies, therefore, found themselves being used as pawns in the struggle against the unions. When National Carpet Workers D.A. 126 attempted to regulate its trade affairs and objected to certain policies of

[7] K. of L., *GA Proc.*, 1887, p. 1360; *Journal of United Labor,* VIII (December 17, 1887), 2543; *The Carpenter,* VIII (January 15, 1888), 4.

[8] *Journal of United Labor,* VIII (April 28, 1888), 2619, (May 12, 1888), 2627; *Cigar Makers' Official Journal,* XII (May, 1887), 8.

[9] K. of L., *GA Proc.*, 1887, pp. 1677, 1733, 1822, 1824.

[10] *Ibid.,* pp. 1278, 1283–84, 1312, 1314, 1326–27, 1330, 1340, 1357, 1374, 1379; *John Swinton's Paper,* February 27, 1887.

[11] Powderly to John O'Keefe, January 3, 1887; Powderly to J. F. Cronin, February 10, 1887; Powderly to John B. Dempsey, April 1, 1887; Powderly to John Devlin, September 14, 1887, TVPLB.

[12] K. of L., *GA Proc.*, 1887, pp. 1528–31.

[13] Powderly to Charles H. Litchman, October 31, 1887, TVPLB; *Journal of United Labor,* VIII (November 12, 1887), 2522, (January 7, 1888), 2555, (January 26, 1888), 2567.

the General Executive Board, its charter was promptly revoked.[14] The Board, moreover, followed a somewhat ambiguous course in granting national trade charters. The rubber workers, for example, had their application for a charter turned down after becoming involved in a dispute with the Board over technical procedures. In a similar case the Board also refused to sanction the establishment of a brickmakers district.[15]

The greatest opposition to national trade assemblies came from the mixed district assemblies, which were instrumental in preventing the newly-organized trade bodies from becoming anything more than paper entities in most cases. McGuire of the Carpenters shrewdly observed that the Knights "are now taking lessons from the trades unions, and are forming themselves on National Trade District lines, which are simply skeletons of trades unions without either their flesh or blood."[16] The General Executive Board, by ruling that local assemblies could not transfer their allegiance from district to national trade assemblies without first receiving the former's "approval and clearance," simply ensured the continued dominance of the mixed organization.[17] Decisions such as this one merely served to block the growth of trade units in the Knights.

On the whole the policy of establishing national trade assemblies to fight the unions proved highly unsuccessful, and by the end of 1888 the Knights had acknowledged this fact, although it continued to support existing assemblies. Powderly, having temporarily suspended his fundamental antipathy toward trade organization in 1887, soon reverted to his earlier attitude. "I will tell you frankly I don't care how quick the National Trade Assemblies go out," he wrote to Hayes early in 1889. "They hinder others from coming to us and I am strongly tempted to advise them all to go it alone on the outside and see how it will go to turn back the wheels of the organization for the benefit of a few men who want to be at the head of something."[18]

The antiunion sentiment of the Order's leadership, together with the hostility of the mixed districts toward their craft counterparts, placed all but insurmountable obstacles in the path of the more successful of the national trade assemblies attempting to remain within the fold. The experiences of the shoe workers were perhaps typical. Long a mainstay of the New England labor movement, the shoe workers had joined the Knights in large numbers following the demise of the Knights of St. Crispin in the middle 1870's and soon came to exercise considerable in-

[14] The Carpenter, VII (January, 1887), 3, (June, 1887), 4; The Craftsman, IV (June 4, 1887), 2.

[15] K. of L., GA Proc., 1887, pp. 1291, 1299–1300.

[16] The Carpenter, VII (October 15, 1887), 4.

[17] K. of L., GA Proc., 1887, p. 1357. See also ibid., pp. 1372, 1418.

[18] Powderly to John W. Hayes, February 9, 1889, cited in Ware, Labor Movement, p. 189. See also Foner, History of the Labor Movement, II, 166; K. of L., GA Proc., 1892, p. 2.

fluence within the Order. Their inability to function efficiently in mixed districts led them to espouse trade districts, and in 1883 the General Assembly agreed to sanction the establishment of shoemakers' districts. Less than a year later thirteen local assemblies withdrew from D.A. 1 in Philadelphia and founded Shoemakers' D.A. 70.[19] Other districts were soon established in Lynn, Massachusetts, and in New York City.[20]

The formation of trade district assemblies gave added impetus to the growing sentiment that only a national organization would meet the needs of the shoe workers. In June, 1885, therefore, one hundred delegates came together in Philadelphia and organized the Executive Council of the Shoe and Leather Workers of the Knights of Labor. In November of the following year some of the more skilled workers established the Boot and Shoe Cutters' International Assembly of the United States and Canada.[21] Finally, through the efforts of D.A. 70 of Philadelphia, National Trade Assembly (N.T.A.) 217, composed of shoe workers, was founded in mid-1887 despite the hostility of the leaders of the Knights.[22] Harry J. Skeffington, prominent since 1876 as a leader of the shoe workers in the Order, became Master Workman.

The new assembly immediately encountered the bitter resistance of mixed districts when it attempted to unify the shoe trade.[23] Matters reached a climax when N.T.A. 217 and D.A. 48 became embroiled in a fight in Cincinnati for control of the trade. The General Executive Board of the Knights undertook an investigation and soon thereafter imposed a settlement which Skeffington refused to obey. For his supposed disobedience he was censured by the General Assembly in 1888. Prior to the meeting of the Assembly, however, the delegates of N.T.A. 217 had empowered their officers to organize a national trade union in the event that the rift with the General Executive Board could not be healed. In February, 1889, therefore, Skeffington issued a circular calling for a new union.[24] "What fool is there," he remarked a few weeks later, "who believes that the shoemakers of the country can be successfully organized and united under the banner of the Knights of Labor . . . The interests

[19] K. of L., *GA Proc.*, 1883, pp. 438, 443, 499, 502; *John Swinton's Paper*, June 15, 1884.

[20] *Union Boot and Shoe Worker*, I (April, 1900), 8; *John Swinton's Paper*, November 22, 1885.

[21] *John Swinton's Paper*, June 7, 1885, November 14, 1886.

[22] *Ibid.*, April 10, June 12, 1887. Powderly was bitterly opposed to both McNeill and Skeffington, the two most prominent leaders in the shoe trade. Powderly to John W. Hayes, April 1, 1887, Powderly-Hayes Correspondence. See also Skeffington's statement in the *Official Book of the American Federation of Labor Issued for the Twelfth Annual Convention . . . 1892* (New York, 1892), not paginated.

[23] See K. of L., *GA Proc.*, 1887, p. 1390.

[24] *Ibid.*, 1888, *Report of the General Executive Board*, pp. 79–82, 119–20, *Proceedings of the General Assembly*, pp. 61, 66, 97; *Union Boot and Shoe Worker*, I (April, 1900), 8; *Shoe Workers' Journal*, XI (July, 1910), 8–11.

of our trade have been trifled with." [25] In June forty-seven unions sent representatives to a convention that organized the Boot and Shoe Workers International Union.

Intermittent warfare continued for the next six years between the shoe workers' union and those who remained faithful to the Knights. A third union, the New England Lasters Protective Union, sought to maintain a middle course between the two warring groups.[26] Not until 1895 did the movement to unify the shoe workers meet with success. Pursuant to a call issued by a committee composed of representatives from the three unions, a convention, meeting in Boston in April, 1895, effected a merger that completely excluded the Knights from the shoe industry.[27]

The shoe workers were by no means the only large group finding the organizational structure and program of the Knights to be incompatible with trade union objectives. The miners, who more than any other group should have found the Order's inclusiveness well-adapted to a trade organized along industrial rather than craft lines, also encountered friction in their relations with the Knights.

Organization among the mine workers had predated the founding of the Knights. The American Miners' Association, established in 1861, set the precedent for the industrial type of unionism in this trade. Unable to survive the postwar period of economic readjustment, it disappeared in the early 1870's. Although other unions arose from the ashes of the American Miners' Association, they were quickly destroyed by the depression of 1873–1878. Having nowhere else to go after 1878, the miners began to join the Knights in large numbers.

The system of mixed districts, however, apparently did not prove satisfactory, and the failure of the Hocking Valley coal strike, which lasted from June, 1884, to March, 1885, convinced many miners that a national organization was absolutely essential.[28] Soon afterwards John McBride, president of the Ohio Miners' State Union and one of the first members of the Knights west of the Alleghenies, issued a call for a convention to meet in Indianapolis in September, 1885, to form a national federation. Out of this meeting came the National Federation of Miners and Mine Laborers. McBride, a delegate to the General Assemblies of 1882 and 1883, probably took this step because of his inability to secure a charter from the Knights for a trade district of miners.[29]

[25] *The Laster,* I (March 15, 1889), 1. See also *ibid.,* II (April 15, 1890), 4.

[26] K. of L., *GA Proc.,* 1892, p. 75; *The Laster,* III (December 15, 1890), 1, IV (September 15, 1891), 1.

[27] *Brauer-Zeitung,* X (May 11, 1895), 1; *The People,* March 31, May 5, 1895; Lasters Protective Union, *Proceedings,* 1895, pp. 8–9, 42–64, 75–76.

[28] Andrew Roy, *A History of the Coal Miners of the United States* (3rd edition: Columbus, Ohio, 1907), pp. 215–26.

[29] See McBride's statement in United Mine Workers of America, *Proceedings,* 1911, I, 581.

While McBride was organizing a national union, there was a similar movement within the Knights to establish a national trade district of miners. In 1885 the General Assembly gave its permission, and in May, 1886, N.T.A. 135, composed of miners and mine laborers, came into existence.[30] Lacking a national organization from 1876 to 1885, the miners suddenly found themselves with two in 1886. The existence of two unions, however, quickly led to jurisdictional rivalries, and relations between the Federation and N.T.A. 135 rapidly deteriorated. At its second convention in the autumn of 1886 the Federation, emphatically opposing any merger with the Knights,[31] refused to accept representatives of N.T.A. 135 into the joint conference of miners and operators. Its Executive Board, furthermore, issued a circular claiming sole jurisdiction over the field and fulminating against those "selfish individuals that are bent upon the destruction of our National Trades' Union." [32] The Knights promptly threatened to refuse to recognize any agreement negotiated by the Federation unless its representatives were admitted on an equal basis, and proceeded to send organizers into the mine fields. The Federation became alarmed and a joint meeting between the two organizations was arranged for June 3, 1887.[33]

Meanwhile, N.T.A. 135 was having its difficulties within the Knights. The mixed district assemblies were bitterly resisting any move to transfer miners to the new trade assembly.[34] William T. Lewis, who succeeded William Bailey as Master Workman of N.T.A. 135 in June, 1887, became incensed at Powderly and made an unsuccessful attempt to take his organization out of the Knights and into the Federation. Lewis charged that Powderly's persistent opposition to trade unionism had undercut the efforts of N.T.A 135 to organize the miners, and that the dual unionism existing in the trade was directly traceable to Powderly's leadership. Lewis, together with a small following, then went into the Federation, which was reorganized as the National Progressive Union.[35]

All of this internecine warfare, however, was having a disastrous effect upon both unions. The annual convention of N.T.A. 135, therefore, instructed its general officers in September, 1889, to issue a call for a meeting of all miners, whether organized or unorganized. The Progressive Union

[30] K. of L., *GA Proc.*, 1885, pp. 126–27, 135; Roy, *History of the Coal Miners*, pp. 243–44.

[31] National Federation of Miners and Mine Laborers, *Proceedings*, 1886.

[32] *Ibid.*, 1887, p. 6. See also the *Cigar Makers' Official Journal*, XI (September, 1886), 6, XII (November, 1886), 5.

[33] Roy, *History of the Coal Miners*, pp. 246–47; National Federation of Miners and Mine Laborers, *Proceedings*, 1887, pp. 6–7.

[34] See K. of L., *GA Proc.*, 1887, pp. 1700–01, 1716, 1814; 1888, *Report of the General Executive Board*, pp. 32, 70–72, 96, 103.

[35] Chris Evans, *History of the United Mine Workers of America* (2 vols: n.p., 1918–1920), I, 385–86; Roy, *History of the Coal Miners*, pp. 248–50; *Journal of United Labor*, IX (December 20, 1888), 2753.

lent its support, and both agreed to send representatives to Columbus, Ohio, in January, 1890, to vote on a merger proposal.[36] The terms of the merger included unification without sacrificing the essential features of either union, maintenance of national, district, and local unions, equal taxation, and one staff of officers. At the Columbus convention the two factions formed the United Mine Workers of America, affiliated with both the Knights and the A.F. of L.

The new organization, cognizant of the danger of being drawn into the rivalry between the Knights and the A.F. of L., attempted at its first convention in February, 1891, to heal the rift between them, but to no avail.[37] The following year McBride became president of the miners. Some months later Powderly, who had apparently been deliberately misled by Hayes, complained that the union was being alienated from the Knights contrary to the terms of the merger, and he suggested to the General Assembly that N.T.A. 135 should leave the Knights. The Assembly then voted to reorganize N.T.A. 135. Twelve months later Powderly withdrew his accusation, but he was defeated for re-election at that time.[38] In 1894 McBride and a companion delegate were excluded from the General Assembly on the grounds that N.T.A. 135 was completely dominated and controlled by the United Mine Workers. An attempted reorganization of this district by the Assembly failed, and both N.T.A. 135 and the United Mine Workers virtually disappeared as functioning organizations after 1894.[39] Thus a decade of rivalry and friction between the Knights and the union had the effect of destroying any influence either might have exerted on behalf of the workers.

The difficulties encountered by the shoemakers and miners in their efforts to function as trade bodies within the Order's framework were by no means isolated or atypical instances. Other workers, also organized along trade lines, met with similar experiences and often they too withdrew in order to form an autonomous union. N.T.A. 198, formed in 1887, left the Knights two years later and became the National Association of Machinists.[40] The United Garment Workers was the successor of N.T.A. 231, and the Carriage and Wagon Workers International Union arose from the ashes of N.T.A. 247.[41] Similarly, the potters seceded from

[36] Roy, *History of the Coal Miners*, pp. 253–54; *Journal of the Knights of Labor*, X (December 26, 1889), 4.

[37] Evans, *History of the United Mine Workers*, II, 87. See also K. of L., *GA Proc.*, 1891, pp. 20–21.

[38] *Journal of the Knights of Labor*, XIII (November 17, 1892), 2; K. of L., *GA Proc.*, 1892, pp. 7–8, 55–56; 1893, *Report of the General Master Workman*, pp. 2–4; Evans, *History of the United Mine Workers*, II, 321–23.

[39] K. of L., *GA Proc.*, 1894, pp. 98–101, 125–26, 130; 1895, p. 29; *Journal of the Knights of Labor*, XV (December 20, 1894), 1, 3, XVI (June 27, 1895), 1.

[40] *Journal of United Labor*, VIII (May 19, 1888), 1; *Journal of the International Association of Machinists*, VII (July, 1895), 238.

[41] *Garment Worker*, III (September, 1896), 4; *Carriage and Wagon Workers Journal*, II (January 1, 1901), 113; United States Industrial Commission, *Report of the Industrial Commission* (19 vols: Washington, D. C., 1900–1902), XVII, 59, 209.

D.A. 160 in 1890 to form the National Brotherhood of Operative Potters.[42] The secession of these groups was largely a consequence of their inability to induce the Knights not to meddle in trade affairs and to support collective bargaining and other union objectives. The trade assemblies also found that the structure of the Knights, with its emphasis on the geographical grouping of all workers irrespective of trade or calling, was incompatible with the trade-union type of organization. But so long as the Order's leaders insisted on pursuing reformist goals and maintaining the dominance of the mixed assembly, it was virtually impossible for the trade assemblies to receive a sympathetic hearing.

III

While the organization of certain national trade assemblies intensified the struggle between trade unionists and reformers within the Knights, the establishment of others antagonized existing unions and led to numerous and bitter disputes. Dual organization in a single trade in itself does not necessarily presuppose conflict, but when the two groups involved refuse to reach a common understanding, friction often becomes inevitable. The conflict between the Knights and the trade unions, however, was in reality less a jurisdictional one and more a basic split over the ultimate goal of the labor movement. The leaders of the unions were not only fearful of the Knights because of the dangers presented by dual organization in a single trade, but also because they recognized that the structure of the Order was inconsistent with collective bargaining and other trade-union goals. "If the K. of L. would only confine itself to its original work of creating 'a healthy public sentiment on the question of labor and all its interests,'" McGuire observed in 1890, "it would have a large field of work without trenching on the militant field of the trade unions. The educational work already done by the Knights, and for which they deserve due credit, will be more than offset if they pursue the disastrous course of encouraging strife and contention among the workers in the movement."[43]

The Knights, however, did not confine its activities to education, and when it reached the economic sphere it stepped on the toes of the unions. The failure of compromise, furthermore, had hardened feelings to such a degree that no common course of action was possible, if indeed it had ever been. Consequently the conflict became more intense after 1886, and throughout the country the two groups locked horns. "Much of the trouble," proclaimed the A.F. of L. in 1889, "has been occasioned by the organization of National trade districts of the K. of L. in crafts where national and international trades unions already exist. Not only has the

[42] Theodore W. Glocker, *The Government of American Trade Unions* (Baltimore, 1913), p. 54.

[43] United Brotherhood of Carpenters and Joiners, *Proceedings*, 1890, p. 22. For similar views see *The Painter*, I (April, 1887), 2; Dayton *Workman*, cited in *The Craftsman*, IV (August 20, 1887), 1; *Bakers' Journal*, VIII (December 17, 1892), 1.

creation of this dual authority been productive of evil results, but too often the National trade district has been made the dumping ground for men who have been branded as unfair by the trade unions." [44]

The Cigar Makers International Union and Cigarmakers N.T.A. 225 clashed, for example, over the label and the use of machines.[45] When the Iron Molders International Union became involved in a struggle with a leading St. Louis firm and its members were locked out, it appealed to the General Executive Board of the Knights for help, since some members of the Order were continuing to make patterns for the firm. The Board, maintaining that the Order was not involved, refused to take any action and instead referred the case to the district assembly in that area.[46] In Chicago the United Brotherhood of Carpenters and Joiners and Knights combined to form the United Carpenters' Council, but this arrangement soon broke down.[47] Another conflict between the Knights and the Amalgamated Association of Iron and Steel Workers developed at a Mingo Junction, Ohio, plant when attempts to set up a joint committee proved fruitless.[48] This struggle was duplicated on a smaller scale at other iron and steel factories throughout the East.[49] Other unions, including the Brotherhood of Painters and Decorators, the Granite Cutters National Union, and the Journeymen Bakers and Confectioners International Union, also clashed with the Order.[50] Thus the policy of the Knights in sanctioning organization in trades where unions already existed simply served to intensify strife and further embittered the unions.

Neither side hesitated to use any weapon that it had at its disposal. "Paid organizers," charged one union journal, "have scoured the country, and every inducement and promise of support has been presented to enlist the masses, and scabs, rats and black listers have been indiscriminately enrolled into Assemblies, to the detriment of the Labor organizations." [51] In 1887 the Knights admitted nonunion printers in Cincinnati, and in New York City it permitted its members to take the places of striking railroad workers.[52] The unions pursued similar tactics. In New York City

[44] A.F. of L., *Proceedings*, 1889, p. 36.

[45] *Journal of United Labor*, IX (July 12, 1888), 2662, (June 13, 1889), 2853; *American Federationist*, III (March, 1896), 8.

[46] *Iron Molders' Journal*, XXIII (May 31, 1887), 9; Iron Molders International Union, *Proceedings*, 1888, pp. 6–8; K. of L., *GA Proc.*, 1887, pp. 1333–34.

[47] United Brotherhood of Carpenters and Joiners, *Proceedings*, 1894, p. 16.

[48] Amalgamated Association of Iron and Steel Workers, *Proceedings*, 1887, pp. 1935–45; K. of L., *GA Proc.*, 1887, pp. 1368–70.

[49] Amalgamated Association of Iron and Steel Workers, *Proceedings*, 1887, pp. 1946, 2093–97; 1888, pp. 2390, 2438–43; 1889, pp. 2662–63; K. of L., *GA Proc.*, 1888, *Report of the General Executive Board*, pp. 42–43.

[50] *The Painter*, II (February, 1888), 2, (April, 1888), 1; A.F. of L., *Proceedings*, 1888, pp. 20–21; *Bakers' Journal*, VIII (October 29, 1892), 1.

[51] *The Painter*, I (May, 1887), 2.

[52] *The Craftsman*, IV (February 12, 1887), 1; *Railroad Brakemen's Journal*, IV (August, 1887), 379–80.

the Carpenters Union refused to recognize carpenters belonging to D.A. 49.[53] Throughout 1887 and 1888 the Carpenters raided the Knights by bringing entire local assemblies into the Brotherhood. Between January and June of 1887 no less than fourteen local assemblies joined the union, and in the single month of February, 1888, six more came in. This practice was condoned by the union's convention, which itself did not hesitate to charter assemblies.[54] The Amalgamated Association of Iron and Steel Workers even went so far as to decree "That on and after April 1, 1888, no person working at or holding any situation in a mill or factory governed by the A. A. of I. and S. W. scale of prices can be a member of the Knights of Labor." [55] Similarly, no members of the Brotherhood of Locomotive Engineers were permitted to belong to the Knights.[56]

The unions were spurred on in their struggle with the Knights by Gompers, who also used the conflict to overcome the suspicions of many unions toward the new Federation. To those unions engaged in disputes with the Order he offered encouragement and help. To others not yet affiliated with the A.F. of L. he offered vitally-needed support as an inducement for joining.[57] When there was dissatisfaction within the Knights, he exploited it to the advantage of the Federation. "You may rest assured," Gompers wrote to a union official, "that I am doing all I can to instill into the minds of disgusted Knights, who . . . propose to leave that Order, the necessity of organization of the working people upon the natural Trade Union basis." [58] When Skeffington, Master Workman of Shoemakers N.T.A. 217, asked the Federation to endorse his organization's label, Gompers refused on the grounds that the assembly was not affiliated with the A.F. of L. Instead he shrewdly suggested that Skeffington send representatives to the following convention of the Federation, thus tacitly encouraging the secession of the shoemakers from the Knights.[59]

Gompers' activities faithfully reflected the A.F. of L.'s official policy. After 1886 the Federation took an increasingly inflexible position toward

---

[53] *John Swinton's Paper*, January 2, 1887.

[54] *The Carpenter*, VII (July, 1887), 4, VIII (January 15, 1888), 4, (March 15, 1888), 1; United Brotherhood of Carpenters and Joiners, *Proceedings*, 1888, pp. 9, 29, 31.

[55] Amalgamated Association of Iron and Steel Workers, *Proceedings*, 1887, p. 2129. This resolution, however, was not strictly enforced. See *ibid.*, 1888, pp. 2338–39.

[56] *Locomotive Engineers' Journal*, XXI (June, 1887), 435.

[57] See Gompers to William Weihe, February 25, 1887; Gompers to P. J. McGuire, February 26, 1887; Gompers to the Officers and Delegates of the National League of Musicians, March 4, 1887; Gompers to P. Fitzpatrick, March 26, 1890; Gompers to the A.F. of L. Executive Council, January 31, 1893, SGLB.

[58] Gompers to William Martin, October 16, 1888. See also Gompers to P. J. McGuire, May 10, 1888, SGLB.

[59] Gompers to H. J. Skeffington, September 14, 1887. See also Gompers to P. J. McGuire, June 7, 1889, SGLB.

the Knights. In 1887 it refused to admit the Washington Federation of Labor to the annual convention because that body was composed of local assemblies. "We recommend," the Executive Council told the delegates, "the utmost resistance on the part of the Federation to all encroachments upon its constituent bodies, irrespective of from whatever quarter they come." [60] A few months later the Council decided against consideration of any protests from the Knights unless they came through the General Executive Board.[61] The hardening of the Federation's attitude toward the Knights was a direct result of pressure from its affiliated unions. By the late 1880's these unions had abandoned all pretexts of friendliness toward dual organization in any trade. "I maintain most firmly," McGuire told the Carpenters' convention in 1888, "that while we should be ever ready to help all other sister labor organizations, and do practically recognize the common fraternity of interests that exist between all branches of honorable toil, yet, in the management of our own trade affairs, we should never make ourselves subordinate to any other organization, nor should we ever allow a dual form of organization to exist in our trade, for if we do, sooner or later, one will be bound to come into conflict with the other, to the disadvantage of the workmen's best interests." [62]

Between 1889 and 1894 the Knights and the A.F. of L. attempted to reach a *modus vivendi* through a series of negotiations. In February, 1889, Gompers and McGuire met with Powderly and Hayes, and the result was a vague circular issued to American workingmen.[63] Six months later another meeting was held because of the Federation's desire to prepare the ground for the eight-hour drive. The final conference in this series took place in October, 1889, when Gompers, McGuire, and the Executive Board of the A.F. of L. met with Powderly, Hayes, and Wright. The Knights could not agree to the eight-hour proposals of the Federation, and suggested instead that a settlement be concluded on the basis of a mutual recognition of working cards and labels, and an affirmation that neither party would accept suspended or expelled members of any labor organization. The Federation offered a counterproposal asking the Knights to discontinue chartering trade assemblies, and in return the Federation would urge its members to join mixed assemblies of the Or-

---

[60] A.F. of L., *Proceedings*, 1887, pp. 8, 26.

[61] *Ibid.*, 1888, p. 33; Gompers to Josiah B. Dyer, October 26, 1888, SGLB.

[62] United Brotherhood of Carpenters and Joiners, *Proceedings*, 1888, pp. 18–19. For similar expressions of opinion see *The Tailor*, I (April, 1888) , 6; International Typographical Union, *Proceedings*, 1887, pp. 54–55; *Brauer-Zeitung*, VII (November 12, 1892) , 1.

[63] K. of L., *GA Proc.*, 1889, *Report of the General Executive Board*, pp. 34–35. After the conference trouble developed when the *Journal of United Labor* printed an editorial that Gompers took offense at. After receiving assurances from Powderly, Gompers agreed to sign it. Gompers to P. J. McGuire, March 11, April 15, May 28, June 27, 1889, SGLB; A.F. of L., *Proceedings*, 1889, p. 13.

der.[64] "Where there exists a dual organization and authority in any trade," Gompers remarked, "a conflict is inevitable and can only end disastrously to all interests." [65] The unions, in other words, were still demanding, as they had been since 1886, unitary control over the economic field. "We . . . assert," the convention of the A.F. of L. proclaimed in December, 1889, "the natural right of the trade unions to occupy the trade union territory. When this right is conceded, discord will end and organized labor be more closely united." [66] The Knights similarly declined to yield to the unions, and the struggle continued unabated. Both groups were as far apart as ever, and the only result was a further exacerbation of the personal relations of their leaders. Exasperated with Gompers and other trade-union leaders, Powderly privately described them as a group of "damn gin guzzling, pot bellied, red nosed, scab faced, dirty shirted, unwashed, leather arsed, empty headed, two faced, rattle headed, itchy palmed scavengers." [67]

Two years later the Knights and the Federation again exchanged similar proposals, with the same result.[68] A final conference was held in 1894, at which the Railroad Brotherhoods were represented. At this meeting the Order came up with some new proposals. It suggested the holding of an annual labor congress that would appoint a committee of arbitration to settle all jurisdictional difficulties and troubles arising from strikes. Any strike involving more than 1,000 workers would require the approval of the Executive Council of the congress. When two organizations existed in a single trade, joint executive committees would arrange wage and hour scales, and there was to be a mutual recognition of working cards. Finally, the workers were called upon to vote against the two major political parties and support the People's party "for the present." Nevertheless, whatever the relative merits of these proposals, the Federation's representatives refused to concede anything and still insisted that a *sine qua non* of settlement had to include a guarantee of the autonomy of every union as well as the elimination of dual unionism.[69]

The conference of 1894 was the final attempt to compromise the issues separating the Knights and the trade unions. Thereafter the A.F. of L. refused even to recognize the right of affiliate members to hold dual membership in the Knights and the Federation. In 1896 it threatened the United Brewery Workers with expulsion unless that union gave up its membership in the Order. Founded in 1886, the Brewery Workers had

---

[64] K. of L., *GA Proc.*, 1889, *Report of the General Executive Board*, pp. 35–36.

[65] A.F. of L., *Proceedings*, 1889, p. 13.

[66] *Ibid.*, p. 37.

[67] Powderly to Tom O'Reilly, December 19, 1889. See also Powderly to Charles H. Litchman, December 3, 1889, TVPLB; *Journal of the Knights of Labor*, XI (April 30, 1891), 2.

[68] A.F. of L., *Proceedings*, 1891, p. 49.

[69] *Ibid.*, 1894, pp. 57–59; K. of L., *GA Proc.*, 1894, pp. 113–16.

affiliated with the A.F. of L. shortly afterwards. As a result of support given by the Knights in the boycott against the Anheuser-Busch Company, the union in 1892 asked the Order and the Federation to act in unison, and it also went on record as endorsing the formation of a national trade assembly of brewery workers. The A.F. of L. warned against taking such a step, but when the Knights agreed to drop its demand that the union leave the Federation, a number of locals formed N.T.A. 35. Trouble immediately developed between the union and the mixed assemblies, and the former asked the General Assembly in 1894 for control over all workers in the trade.[70] Soon afterwards the Federation refused to support either the union's label or its boycott against the Pittsburgh employers unless it gave up its membership in the Knights. The Brewery Workers, although protesting this decision, finally gave in and dissolved N.T.A. 35 in 1896.[71] In a similar situation the A.F. of L. Executive Council supported the decision of the Trade and Labor Union of St. Louis in expelling any organization maintaining its affiliation with the Knights.[72]

IV

By 1895 the Knights of Labor was no longer a force to be reckoned with in the labor movement. Defeated in the struggle with the trade unions, it was also torn apart internally by the rivalry of dissident factions. In 1893 Powderly's long tenure as General Master Workman suddenly came to an end as a result of charges brought against him by Hayes and the formation of an alliance between western agrarians led by James R. Sovereign of Iowa and eastern socialists led by Daniel DeLeon of New York City. When Powderly, who had the constitutional power to present to the General Assembly nominees for election to the General Executive Board, refused to present men acceptable to the delegates, he was defeated and Sovereign was elected in his place.[73] The alliance between the agrarians and the socialists, however, proved short-lived. After Sovereign apparently reneged on his promise to give the socialists the editorship of

[70] Hermann Schlüter, *The Brewing Industry and Brewery Workers' Movement in America* (Cincinnati, Ohio, 1910), pp. 212–17.

[71] *Brauer-Zeitung*, X (April 27, 1895), 1, (June 1, 1895), 1, XI (October 10, 1896), 1; *American Federationist*, II (May, 1895), 51, (July, 1895), 88–89, III (November 1896), 197–98.

[72] Gompers to David A. Kreyling, March 24, 1896, SGLB; *American Federationist*, III (April, 1896), 36, (May, 1896), 55.

[73] K. of L., *GA Proc.*, 1893, pp. 45–48, 53–61. Powderly's actions at this Assembly led one delegate to remark: "I have become convinced, since the opening of this session, that the General Master Workman holds as his enemy every delegate who does not vote in accordance with his (the General Master Workman) views on all questions, and appears unwilling to place in nomination for the General Executive Board any man who is likely to stand up for his own opinions when they happen to conflict with those of his chief." *Ibid.*, p. 60.

the *Journal of the Knights of Labor,* they left the Order and organized a rival assembly in New York City.[74] By this time, however, the membership of the Knights was well under 50,000 and its influence on the labor movement was practically negligible.

The defeat of the Knights by the trade unions was undoubtedly one of the most significant events in the history of the American labor movement. Clashes between rival unions have not been uncommon, but generally these struggles have revolved around such problems as jurisdiction, personalities, or power. The conflict between the Knights and the trade unions, however, had much deeper roots. In a sense, it was the culmination of more than a half-century of historical development. The intellectual roots of the Knights dated from the age of Jackson and the humanitarian and reform movements of the 1830's and 1840's. Paralleling the persistence of reform unionism in the post-bellum decades, on the other hand, was a new form of organization—the trade union—which more nearly mirrored the emerging American acquisitive industrial society. The gradual acceptance of trade unionism by the workers implied a complete shift in aims and objectives. Discarding the idea of the reform of society, the trade unions began to develop a job- and wage-conscious program that was well-adapted to a dynamic and expanding environment. Although at first confined to the skilled workers, trade unionism, which was more a philosophy of labor than a system of organization, was capable of expansion. Indeed, many trade unions later became craft-industrial organizations.

The conflict between the Knights and the trade unions, therefore, was not simply one between rival organizations. It was rather a fight between two fundamentally different ideologies (each having a different structural form) over the future direction of the American labor movement. Why, then, did the Knights of Labor, after such promising beginnings, fail so dismally in the end? Perhaps the most important reason for the Order's decline was the fact that nineteenth-century reform unionism had been rendered obsolete by technological advance. As a result, the reform program of the leaders of the Knights did not harmonize with their environment, for the *raison d'être* had been cut away from many of the old objectives. The technology and organization of society had made the co-operative workshop something of an anachronism, and the ideal of the small producer was technologically obsolete. Under the pressure of new forces the working class slowly began to abandon its dream of independence. Obviously an idealized America based on the sturdy individual entrepreneur offered much more to the workers than did the impersonal factory, but one was ideal, the other, real. Workers were willing to join

[74] *The People,* December 1, 1895; Nathan Fine, *Labor and Farmer Parties in the United States 1828–1928* (New York, 1928), pp. 154–56; *Fifteenth Annual Official Hand-Book District Assembly 49 Knights of Labor and Affiliated Trades* (New York, n.d.), not paginated.

the Knights; whether or not they retained their membership depended largely on the degree to which their interests were served. "During the flood-tide of 1886–7," John Swinton observed, "tens of thousands rushed into the Order with a vague expectation that it would somehow bring them immediate advantages; that it would at once shorten their hours, raise their wages, improve their condition, and subdue their adversaries." [75]

These, however, were the very goals that leaders like Powderly refused to fight for, because the effort would have meant a diversion from the main goal of reforming society. The irony of the situation was even evident to Powderly, who remarked in 1893:

> I have held a most anomalous position before the public for the last 20 years. All of this time I have opposed strikes and boycotts; I have contended that the wage question was of secondary consideration; I have contended that the short-hour question was not the end but merely the means to an end . . . but all of this time I have been fighting for a raise in wages, a reduction in the hours of labor or some paltry demand of the trade element to the exclusion of the very work that I have constantly advocated. Just think of it! opposing strikes and always striking; opposing a battle for short hours and lacking the time to devote to anything else. Battling with my pen in the leading journals and magazines of the day for the grand things we are educating the people on, and fighting with might and main for the little things. Our Order has held me up to the present position I hold because of the reputation I have won in the nation at large by taking high ground, and yet the trade element in the Order has always kept me busy at the base of the breast works throwing up the earth which they trampled down. Again, no man in this country has so many domineering bosses as I have, for every member feels it to be his right to sit down and abuse me if he pleases or order me around to do as he likes and not as I think. . . . On the other hand my relations with my brother officers . . . are not pleasant . . . I who have been preaching independence for others have been the slave of thousands, and as my reward am as little understood by the people I work for as Hoke Smith or Dink Botts.[76]

Powderly's observations illuminated the internal contradictions of his organization. At the national level the emphasis was on the fundamental reform of society. Members at the local level, however, while initially attracted by the promises of their leaders, generally became engaged in other matters as time progressed. While still paying homage to the vision of a new society, they began increasingly to emphasize such goals as higher wages, shorter hours, and job control. This served to create a tension within the Knights, and on such vital issues as collective bargaining, strikes, and the eight-hour day, the national leadership became more and more alienated from the rank and file. The result was an internal struggle

[75] *John Swinton's Paper,* August 7, 1887.
[76] Powderly to Mrs. A. P. Stevens, April 11, 1893, TVPLB.

for power, and the trade element, because of the structural heterogeneity and geographical orientation of the Knights, found itself a perpetual minority. A mass exodus from the Knights ensued, fatally weakening that organization. Becoming also embroiled in a protracted struggle with the trade unions, the Order found itself on the losing side because its reform ideology conflicted with economic and technological developments. The career of the Knights might have followed a different course had its leaders encouraged the formation of trade or industrial assemblies. Their reluctance to modify any basic concepts and reliance upon the mixed assembly as the ideal unit of organization, however, proved too great an obstacle, and trade assemblies within the Knights never enjoyed any degree of success.

Preoccupation with reform also led to neglect of those features of labor organizations that might have acted as stabilizing factors. A case in point was the Order's almost total neglect of any benefit system. During the 1880's the trade unions began to experiment with such systems in the hope of institutionalizing their structures, thus providing members with an incentive to remain in good standing. Within the Knights there also was much sentiment in favor of such a plan, and in 1881 the General Assembly established a voluntary Insurance Association. Response was meager, and two years later only 655 members were participants. Up until 1886 $31,270 had been paid out in benefits.[77] Considering that the Knights had over 700,000 members at this time, it was obvious that the plan had not proved a success. In succeeding years the Insurance Association declined still further. Failure to integrate the benefit system into the functioning structure of the Knights proved an important source of weakness. The lackadaisical and unenthusiastic attitude of the Order's leadership was another cause of failure. "Experience has demonstrated," Powderly once remarked, "that the insurance feature does not succeed in a labor organization . . . Many years ago the progressive members of the trade unions became convinced that the organization which expended all its time and energy in attempting to elevate the condition of the workingman by raising his wages and shortening his hours of labor must ultimately fail." [78]

Aside from its immersion in reform to the exclusion of other objectives, the Order was further weakened by the character of its leaders and internal rivalries. Powderly, for example, had certain traits in his personality that created numerous difficulties during his long tenure as head of the Knights. A typical nineteenth-century reformer, he regarded the Order as his private domain and equated disagreement with disloyalty. Thus he was instrumental in having such leading Knights as Joseph R. Buchanan and Thomas B. Barry expelled because of their opposition to

[77] K. of L., *GA Proc.*, 1881, pp. 315–16; 1883, pp. 419–20; 1886, p. 59.
[78] *Journal of the Knights of Labor*, XIII (May 4, 1893), 5.

certain of his policies.[79] Endowed with an exaggerated notion of his own abilities, Powderly also tended to magnify the relative importance of his office. His feeling of indispensability led him to submit his resignation as General Master Workman more than a dozen times, knowing that it would not be accepted by the General Executive Board. Powderly constantly reiterated his firm belief that the "President of the United States has a light task in comparison to that which falls to my lot each day." [80]

In the administration of the Knights, Powderly was unable to delegate responsibility and often insisted upon supervising even minute details. His relations with the General Executive Board were not always close. While the Board worked under a common roof in Philadelphia, Powderly remained a hundred miles distant in Scranton, journeying only infrequently for meetings with the Board. He spent much of his time writing letters, many of which expressed dissatisfaction with his heavy burdens.[81] When events moved rapidly, Powderly frequently manifested a lack of adaptability, often offering the poor state of his health as an excuse for inaction.[82] Moreover, when hundreds of thousands of workingmen flocked to the Order's banner in the feverish years of 1885 and 1886, Powderly did little more than issue complaint after complaint. He insisted that striking workingmen could not be admitted to membership, that such rapid growth was unhealthy, and that he could not possibly keep pace with ensuing developments. On more than one occasion he suggested that the General Executive Board prohibit strikes altogether and recall the charters of those assemblies that disobeyed the order.[83]

The actions of other high individuals also served to cause internal friction and discredit the Order among the rank and file. Litchman, to cite one case, was usually spending the Order's money without authorization or else using his position to advance his personal political ambitions. Hayes was an adventurer who looked upon the Knights as a vehicle for his own advancement. The Home Club of D.A. 49 of New York City, composed of a group of socialists bent on fighting the trade unions and gaining unbridled control over the Knights, was forever engaging in various intrigues, to the detriment of the parent body. Finally, the diffi-

[79] See Powderly to Edward Enbody, October 11, 1888, TVPLB; *Journal of United Labor*, IX (October 18, 1888), 2717–18, VIII (June 2, 1888), 2638; Buchanan, *Story of a Labor Agitator*, pp. 359–69.

[80] Powderly to Frederick Turner, December 31, 1885. See also Powderly to John J. Roche, August 12, 1887, TVPLB.

[81] Powderly to John W. Hayes, April 29, 1887, TVPLB.

[82] See, for example, Powderly to John W. Hayes, January 13, 1888, TVPLB.

[83] Powderly to Edward B. Irving, December 4, 1885; Powderly to Frederick Turner, December 31, 1885, March 25, 1886; Powderly to Dan F. Tomson, January 23, 1886; Powderly to Michael Healy, December 1, 1886, TVPLB. See also Powderly's secret circular of March 13, 1886, reprinted in Missouri Bureau of Labor Statistics and Inspection, *Official History of the Great Strike*, pp. 69–75.

culties with the Catholic Church was also a weakening factor.[84] Consequently much of the Order's energies were expended in wasteful and useless activities.

Ultimately the Knights of Labor came to an inglorious end. Whatever the reasons for its failure, however, one fact was evident. That fact was that the reform unionism of the nineteenth century, for over five decades the dominant force in the American labor movement, was at last dead, and organized labor was henceforth to follow a different path. Yet the passing of the Knights did not mean that all of the things it had stood for were dead or forgotten. To future labor leaders its insistence upon the solidarity of labor regardless of color, sex, or degree of skill, was to stand as an inspiring example. The Knights of Labor, to the benefit of future generations, made a significant contribution to the democratization of the American labor movement. In this sense it carved out for itself an important niche in the history of American labor.

[84] For a brief summary of the relations between the Knights and the Catholic Church see Chapter Three, fn. 14. Henry David has discounted the impact of the Haymarket Affair upon the decline of the Knights, a point of view that this author subscribes to. See David, *The History of the Haymarket Affair* (New York, 1936), p. 536.

CHAPTER EIGHT

The Establishment of the American Federation of Labor, 1886–1896

I

♧ THE DEFEAT OF REFORM UNIONISM in the late 1880's did not necessarily imply that the trade unions would automatically pre-empt the field to the exclusion of all other forms of organizations and ideologies. Indeed, after 1890 various socialist factions made determined efforts to turn the labor movement toward an endorsement of their peculiar brand of socialism, and even within the ranks of the trade unions there was some uncertainty as to the proper course of action. Yet in spite of the factionalism and ideological differences that divided the working class in the last decades of the nineteenth century, the basic structure and philosophy of trade unionism was institutionalized and made permanent in the decade after the founding of the American Federation of Labor.

The establishment of the A.F. of L. in 1886 marked the culmination of two decades of agitation for a national federation of labor. For a brief time the trade unions had supported the National Labor Union before that organization turned to politics and reform. During the early 1870's many unions espoused such a federation,[1] but the depression of 1873–1878 prevented any further action from being taken. In 1879 the International Typographical Union took the lead in the movement to establish an association of trade unions, and in August, 1881, twenty-one delegates from thirteen unions were present at a meeting called by the Typographical Union in Terre Haute, Indiana.[2] Because of the small number of unions that heeded the call, the delegates agreed to issue another summons for a "national labor congress" that would meet in Pitts-

---

[1] For trade union sentiment favoring a federation see the *Coopers' Journal*, III (October, 1872), 598–600; International Typographical Union, *Proceedings*, 1873, p. 13.

[2] International Typographical Union, *Proceedings*, 1879, pp. 39–40; 1880, pp. 63–64; 1881, pp. 25–27.

burgh on November 15, 1881.³ Out of the November meeting came the establishment of the Federation of Organized Trades and Labor Unions of the United States and Canada.

Although it held six annual conventions between 1881 and 1886, the Federation of Organized Trades and Labor Unions was not a success. Its sole claim to fame was its passage of a resolution in 1884 setting in motion the eight-hour movement of 1886. Yet the Federation took no further action and gave no leadership or direction to the movement. The lack of an adequate revenue and the apathy of the constituent unions, furthermore, contributed in no small measure to the Federation's weakness. The fact that the unions were wary of giving a national organization any substantial degree of authority also prevented it from becoming much more than a paper body. "Never was it the thought," McGuire observed in 1884, "that the Federation should be the head centre, from which should emanate all power and authority. . . . The general movement of all trades must be organically federative and voluntary, and not centralized and autocratic. The Federation can be simply representative and reflect the sentiments of its constituencies—nothing more. It can not go very far in advance of them, but it can at least offer suggestions." ⁴

The expansion of the Knights between 1885 and 1886 into the jurisdiction claimed by the unions, however, served to stimulate interest in a federation that would be able to represent the interests of the national unions. The unwillingness of union leaders to utilize the Federation of Organized Trades and Labor Unions for this purpose probably can be attributed to their reluctance to associate themselves with an organization whose past had not been characterized by success. After the failure of the negotiations between representatives of the Knights and the unions between May and October of 1886, the union committee (Weihe, McGuire, Evans, Fitzpatrick, and Strasser) issued a call for a trade-union convention to meet in Columbus, Ohio, on December 8, 1886.⁵ Out of this meeting came the American Federation of Labor.

II

Completely unlike the National Labor Union or Knights of Labor, the A.F. of L. represented a new departure from the traditional reformism that had dominated the labor movement since the Jacksonian era. Essen-

---

³ The call for the November meeting can be found in the Federation of Organized Trades and Labor Unions of the United States and Canada, *Proceedings*, 1881, pp. 6–7.

⁴ *The Carpenter*, IV (September, 1884), 4.

⁵ *Ibid.*, VI (November, 1886), 3; Bricklayers and Masons International Union, *Proceedings*, 1887, pp. 79–80. The Federation of Organized Trades and Labor Unions of the United States and Canada changed its annual meeting so as to coincide with the trade-union convention, and it merged with the newly-formed A.F. of L. on December 9, 1886.

tially a response to the social and economic forces that were transforming the United States from a rural and agrarian nation into an urban and industrialized one, the rise of the Federation, by symbolizing the supremacy of the trade union, opened a new chapter in the history of American labor. Eschewing the reform of society, its leaders abandoned the concept that the working class was the only legitimate group in the community. "The fact is being fast forced upon the consciousness of the wage-workers of this continent," Gompers observed in 1888, "that they are a distinct and practically permanent class of modern society; and, consequently, have distinct and permanent common interests." [6] He therefore insisted that only bona fide workers could belong to unions. Decrying the policy of the Knights in admitting employers, Gompers held it to be self-evident that the emancipation of the working class must be achieved by the working class. "There is no doubt that men with the best intentions outside of the ranks of labor can aid in this movement," he wrote, "but [we] cannot give into their hands the direction of the affairs which rightfully belong to and must be exercised by the wage-workers." [7]

Structurally dissimilar from the Knights, the A.F. of L. was not a sovereign independent body but relied upon the national and international unions for its power. Consequently, the new Federation reflected its constituents' preoccupation with collective bargaining, and it paid little attention to reform panaceas. After their experiences with the Knights, the unions were highly suspicious of any proposals to create a powerful centralized national federation. The autonomy of the member unions, therefore, quickly became the most fundamental principle of the Federation.[8] Composed of sovereign affiliates, the Federation had no real power of compulsion, especially against the more important national unions. It could not dictate membership or admission requirements of its affiliates; it had no voice in the internal government of a union; its ability to intercede in strikes was practically nonexistent; and it exercised no control over the collective-bargaining activities of its affiliates. Its only punitive power was expulsion—a remedy that could be deadlier than the disease. The Federation, therefore, had to adopt a cautious policy that would be acceptable to a large majority of its members. In practice this was tantamount to the supremacy of the stronger affiliates. The result was that while many critics attacked the inherent conservatism of the A.F. of L.,

[6] Gompers to the Trade and Labor Unions of San Francisco, June 13, 1888, SGLB.

[7] Gompers to S. R. Holmes, October 8, 1890. See also Gompers to Charles E. Miller, February 1, 1889; Gompers to Claude F. Drake, May 24, 1890; Chris Evans to C. Boesche, April 4, 1891; Gompers to H. P. Kimball, September 5, 1891; Gompers to William P. Effinger, April 29, 1892; Gompers to Eva McDonald Valesh, August 4, 1893, SGLB; John Mitchell, *Organized Labor* (Philadelphia, 1903), p. ix.

[8] Gompers to P. M. Arthur, September 11, October 9, 1888; Gompers to P. F. Fitzpatrick, July 20, 1889; Gompers to Frank P. Sargent and Eugene V. Debs, August 30, 1890, SGLB.

it was this very conservatism that proved the greatest centripetal force.

The supremacy of the member national unions was protected in many ways. Each national union, for example, was permitted one delegate to the national convention for every 4,000 members, while all local unions or federated bodies were limited to one. In 1887, moreover, the method of voting at the annual convention was changed so as to enhance further the power of the national unions. If a roll call was demanded (although questions could also be decided by a show of hands), each delegate would cast one vote for every hundred members, but city or state federations still would cast only one vote.[9] This system of balloting served to formalize the dominance of the national union over the more politically-minded city and state federations. The locus of power thus led the Federation to emphasize trade problems above all others.

The dominance of the national union, however, did not imply the exclusion of the unskilled worker from the labor movement. "I have always maintained that a trade union could be organized from all classes of wage-workers of any particular trade or calling whether skilled or unskilled," observed Gompers.[10] Organization along trade lines was a natural outgrowth of nineteenth-century experience. Conditioned to think in terms of the skilled craftsman rather than the general factory worker, trade unionism seemed the most logical approach to the problem. A.F. of L. leaders were not unaware of the leveling influence of technology upon skill, and in 1888 Gompers suggested organization into industrial divisions.[11] Nothing came of this proposal. Since the skilled workers had taken the lead in organizing, the trade union remained the dominant form of organization, even though jurisdictional lines became blurred by the advances of technology. Nevertheless, the A.F. of L. was not necessarily committed to any specific structural form. Thus the United Mine Workers functioned as an industrial rather than a trade union, while other unions represented an amalgamation of jurisdictions.

The fundamental character of American trade unionism, however, lay not in its structure or form of organization. Indeed, few unions have ever been characterized by structural purity. More often they have afforded themselves substantial leeway and room for maneuverability in order to meet changing conditions. Thus most of them represent a curious blend of trade-industrial jurisdictions. More than anything else, American trade unionism was a philosophy of action and a state of mind. It paid little attention to theories of reform and social transformation. "I do not un-

[9] A.F. of L., *Proceedings*, 1886, p. 3; 1887, p. 3. City and state federations were granted one minor concession in 1888 when the convention amended the constitution so as to permit a roll call only when demanded by one-fifth of the delegates, but this did not in any way impair the supremacy of the national unions. *Ibid.*, 1888, p. 3.

[10] Gompers to Frank D. Hamlin, May 6, 1890. See also Gompers to Albert C. Stevens, November 1, 1889; Gompers to George H. Daggett, January 4, 1896, SGLB.

[11] A.F. of L., *Proceedings*, 1888, p. 14. See also Gompers, "To Organize Unskilled Labor," *American Federationist*, III (February, 1897), 256–57.

derstand that trades unionism is a theory reduced into practicality,"
Frank K. Foster, a leading unionist, testified before a Senate committee
in 1883. "I understand rather that the theory is evolved from the necessities of the circumstances surrounding labor organizations." [12] Instead of
abstractions, union leaders devoted themselves to the development of
wage and hour policies, work rules, and membership standards.

Stated in its broadest terms, the A.F. of L.—in Gompers' words—had
a "practical" rather than a theoretical function. "We propose to organize
our fellows, we propose to improve the condition of our fellow-working
men and women, to raise men upon a higher standard of life, a higher
plane of the social structure in which we live." [13] Throughout its early
history the Federation's activities revolved around such problems as organization, jurisdiction, eight hours, assessments, and strike policies. This
is not to imply that it took no interest in many of the broader social,
economic, and political questions of the day. On the contrary, the Federation often took stands upon nonlabor issues. Generally, however, it directed its major energies toward building and strengthening the trade-
union movement.

III

Yet the success of the A.F. of L. in its early years was by no means assured, and it had to overcome many formidable obstacles. One of the
greatest impediments was the fear of the national unions that the Federation would usurp their prerogatives. Within the International Typographical Union, for example, a hard core of unrelenting opposition to
the A.F. of L. persisted for nearly four years. After a lengthy debate at
its convention in 1887, the union finally agreed to affiliate, although a
personal appearance by Gompers was necessary to achieve this.[14] Even
while joining, however, the Typographical delegates also voted to with-
hold payment of the per capita tax of one cent per month due the
Federation. Instead, they supported a plan whereby each union would
contribute money to meet the expense of the Federation's annual convention.[15] The refusal of the union to pay the tax placed Gompers in a
delicate position. "The I.T.U. have not paid a solitary cent to the Federation in nearly three years," he complained at the end of 1888.[16] An agree-

---

[12] *Report of the Committee of the Senate Upon the Relations Between Labor and
Capital, and Testimony Taken by the Committee* (4 vols: Washington, D. C., 1885), I,
667. See also *ibid.*, p. 1160; *Granite Cutters' Journal*, XIX (March, 1896), 1.

[13] A.F. of L., *Proceedings*, 1889, p. 10. See also *ibid.*, 1890, p. 13; Gompers to J. E. A.
Hall, August 6, 1891; Gompers to Benjamin Boden, April 28, 1896, SGLB; *Cigar
Makers' Official Journal*, XXIII (January, 1898), 9.

[14] *Printers' Circular*, XXII (June, 1887), 68.

[15] International Typographical Union, *Proceedings*, 1887, p. 112. See also *ibid.*, 1888,
p. 157.

[16] Gompers to Frank K. Foster, November 13, 1888, SGLB.

ment was finally reached whereby the union undertook to pay the tax in return for the cancellation of the debt it had incurred up to December, 1887.[17]

While the Typographical Union was the only organization taking formal action against paying the per capita tax, others simply failed to remit their share. When the Molders Union was dilatory in paying the tax, Gompers, fearing that the union would not send representatives to the Federation's annual convention, hastened to assure the president of the Molders that if the tax was too great a burden the union could probably be exempted from part of it.[18] Even Gompers' own union—the Cigar Makers International Union—did not bother to pay its portion. "You can well imagine," Gompers wrote to Strasser, "that if organizations such as the C.M.I.U.—which decidedly recognizes the necessity of the federation of Trades Unions—fail to pay the per capita, then others which look with greater indifference upon the movement become more lax in their duties." [19] A year later an exasperated Gompers was threatening the union with suspension. "Either we shall have a Federation capable of doing some work or none at all." [20] The Cigar Makers, after much cajolery on Gompers' part, finally paid up most of its indebtedness.

Lack of a steady and sufficient revenue severely curtailed the Federation's activities in its beginning years. It was unable, for example, to send paid organizers into areas requiring them.[21] Much of Gompers' time was taken up in routine office duties, such as addressing wrappers, and he appealed to the Executive Council for authority to hire a boy at a weekly wage of $3.50.[22] Often spending his own money for the Federation, Gompers frequently complained that he could not support his family unless he received the salary that was due him.[23] By the end of November, 1887, the Federation had collected $2,100.34 and had expended $2,074.39, leaving a balance in the treasury of just under $26. From this time on revenue began to increase as unions met their obligations and membership rose, and in 1888 the Federation doubled its income. Yet even as late as 1896 its income (from the per capita tax) was still only slightly over $16,000.[24]

[17] Gompers to Edward Ives, November 16, 1888; Gompers to W. S. McCleevy, November 21, 1888, SGLB.

[18] Gompers to P. F. Fitzpatrick, November 17, 1887, SGLB.

[19] Gompers to Adolph Strasser, March 10, 1888. See also Gompers to Strasser, April 7, 1888; Gompers to George W. Perkins, September 13, 1888, SGLB.

[20] Gompers to Strasser, February 25, 1889, SGLB.

[21] Gompers to H. Streifler, March 20, 1888, SGLB.

[22] Gompers to the A.F. of L. Executive Council, March 14, 1887, SGLB. The Council granted Gompers' request.

[23] Gompers to G. Edmondston, April 22, 1887; Gompers to the A.F. of L. Executive Council, November 17, 1888, SGLB.

[24] A.F. of L., *Proceedings*, 1887, p. 15; 1888, p. 39; 1896, p. 28; Gompers to Edward Harvey, June 21, 1888, SGLB.

Despite all these early obstacles, the A.F. of L. succeeded in weathering its early trials, and by 1890 was established on a firm foundation. To Gompers and McGuire is due much of the credit for this fact. To both men the labor movement was not simply an economic movement nor a vehicle for personal advancement; it was, rather, a religious crusade on behalf of the downtrodden and oppressed. Into this crusade they poured their meager funds, their time, their energy, and, indeed, their health. Disregarding personal comfort and the welfare of their families, they made the labor movement their life's work.

Born in London's East End in 1850, Gompers migrated to the United States when he was thirteen years old. He joined the New York City Cigar Makers Union the following year, and soon became active in the labor movement. In the late 1870's and 1880's Gompers played a prominent role in assisting Strasser in the reorganization of the Cigar Makers International Union. New York City at this time was a breeding ground for radicals of all persuasions, and early in life Gompers became familiar with socialist thought.[25] Although never joining the Marxian First International, he was sympathetic toward its aims and attended its meetings. A young and impetuous man, Gompers was fired with visionary dreams of reforming the world according to vague socialist principles. At this point he came under the influence of Karl Ferdinand Laurrell, a political exile who had been expelled from Denmark in the 1870's because of radical activities. Laurrell, like so many other trade unionists, had also been a socialist who had left the fold, but had retained the Marxian faith in the prime importance of economic action through trade unionism. Under his influence Gompers began to put more faith in immediate objectives through trade-union economic action and less in ultimate goals. Gompers' acceptance of the "ultimate emancipation of labor," at best a vague faith, receded further and further into the background as he became immersed in the every-day problems of running a union. "I believe with the most advanced thinkers as to ultimate ends, including the abolition of the wage system," he observed in 1887. "But I hold it as a self-evident proposition, that no successful attempt can be made to reach those ends without first improving present conditions." [26] Although abandoning his early be-

[25] See Gompers to Florence K. Wischnewetzky (Florence Kelley), October 17, 1888; Gompers to Frank O. Green, March 14, 1889; Gompers to William Trant, May 16, 1889, SGLB. These letters indicate that Gompers had read Friedrich Engels, Herbert Spencer, and Thorold Rogers. Benjamin Stolberg, a personal acquaintance, claimed that Gompers had "read a good deal in the social sciences, but always to prove his own prejudices." Stolberg further asserted that Gompers had never read Marx, Bakunin, Kautsky, or Lenin. Stolberg, "What Manner of Man Was Gompers?," *Atlantic Monthly*, CXXXV (March, 1925), 408. But see Gompers' auto-biography, *Seventy Years*, I, 82–83, and John R. Commons, "Karl Marx and Samuel Gompers," *Political Science Quarterly*, XLI (June, 1926), 281–86.

[26] *John Swinton's Paper*, July 31, 1887. See also Gompers, *Seventy Years*, I, 57, 70–88, 97–98, 127, 216, 223; *Report of the Committee of the Senate Upon the Relations Between Labor and Capital*, I, 374; Gompers to August S. Leitch, January 25, 1892, SGLB.

lief in doctrinaire socialism, Gompers always retained his faith in the efficacy of economic action by the working class.

Well-versed in trade-union tactics and philosophy, Gompers was un-yielding in his opposition to the reform unionism of the National Labor Union and Knights of Labor, as well as to union partisan political action. Spending most of his early years in a trade where he became familiar with all shades of imported radicalism, he was not influenced by ante-bellum reformism. Consequently his outlook differed markedly from native leaders like Sylvis and Powderly.

A shrewd and able individual, Gompers was cognizant of the limitations of his position within the A.F. of L., and was able to get along with most of his opponents. Recognizing the dependence of the Federation on the national and international unions, he shaped policy so as to lessen any potential tensions between the two. A tireless worker, he untertook long trips covering thousands of miles on behalf of the labor movement, often at the cost of both his money and health. When his services were sought by various unions, he asked only for expense money.[27]

Elected to the presidency of the A.F. of L. in 1886 because other more prominent union leaders did not seek such an unpromising position, Gompers brought to the post a long record of experience in the labor movement. First as a worker, then as a member and officer of the Cigar Makers International Union, he had also been active in the Federation of Organized Trades and Labor Unions, serving in various capacities. From 1886 until his death in 1924 Gompers managed to retain his position as president of the A.F. of L. (except for the year 1895, when he was defeated for re-election because of socialist opposition). His long tenure in office was due largely to his ability to analyze the environment within which the labor movement was operating. Recognizing that the rank and file regarded themselves as potential members of the middle class, and that their goals were defined largely in material terms, Gompers directed the Federation in such a way as to make it the vehicle through which its members could realize their aims. He was not the type of leader who through force of personality and technique and originality of thought could bring his followers around to his way of thinking. Rather Gompers' success as a labor leader lay in the fact that he could understand his constituents and formulate policy accordingly. Basically he was a compro-miser and moderator. Aware of the limited authority of his own position, he labored unceasingly to minimize internal conflicts and develop a policy that would satisfy the rank and file as well as fulfill some of their demands. In many respects he was the most able of all of the trade-union leaders of his generation.

Gompers was fortunate in having Peter J. McGuire as a friend, adviser, and co-worker. Born in 1852 in New York's Lower East Side, McGuire

---

[27] Gompers to Frank J. Dignan, August 10, 1887; Gompers to the A.F. of L. Executive Council, February 28, November 17, 1888; Gompers to L. H. Banford, August 11, 1888; Gompers to Eva McDonald Valesh, February 28, 1896, SGLB.

became apprenticed as a joiner when he was fifteen. During the late 1860's he wandered in and out of the labyrinths of radicalism then in vogue in cosmopolitan New York City. Outraged at police brutality during the Tomkins Square parade in 1874, he was one of the leaders who helped establish the Social Democratic party of North America (later the Socialist Labor party) . Influenced by the teachings of Ferdinand Lassalle, he eventually arrived at the shrine of trade unionism. McGuire's radicalism, which he never abandoned, did not in any way deter him from establishing and building the United Brotherhood of Carpenters and Joiners into one of the foremost trade unions in the United States. His genius, however, lay not in administration, but in agitation and education. Later, after his union had been established on a firm foundation, he and his brand of ideological unionism were shunted aside to make room for the professional trade unionists.[28] Yet McGuire's part in building the labor movement in the 1880's and 1890's can scarcely be exaggerated. Working to the point of total exhaustion, he freely offered his services where they were required and was instrumental in establishing a number of unions as well as helping others in distress.

The work of Gompers and McGuire in establishing the A.F. of L. on a firm and stable base reflected the activities of other trade-union leaders. Immersed in the day-to-day problems of their particular organizations, they devoted little time or effort to the ultimate reform of society. Many of them—Chris Evans, Daniel McLaughlin, John Pollack, William T. Lewis, and Patrick McBryde of the coal miners, Robert Howard, James Tansey, and John Golden of the textile workers, John Jarrett and William Martin of the steel workers, Josiah B. Dyer and James Duncan of the granite cutters, Adolph Strasser of the cigarmakers, Ernest Kurzenknabe and Charles F. Bechtold of the brewery workers—were foreign-born and therefore little influenced by the antimonopolism and reformism of American radicalism. Furthermore, the labor movement held great attraction for the perceptive and gifted immigrant who was barred from holding managerial or political positions because of philosophy or language difficulties.[29] Other native unionists, like McGuire, had spent their youth among European socialists who had migrated to the United States, and were to all intents and purposes divorced from the mainstream of ante-bellum radicalism.

Eschewing the tradition of labor reform, disillusioned with the interminable disputes of the various sectarian schools of socialist theory, and influenced by their own experiences in the shops and factories, union leaders developed their own peculiar ideology. "I have been brought up

---

[28] There is an excellent account of McGuire in Christie, *Empire in Wood*, pp. 29–37, 91–105. See also McGuire's testimony in 1883 in *Report of the Committee of the Senate Upon the Relations Between Labor and Capital*, I, 315–61, 808–13, 820–21.

[29] Sumner H. Slichter, "The Worker in Modern Economic Society," *Journal of Political Economy*, XXXIV (February, 1926) , 120.

in the hard, cold cruel school of the trade unions whose very existence demands that men who take a leading part in shaping its work shall be more than mere word mongers," Gompers remarked in 1892 in words that might have easily been spoken by any of his co-workers. "I am not a trade unionist from mere choice or whim or for revenue. I am a trade unionist from rearing and conviction." [30] Although lacking the perfection of a completed philosophical system, the ideas of the trade unionists had the great advantage of being solidly grounded on facts and not on theories. By accepting concentration of economic power as an inevitable conse-quence of industrialism, union leaders sought not to change the system, but rather to develop the economic power inherently possessed by the working class. In an abundant and expanding economy marked by a relative scarcity of labor and an absence of feudal restrictions, they found a favorable environment for their work. Disowning any revolutionary intentions, they sought to use their economic power as others had done and were doing. "We have no ultimate ends," Strasser told a Senate com-mittee in 1883. "We are going on from day to day. We are fighting only for immediate objects—objects that can be realized in a few years." [31] The changing cultural milieu of the postwar decades, as well as the influx of millions of immigrants was also bringing about a transformation among the rank and file of workers. Abandoning their absorption in reform, the working class began to look upon trade unionism with increasing favor, and this fact was reflected in the decline of the Knights and rise of the A.F. of L.

IV

The importance attached by the unions to economic power had im-portant consequences for the entire labor movement. While the National Labor Union and Knights of Labor had condemned strikes in no uncer-tain terms, the unions proceeded to elevate the strike to a position of primary importance—a direct result of the emphasis on economic power. This was not to say that union leaders favored indiscriminate striking. On the contrary, they clearly distinguished between strikes that could probably be won and those that could not. Nevertheless, they recognized that in the final analysis the strike—actual or potential—was one of their most potent weapons.[32]

To make the most of their strongest weapon, the national unions dur-ing the last two decades of the nineteenth century began to develop a

[30] Gompers to E. H. Cherry, February 10, 1892, SGLB.

[31] *Report of the Committee of the Senate Upon the Relations Between Labor and Capital,* I, 460.

[32] For the attitude of the trade unions toward the strike see the following: Adolph Strasser, "Strikes," *American Federationist,* I (September, 1894), 140; *Cigar Makers' Official Journal,* VI (April 10, 1881), 1; Gompers to William J. Smith, September 28, 1894; Gompers to James E. Cory, May 4, 1896; Gompers to E. E. Dilleter, December 31, 1896, SGLB.

rational strike policy based on centralized control of large strike funds. The question then arose as to whether or not the A.F. of L. should maintain its own assistance fund. After defeating one plan in 1887, the convention of the A.F. of L. which met in 1889 adopted a rather weak plan, and all attempts at subsequent conventions to strengthen it failed.[33] While Gompers was keenly disappointed at the Federation's inability to provide more financial assistance to distressed affiliates, many unions felt themselves justified in opposing a central fund.[34] After their experiences with the Knights, they were suspicious of any centralized authority and hence voted against measures that might have created an overly-strong and independent A.F. of L. Furthermore, many unions were too weak to provide strike benefits even for their own members, while others feared that assessments might be imposed when they themselves were engaged in trade disputes.[35]

Although its ability to raise money for affiliated unions was strictly circumscribed, the A.F. of L. offered support in other ways. In contrast to the strike policies of Powderly and other officials of the Knights, Gompers always sustained striking workers whether or not he believed in the wisdom of their course. During the Homestead strike in 1892 he attempted to help the steel workers by preventing the importation of strikebreakers, and the Federation raised over $7,000 to defend workers indicted for murdering Pinkerton guards.[36] When the massive powers of the federal government were arrayed against Eugene Debs and the American Railway Union during the Pullman strike of 1894, Gompers raised his voice in protest. Soon afterwards he called the A.F. of L. Executive Council to a meeting in Chicago. After the strike was lost and Debs faced prosecution, the Federation raised money for his defense, and the convention, which included many socialist delegates hostile to Gompers, unanimously endorsed the actions of its officers.[37]

Leaving strikes in the hands of its affiliates, the A.F. of L. devoted much of its time and money to strengthening and rebuilding the labor movement in order to enhance the economic power of the working class. Unlike the Knights, the Federation paid comparatively little attention to elaborating or publicizing a particular system or ideology. The most

[33] A.F. of L., *Proceedings*, 1887, pp. 22–23; 1888, pp. 10–11, 17–18, 21; 1889, pp. 31–32; 1892, pp. 15, 22, 30–31, 33–34; 1893, pp. 15, 43–44.

[34] See Gompers to Thomas Holland, June 30, 1888; Gompers to Patrick Needham, May 9, 1892, SGLB; A.F. of L., *Proceedings*, 1896, p. 22.

[35] See the statement of John B. Lennon, A.F. of L. treasurer, concerning strike funds, in A.F. of L., *Proceedings*, 1891, p. 22.

[36] Gompers to the A.F. of L. Executive Council, July 7, 1892; Gompers to M. Dampf, July 8, 1892; Gompers to M. M. Garland, March 21, 1893, SGLB; A.F. of L., *Proceedings*, 1892, p. 11; 1893, pp. 17–21.

[37] Gompers to Eugene V. Debs, July 5, August 16, 1894; Gompers to P. J. McGuire, July 9, 1894; Gompers to Thomas I. Kidd, July 9, 1894; Gompers to M. M. Garland, July 9, 1894; A.F. of L., *Proceedings*, 1894, pp. 11, 28–29.

pressing need of the last decades of the nineteenth century was a more widespread organization of the working class. Even by its own estimates the Federation was woefully weak, having only 160,000 members in 1887 and 265,000 in 1896.[38] The obstacles it had to overcome were indeed formidable. A biased press, a fearful public, a hostile government, ethnic and racial differences, and, above all, the obstinate refusal of employers to accept collective bargaining—all these combined in stubborn opposition to organized labor. While progress was slow and arduous, the persistency of the A.F. of L. began to pay dividends, and by 1904 it claimed a membership of almost 1,700,000.

One of the earliest organizational campaigns undertaken by the A.F. of L. revolved around the eight-hour movement of 1888–1891. Remembering the enthusiastic reception accorded the earlier movement of 1884–1886, and seeking to offset the ensuing psychological letdown, the convention of the A.F. of L. in 1888 set May 1, 1890, as the date to inaugurate the eight-hour workday.[39] "It does not necessarily follow that because we are agitating the subject," Gompers observed, "that all Unions must strike for it May 1st 1890. The agitation will do us good. It will wake up the millions of workers from their present lethargy. Upon it all men of labor, however much they may differ upon other matters, can unite upon this." [40] Gompers was as much concerned with the movement's organizational possibilities as he was with achieving a reduction of hours. "I am confident," he wrote to a fellow unionist, "that if you were to take an active part in our Eight Hour movement and bring it to the notice of your members and your trade generally that would prove a rallying cry and that although you might not achieve Eight Hours in your trade at the appointed time yet they would organize in your Union and achieve some success." [41]

Unlike the Federation of Organized Trades and Labor Unions, which gave only nominal direction to the earlier movement of 1884–1886, the A.F. of L. undertook an organized campaign to win eight hours. It issued a number of pamphlets explaining the significance of the movement,[42]

---

[38] A. F. of L., *Proceedings*, 1904, p. 16; Leo Wolman, *The Growth of American Trade Unions 1880–1923* (New York, 1924), p. 32.

[39] A.F. of L., *Proceedings*, 1888, pp. 25–26.

[40] Gompers to John O'Brien, February 7, 1889. See also Gompers to August Delebar, January 25, 1889; Gompers to John S. Kirchner, February 28, 1889; Gompers to August Keufer, May 9, 1890, SGLB.

[41] Gompers to August Schmidt, February 23, 1889, SGLB.

[42] George Gunton, *The Economic and Social Importance of the Eight-Hour Movement* (Washington, D. C., 1889); George E. McNeill, *The Eight Hour Primer* (New York, 1889); Lemuel Danryid, *History and Philosophy of the Eight-Hour Movement* (New York, 1889). The main argument on behalf of eight hours was that it would help solve the unemployment problem, although Ira Steward's theories still exercised considerable influence. Gompers never regarded the eight-hour movement as an end in itself, but rather as a means to an end. See Gompers to Edward T. Plank, May 20, 1889; Gompers to H. Donnally, March 8, 1890, SGLB.

and leading unionists and organizers spoke at mass meetings on behalf of the cause. On February 22, 1889, no less than 240 meetings took place; on July 4, 1889, 311; and on September 2, 1889, 420.[43]

Despite the enthusiasm generated by such efforts, it soon became evident that not all unions were prepared to enforce the adoption of eight hours on May 1, 1890. Gompers, cognizant of the inability of many member unions to undertake any militant action in order to achieve eight hours, then began to recede slowly from the broad position that he and the Federation had taken at the convention of 1888. He denied that affiliated unions were required to strike for eight hours in 1890 and suggested instead that aid be extended to those organizations that were prepared to take action on the issue. "Every man," he pointed out, "who succeeds in reducing his hours of labor makes it easier for every other man to reduce his." [44] The convention of the A.F. of L. in 1889 narrowed the scope of the movement by empowering the Executive Council "to select such trade or trades . . . best prepared to achieve success" to take the lead.[45] Shortly thereafter the Council chose the United Brotherhood of Carpenters and Joiners, the largest union then affiliated with the A.F. of L., to lead the movement on May 1, 1890.[46]

Meanwhile, the Federation kept up its program of agitation and mass meetings, besides raising over $12,000 for the use of the Carpenters.[47] While the Carpenters did not win the eight-hour day, they did succeed in appreciably shortening their hours in many cities. Furthermore, the union increased its membership from 31,494 to 53,769 during 1890, as compared with an increase of only 3,078 in 1889.[48] "The agitation for the Eight Hour movement," Gompers reported, "not only has had the effect of gaining this immense advantage for the Carpenters and Joiners of America, but it has given courage and hope to the working people who for years were disheartened and acting on the defensive against the encroachments of the employing class. Every trade and labor union of the country has vastly increased its membership and obtained improved conditions." [49]

[43] A.F. of L., *Proceedings*, 1889, p. 14. See also Gompers to Richard Eisner, February 25, 1889; Gompers to W. W. Wood, February 28, 1889; Gompers to E. H. McAuinch, February 28, 1889; Gompers to the General Assembly of the Knights of Labor, November 9, 1889, SGLB.

[44] Gompers to Edmund Kraft, February 8, 1889. See also Gompers to James H. Perry, January 22, 1889; Gompers to Edward T. Plank, May 20, 1889; Gompers to O. R. Lake, May 20, 1889, SGLB.

[45] A.F. of L., *Proceedings*, 1889, pp. 29–30.

[46] Gompers to P. J. McGuire, March 20, 1890, SGLB.

[47] Gompers to Adam Menche, March 14, 1890; Gompers to L. C. Tosse, July 14, 1890, SGLB.

[48] United Brotherhood of Carpenters and Joiners, *Proceedings*, 1900, p. 48.

[49] Gompers to August Keufer, May 9, 1890. See also Gompers to L. C. Tosse, July 14, 1890; Gompers to the Editors of the "Labor Tribune," July 28, 1890, SGLB; A.F. of L., *Proceedings*, 1890, p. 13.

The Federation then expected the United Mine Workers, which had declared its intention to enforce the eight-hour day at its convention in January, 1890, to follow the Carpenters in the movement. The Miners' Executive Board instead decided that because of contractual obligations it could not take any action before May 1, 1891.[50] The weakness of this newly-established organization, however, made it a poor choice to press for shorter hours. Although the miners commenced preparations for the drive, a disturbing factor arose when a strike began among its members in the Connellsville region of Pennsylvania. A shortage of funds and the defection of at least one important region from the movement then led the union to postpone its plans.[51]

The poor showing made by the miners in 1891 marked the end of the movement. Although the A.F. of L. convention in 1891 empowered its Executive Council to choose a trade to press for eight hours in 1892, it refused to endorse applications by the International Typographical Union and Journeymen Bakers and Confectioners National Union, and the Executive Council took no further action.[52] After 1891 each union was left free to pursue its own tactics, and the Federation never again attempted to exercise any centralized control over the movement. Nevertheless, it had succeeded in identifying the eight-hour cause with the trade unions. In so doing it laid claim to an issue that proved valuable in future organizational campaigns.

After surrendering its leadership in the shorter hours crusade, the A.F. of L. concentrated much of its energies on purely organizational work. It carried on its activities in this area at several different levels. At the local level it established "federal labor unions," which after 1893 included workers of all trades.[53] These units were recruiting grounds for the trade unions, for as soon as there were enough workers of the same occupation, they were expected to form regular trade unions. When enough local unions of a particular occupation existed, the Federation's officers would attempt to bring them together to form a national union. Local unions affiliated directly with the A.F. of L. were required to join the national organization of their trade as soon as the latter was formed.[54] In some cases the Federation was directly responsible for the establishment of national unions, and in others it gave existing national unions help in organizing their trade. During 1891 the A.F. of L. aided in resuscitating the Coopers International Union and formed the Electrical Workers into a national union out of affiliated locals.[55]

[50] A.F. of L., *Proceedings*, 1890, pp. 14, 43; Evans, *History of the United Mine Workers*, II, 17, 41; Gompers to Robert Watchorn, May 28, 1890, SGLB.
[51] Evans, *History of the United Mine Workers*, II, 94–96, 106–08, 114–17, 122–26.
[52] A.F. of L., *Proceedings*, 1891, p. 47.
[53] *Ibid.*, 1893, pp. 43–44.
[54] *Ibid.*, 1890, p. 14.
[55] *Ibid.*, 1891, p. 12.

The Federation's organizational abilities were fully recognized by its affiliates, who often appealed for the parent body's help in organizing their trade. Generally the annual conventions of the A.F. of L. responded favorably to these requests.[56] But lack of funds hindered the Federation's organizational campaigns in its early years, and it was forced to rely on unpaid volunteer unionists to act as organizers.[57] A.F. of L. officials were often hard pressed to carry out the convention's instructions to organize or help national unions. In 1894 the Federation spent only $448.49 for organizing, while in 1896 it spent $183.44 for organizing and an additional $450.83 for organizational literature. As it grew stronger, however, it appropriated more and more of its income to further the work of organizing, and by 1905 was using nearly 30 per cent of its revenue—$61,694.29—for this purpose.[58]

A depression, beginning in 1893, temporarily threw the A.F. of L. on the defensive. But despite all obstacles, it continued to organize the working class, and between 1896 and 1901 formed no less than thirty-five international unions out of directly chartered federal and trade unions.[59] By the turn of the century the great majority of national unions (except the Railroad Brotherhoods) had accepted the A.F. of L. as their official spokesman. By leaving the unions free to pursue their particular interests, and by concentrating on labor's common goals, the A.F. of L. had established itself as an important working-class institution. As Gompers told the convention of 1892:

> It is our purpose and a large part of our work has been devoted to gathering and concentrating the forces of labor into the compact National Unions, and that work has been crowned with a success never before equalled. The Trade Unions are realizing more clearly that the interests of all are best subserved by the underlying principles of the A.F. of L., and that their autonomy and independence is safe at the hands of and best promoted by affiliation with the A.F. of L. We want to make the trade union movement under the A.F. of L. as distinct as the billows, yet one as the sea.[60]

V

The A.F. of L.'s preoccupation with organizational activities was simply a reflection of the dominance of the national union in the labor movement. These unions were reluctant to surrender any portion of their

[56] *Ibid.*, 1893, pp. 39–40; 1894, pp. 33–34.

[57] Gompers to the A.F. of L. Executive Council, January 24, 1888; Gompers to John T. Elliott, January 28, 1888; Hugh McGregor to Gompers, February 1, 1888; Gompers to E. J. Lake, March 20, 1888, SGLB; A.F. of L., *Proceedings*, 1888, p. 12.

[58] A.F. of L., *Proceedings*, 1894, p. 18; 1896, p. 27; Philip Taft, *The A.F. of L. in the Time of Gompers* (New York, 1957), p. 100.

[59] Taft, *The A.F. of L.*, p. 98.

[60] A.F. of L., *Proceedings*, 1892, p. 16.

autonomy or independence because of their earlier conflict with the more highly-centralized Knights. This in turn prevented the Federation from exercising more than nominal control over its affiliates. The A.F. of L., therefore, became in practice more of an arbiter than a genuine governing body. While hoping that the broader interests of labor would govern the decisions of its affiliated unions, the Federation's officials were forced to recognize that special interests often prevailed. Rather than provoke a schism in the movement, they often preferred to retain the theoretical principle while accepting the contradictory practice. This attitude of compromise, based upon a recognition of the Federation's limited power, was usually the only course that its responsible leaders could pursue. Thus many of the A.F. of L.'s policies were determined not necessarily on the basis of the general welfare of the labor movement, but rather on the basis of what was practical and possible.

In organizing Negro workers, for example, the A.F. of L. had to face the fact of racial animosity among its affiliates, some of which had enacted constitutional barriers against colored membership. The exclusion of Negroes from unions had important repercussions, especially for the Southern labor movement, which was thereby weakened and divided. The Federation, on the other hand, in 1893 reaffirmed its belief that the working class had to unite regardless of "creed, color, sex, nationality or politics." [61] Gompers held similar views. "Your employers care nothing for you as a rule," he wrote to the president of a Nebraska local union in 1889, "except as to who will work the cheapest; white or black is immaterial to them, and the first consideration that should engage your attention is unity [of] purpose regardless of color." [62] Gompers also drew no distinction between Negro and white workers, for in his eyes both were members of the same economic class. "It isn't a question of social or even any other kind of equality," he wrote to a Federation organizer. "It is one of absolute necessity. . . . If we do not make friends of the colored men they will of necessity be justified in proving themselves our enemies, and they will be utilized upon every occasion to frustrate our every effort for economic, social and political improvement." [63]

Yet race prejudice did exist among white workers, and Gompers was forced to recognize its existence. In response to numerous complaints that particular locals were refusing to accept Negroes, Gompers answered that he stood ready to grant charters to all-colored locals.[64] This was not to say that a segregated labor movement was in any way desirable, for Gompers

[61] A.F. of L., *Proceedings*, 1893, p. 56.

[62] Gompers to James H. White, September 14, 1889. See also Gompers to Fred J. Carr, December 8, 1891; Gompers to Charles E. Archer, June 1, 1894, SGLB.

[63] Gompers to Jerome Jones, March 8, 1893, SGLB.

[64] Gompers to Louis F. Klinger, July 18, 1891. See also Gompers to William H. Luchtenburg, May 9, 1892; Gompers to A. D. Bauer, June 13, 1892; Gompers to H. M. Ives, November 10, 1892; Gompers to E. M. McGruder, April 3, 1893, SGLB.

was pledged to an elimination of the color line. When issuing charters, for example, Gompers steadfastly refused to include either a "white" or "colored" designation in the title, for that was to give official recognition to the existence of the color barrier.[65] But, as he informed the secretary of a local union in 1893, "It is useless to deny the fact that there is a great amount of race prejudice still existing among white workmen, and it is well for us to keep this fact in mind. . . . It is useless to be simply trying to ram our heads through stone walls; recognizing the conditions which exist is the best way we can secure the organization of all in a way which must ultimately bring about a unity of feeling and action among all toilers." [66]

The problem of discrimination first arose in a practical way when the National Association of Machinists included a clause excluding Negroes from membership in its constitution. In 1890 there was a movement to have the union affiliate with the Federation. Gompers attempted to induce the union to eliminate the disputed clause and even hinted at dual organization should it refuse to do so. The convention of the A.F. of L. meeting in 1890 also urged the union to abrogate the disputed clause and instructed its Executive Council to issue a call for a convention of all organized machinists to form a single national organization.[67]

Shortly thereafter Gompers visited the Machinists' convention and formally requested the removal of the color line. The convention replied that it was "inexpedient at that time" to comply, but that it would "in all probability" do so at its next session. Gompers and the Executive Council then called a convention and organized a rival union known as the International Machinists' Union of America. That this action met with resistance was demonstrated when an A.F. of L. committee stated that the organization of the rival union had been "premature." Forced to deny the charge that the Federation was dictating standards of admission to its affiliates, Gompers expressed the belief that the International Association of Machinists would be admitted if it abrogated the anti-Negro clause.[68]

In 1892 the president of the Machinists told a Federation committee that he was satisfied with the position taken by the A.F. of L. Executive Council; and he assured the committee that the color line would be eliminated at the Machinists' next convention.[69] Within the union, how-

[65] Gompers to Henry J. Spaeter, November 10, 1893; Gompers to Julius Friedman, March 31, 1894, SGLB.

[66] Gompers to David Watkins, July 17, 1893, SGLB.

[67] Gompers to T. N. Talbot, April 15, 1890; Gompers to Frank D. Hamlin, April 30, 1890; Gompers to J. J. Creamer, November 10, 1890; Gompers to Harry E. Easton, April 30, 1891, SGLB; A.F. of L., *Proceedings*, 1890, pp. 31–32. Shortly afterwards the union changed its name to the International Association of Machinists.

[68] A.F. of L., *Proceedings*, 1891, pp. 12, 39–41; Gompers to R. T. Coles, April 28, 1891; Gompers to the International Association of Machinists' Delegates, May 7, 1892, SGLB.

[69] A.F. of L., *Proceedings*, 1892, p. 40.

ever, the question of removing the exclusion clause had aroused strong feelings, especially in the South. Gompers was accused of following a "rule or ruin policy." [70] While some members favored removal of the color line,[71] others vigorously opposed it. "I would like to say," one Georgia member strongly stated, "that I never had any preference for negro hand-shaking, and can't possibly conceive how I could bind myself by any oath to trail in the dust the most endearing term known in modern language—*brother*. Let us not only keep the I.A. of M. *white*, but let each member start out with the determination to make it *whiter*, and the ascent that is necessarily bound to follow will be the greatest achievement of a future day." [72]

In 1895 James Duncan, who acted as president of the A.F. of L. for several months while John McBride was ill (this was the only time between 1886 and 1924 that Gompers failed to be re-elected to the presidency of the Federation), suggested that the International Association of Machinists drop the disputed clause from its constitution and leave the admission of Negroes to its locals (where exclusion was the rule).[73] Soon afterward the union adopted this procedure and became affiliated with the Federation, although as late as 1902 it had practically no Negro members.[74]

In a similar case Gompers used the threat of a rival union as a lever to compel the abrogation of an exclusionist policy.[75] But the more Gompers attempted to induce organizations to accept colored workers, the stronger and more intense the opposition grew. When he appointed two Negro organizers in the early 1890's to work in the South, they met with fierce resistance from white unionists.[76] In 1896, while trying to persuade the Brotherhood of Locomotive Firemen to affiliate with the Federation, Gompers denied that the A.F. of L. compelled its affiliates to accept Negroes. "What the A.F. of L. declares by its policy," he informed the union, is "that organization should not declare *against* accepting the colored man *because he is colored*." [77] Gompers conceded that the Firemen were justified in excluding Negroes working for substandard wages.[78] This fact, he implied, simply demonstrated the pressing need for organization. Gompers decried the fact that the race question was being used to

[70] Gompers to the A.F. of L. Executive Council, May 17, 1893, SGLB; *Journal of the International Association of Machinists*, V (May, 1893), 136.

[71] *Journal of the International Association of Machinists*, VI (April, 1894), 115.

[72] *Ibid.*, VI (May, 1894), 154.

[73] James Duncan to James O'Connell, March 27, 1895, SGLB.

[74] John McBride to T. J. Morgan, May 16, 1895, SGLB; W. E. Burghardt DuBois, ed., *The Negro Artisan* (Atlanta, 1902), pp. 167, 169–70.

[75] Gompers to John C. Knight, March 6, 1893, SGLB.

[76] Gompers to George L. Norton, May 16, 17, 24, 1892; Gompers to John M. Callahan, May 17, 24, 1892; Gompers to Joseph Amstead, October 18, November 4, 1892, February 2, 27, 1893; Gompers to J. Geggie, October 18, 27, November 4, 1892, SGLB.

[77] *Locomotive Firemen's Magazine*, XXI (July, 1896), 65.

[78] Gompers to F. P. Sargent, August 17, 1896, SGLB.

split the ranks of labor, referring to it in 1897 as "a bugaboo urged among some workingmen to frighten them from performing their duties." [79]

As opposition increased Gompers began to retreat from his earlier views. Urging moderation, he declared that the unionization of the white worker was more important than an issue that might well split the entire labor movement.[80] More and more Gompers began to say that the best solution was the organization of colored locals, at least for the time being.[81] When confronted with the problem of whether a charter should be issued to a Central Labor Union representing the New Orleans' colored workers, Gompers replied in a typical letter. "Of course I am free to say that I should prefer that there should be unity of organization as well as unity of purpose. However there is no use kicking against the pricks, and we cannot overcome prejudice in a day. Under these circumstances, I should have no hesitation in approving the formation of a Central Body composed of the unions of colored workmen." [82]

In 1900 the constitution of the A.F. of L. was amended so as to permit the chartering of separate colored central labor unions, local unions, and federal labor unions—if it seemed "advisable and to the best interest of the trade union movement to do so." [83] Thus by 1900 the Federation had accepted or at least acquiesed in the exclusionist policy of many of its affiliates.[84]

[79] Gompers to W. D. Lewis, April 9, 1897, SGLB. The Brotherhood of Locomotive Firemen failed to join the Federation when a referendum on the abrogation of the clause excluding Negroes did not obtain a two-thirds majority.

[80] Gompers to H. M. Ives, November 10, 1892; Gompers to James Leonard, June 28, 1900, SGLB.

[81] Gompers to W. S. Griscom, April 16, 1897; Gompers to J. W. Crow, September 26, 1900, SGLB.

[82] Gompers to J. E. Porter, May 23, 1900, SGLB.

[83] A.F. of L., Proceedings, 1900, pp. 22–23, 112, 129.

[84] A study made in 1900 indicated that nineteen national unions, with a total membership of nearly 400,000, had about 33,000 Negroes. Eleven more with almost 100,000 workers had a negligible proportion of colored members. Twenty-three other unions reported having no colored workers, while one was undecided and another had no record. Fully thirteen national organizations excluded Negroes outright. DuBois, Negro Artisan, pp. 158, 164, 167.

Why did the glittering hopes of the 1880's fade into the discriminatory practices of the 1890's and early twentieth century? Bernard Mandel, writing from a Marxist viewpoint, condemns Gompers for sacrificing "both his principles and the Negro workingmen, as well as the broader interests of the whole labor movement, to the short-sighted and selfish demands of the aristocratic officialdom of the craft unions, whose spokesman he had agreed to be." Mandel, "Samuel Gompers and the Negro Workers, 1886–1914," Journal of Negro History, XL (January, 1955), 60. A more plausible explanation of the renewed persistence of prejudice in the labor movement, however, is to be found in the course of Southern history in the 1890's, and especially the frustration of Southern Populism through the utilization of Negroes by Southern conservatives. The rise of Jim Crowism and segregation were outgrowths of the 1890's, and they also had an important impact upon the labor movement. See especially C. Vann Woodward's works, The Strange Career of Jim Crow (New York, 1955), and Origins of the New South 1877–1913 (Baton Rouge, Louisiana, 1951).

In a sense the A.F. of L. was caught in an historical dilemma. The only effective weapons against an exclusionist policy—rival unionism and expulsion—were impossible because of their inherent danger to the well-being of the whole labor movement. Moreover, it is doubtful whether either weapon would have been effective. The A.F. of L. was never itself guilty of enacting any discriminatory clauses or of refusing to admit Negroes, but it was forced to approve what it regarded as the lesser of two evils. Since it was attempting to build a strong labor movement in the South, it hesitated to push a policy of integration that might have defeated the larger goal. So it accepted what it regarded as an unfortunate situation, hoping that time would heal an unwelcome division and make possible the organization of labor on a nonracial basis.

Inability to compel acceptance of the Negro, however, was not the only example of the limited nature of the Federation's authority over its affiliates. In almost all its dealings the A.F. of L. was forced to seek workable compromises acceptable to its constituent members.

Disputes over jurisdiction, for example, evoked some of the A.F. of L.'s most difficult problems. Although it was responsible for founding many unions, the Federation had virtually no control over the delineation of the various jurisdictions claimed by each. While the principle of one organization in each trade was endorsed by nearly all unions, conflicts often arose over its application. Union jurisdictional claims were generally phrased in broad terms, leading to some duplication and overlapping. Technological innovation often served to obliterate trade lines, thus causing additional friction. The fact that most unions represented a blend of trade and industrial jurisdictions was another source of difficulty. Inevitably, A.F. of L. affiliates were constantly engaged in jurisdictional disputes.

The Federation was first confronted with the problem of jurisdiction in 1888, when the Amalgamated Society of Carpenters and Joiners, an American branch of an English union, applied for a charter. The United Brotherhood of Carpenters and Joiners objected, and the convention of the A.F. of L. refused to grant the charter on the ground that it would be "detrimental to the interests of labor to have any more than one organization in any trade." [85] The delegates then instructed the Executive Council to do all in its power to effect an amalgamation if more than one organization existed in any trade.[86] Even at this early date Gompers was cognizant of the limitations of the Federation, and when asked to rule on a jurisdictional dispute, replied: "I am loath to give decisions in matters

---

[85] Gompers to P. J. McGuire, September 13, 1888; Gompers to Thomas Shaw, November 10, December 6, 1888, SGLB; A.F. of L., *Proceedings*, 1888, pp. 7, 19. Two years later, however, the Federation admitted the Amalgamated Society of Carpenters and Joiners. Never having more than 9,000 members, the Amalgamated was finally absorbed by the United Brotherhood of Carpenters and Joiners in 1915.

[86] A.F. of L., *Proceedings*, 1888, p. 27. See also *ibid.*, 1889, p. 20.

that arise between organizations, it seems to me to partake too much of a dictatorship. Hence [I] do not decide when other means accomplish the same purpose."[87] Generally Gompers attempted to act as a moderator by bringing both parties together.[88]

When a conflict developed between two strong organizations, the A.F. of L. often demonstrated reluctance to become involved and attempted instead to have the dispute settled by the two interested parties. In 1889 a disagreement between the Carpenters and the Furniture Workers International Union came before the A.F. of L. Since two prominent unions were involved, the convention simply proposed the mutual adoption of a system of working rules that would obviate all future conflicts. When a similar disagreement arose three years later, the convention adopted practically the same recommendation. In 1895 the convention also refused to intervene in a jurisdictional conflict between the International Typographical Union and the International Association of Machinists and persuaded the two unions to work out a settlement by themselves.[89] Even after the Federation had adopted a resolution apparently clarifying the jurisdictional claims of the Journeymen Tailors National Union and the United Garment Workers of America,[90] Gompers was called upon by the latter's secretary to arbitrate the dispute. Recognizing the dangers involved, Gompers replied judiciously:

> I beg to say that I do not look upon this position [of umpire or arbitrator] as a very enviable one and would have much preferred that the matter in dispute might have been adjusted amicably between yourself and Mr. Lennon. I am sure that you are both as competent to arrive at a just conclusion as I am. I realize, too, that the position of umpire or arbitrator is more than likely to have unpleasant results. Men are not accustomed to take kindly to those who decide against them, and that refers equally to the one as to the other side in the dispute. I have suggested to Mr. Lennon, and I now make the suggestion to you, that a renewed effort be made by you both for the purpose of coming to an agreement. If the same has not been accomplished within two weeks from the date of this letter, then the matter be submitted to me for arbitration and decision. The condition that I impose in accepting the position is that each side will declare its willingness to abide by the decision rendered.[91]

On the other hand, when the dispute was between a strong and a weak union, the A.F. of L. frequently sided with the stronger simply as a matter

[87] Gompers to Charles E. Miller, May 11, 1888, SGLB.

[88] See Gompers to the Officers and Members of the Operative Painters Protective and Benevolent Union, June 27, 1890, SGLB.

[89] A.F. of L., *Proceedings*, 1889, p. 34; 1892, pp. 34–35; 1895, pp. 44–45, 76. One of the only times the Federation ruled against the Carpenters occurred in 1893, when the convention requested that the Carpenters prevent its members from infringing on the work done by the Tin, Sheet Iron and Cornice Workers International Union. *Ibid.*, 1893, p. 45.

[90] *Ibid.*, 1896, p. 48.

[91] Gompers to Henry White, June 16, 1897, SGLB.

of self-interest. Sanctions against a weak organization could be made effective; sanctions against a strong one were simply unfeasible and dangerous. Thus when two locals complained to Gompers about certain activities of the Carpenters, Gompers forwarded the letters to McGuire. "You will of course understand," he added, "that I have no desire to interfere with the affairs of your organization in deciding the questions that so intimately concern you, and I do not attempt it even in these instances." [92] In 1891 a long-standing dispute between the Iron Molders International Union and the International Brotherhood of Machinery Molders was referred to the Federation. Gompers, unhappy about the seemingly indefinite subdivisions of the trade-union movement, sided with the Iron Molders and urged the Machinery Molders to amalgamate with the stronger organization. When the Machinery Molders refused, its delegate was denied admission to the convention of the A.F. of L. in 1892.[93] In 1896 the Federation expelled the Tin, Sheet Iron and Cornice Workers after the Iron Molders had complained that the Tin Workers were initiating unfair workers.[94] Similarly, the convention supported the Amalgamated Wood Workers in its conflict with the United Order of Box Makers and Sawyers of Chicago, the Electrical Workers over the Theatrical Stage Employees, and the International Association of Machinists over the Die Sinkers and Drop Forgers Protective Union.[95]

Since few of the strong national unions evinced willingness to permit a central organization to define jurisdictional boundaries, the A.F. of L. had to acquiesce in the reality of the situation and follow a policy that harmonized with the locus of power in the labor movement. As the two delegates of the Granite Cutters National Union to a convention of the A.F. of L. astutely observed:

> As the trade union movement advances, it is evident that one of the most difficult things to contend with is the question of jurisdiction. The sub-divisions of work and labor-saving devices have brought what was considered skilled workmanship within the reach of men following other kinds of employment, and annually unions send their grievances to the American Federation of Labor conventions in hope that decisions may be rendered which will for all time give them the advantage their propositions seek. . . . In connection with the desire for lasting decisions by the convention, it should be borne in mind that the American Federation of Labor is a voluntary body in which the constitutional laws of the different organizations are respected and is not a supreme body. The unions affiliated maintain the supremacy and the Ameri-

[92] Gompers to P. J. McGuire, July 26, 1889. See also Gompers to George N. Lawrence, October 3, 1889, SGLB.

[93] Gompers to John A. Penton, June 26, 1891; Gompers to Thomas I. Kidd, June 21, 1892, SGLB; A.F. of L., *Proceedings*, 1892, p. 28.

[94] A.F. of L., *Proceedings*, 1895, pp. 35, 68; 1896, p. 33. The union was readmitted in 1897. *Ibid.*, 1897, p. 17.

[95] *Ibid.*, 1896, pp. 66–67, 83–85.

can Federation of Labor acts as per the best judgment of the whole combined. This being a fact, when decisions are not rendered in favor of one or the other unions, the one most aggrieved sometimes sends out an alarm that the American Federation of Labor is not a useful organization, but it is from its voluntary nature and because at all times it has given its best services to settle disputes between organizations without following dictatorial lines, that it has been so successful.[96]

Both Gompers and the Federation recognized that jurisdiction could be divided ad infinitum and that trade unionism could be carried to an illogical extreme. "There are too many of our fellow-workers who prefer division rather than unity in the trade union movement," Gompers complained. "When I say this I mean that every little division or subdivision in a trade wants to organize as a distinct national union." [97] He therefore attempted to induce related organizations having similar interests to amalgamate voluntarily.[98] Similarly, the A.F. of L. sought to further trade amalgamation wherever possible, and adopted a strong resolution on this subject in 1893. When two unions claimed jurisdiction over a particular trade, it stipulated, the Executive Council was to attempt to bring about an amalgamation. Failing to effect union amicably, the Council might then "draw up a plan of amalgamation which shall be binding upon both national organizations." [99] This resolution, however, presupposed that all affiliated unions would be willing to accept the Federation's rulings in such cases—an unlikely event. As Frank Duffy of the Carpenters remarked at a later date: "We reserve the right to say what our jurisdictional claims shall cover, and we don't propose that they shall be curtailed, altered, or amended through any other agency." [100] Lacking means of enforcement, the resolution of 1893 quickly became a dead letter, and the A.F. of L. continued to settle jurisdictional disputes in a voluntary manner.[101]

The A.F. of L. was also cautious about intervening in conflicts within unions. When the Brotherhood of Painters and Decorators split into two rival groups, the Federation undertook to heal the schism and succeeded after nearly six years of long and patient effort in unifying the dissident groups.[102] Gompers frequently offered advice, but never in such a way as to leave himself open to the charge of interfering in a union's internal affairs. Even when charges of corruption were brought against officials of the Waiters Union, he hesitated to act. While not denying the existence

[96] Granite Cutters' Journal, XXIV (February, 1901), 4.
[97] Gompers to J. M. Vale, March 14, 1896, SGLB.
[98] See Gompers to Charles W. Nelson, April 29, 1892, SGLB.
[99] A.F. of L., Proceedings, 1893, pp. 67–68.
[100] Frank Duffy, "Our So-called Unwarranted Jurisdictional Claims," The Carpenter, XXVI (March, 1916), 5–6, cited in Christie, Empire in Wood, p. 111.
[101] Sometimes the A.F. of L. was able to bring about a voluntary amalgamation. See, for example, A.F. of L., Proceedings, 1895, pp. 28, 34–35, 84; 1896, p. 33.
[102] Taft, The A.F. of L., pp. 107–09.

of corruption, Gompers steadfastly maintained that the members themselves had to effect a change. "The administration of the affairs of the National union is as good as the membership," he remarked. "No, neither as an individual or as a union man, or President of the American Federation of Labor, will I give any encouragement to division, secession or rivalry in the labor movement." [103]

VI

Despite its limited and circumscribed power, the A.F. of L. succeeded in becoming the recognized spokesman of the working class in the United States. This paradoxical and startling fact, however, provides the key to an understanding of its success. Completely dependent upon its sovereign affiliates, the A.F. of L. came to reflect the interests of its constituents. In turn the member unions were influenced by the economic, social, and political milieu in which they operated, and their survival depended in large part on their ability to keep pace with changing developments. Thus while the unions were forging the complicated apparatus of collective bargaining and laying the foundation for industrial government, the Federation was creating an institutional framework in which they could operate.

Critics of the A.F. of L. have often stressed its inconsistencies and what it failed to accomplish. Such criticism, while partially justified, nevertheless avoids the basic problem. While the broad interests of workers were basically similar, there were often differences on specific issues. Functioning within and not above the labor movement, the leaders of the Federation were forced to deal realistically with such internal stresses and tensions. They never forgot their long-range goals, but in achieving them they also had to take peculiar immediate conditions and the existing balance of power into account; and they always had to remember that what was suitable for one union might be disastrous for another. Consequently, the A.F. of L. never insisted on a monolithic approach to specific problems but was content to develop individual policies to meet individual problems.

The A.F. of L., furthermore, reflected the dominant features of the rapidly changing environment in which it operated. In the last quarter of the nineteenth century the American *Zeitgeist* emphasized individualism and advancement and interpreted these goals primarily in terms of wealth and power. "The word 'enough,'" observed a French visitor, "is the loneliest, and the least often employed, word in the American vocabulary. There is no diversity of striving; all are striving for money, money, money. This makes the race fast and furious, and competition and rivalry bitter,

[103] Gompers to Jerry O'Sullivan, September 24, 1897, SGLB.

and not always honorable. Money here is tyrant, as it is tyrant nowhere else." [104]

For its part, the Federation sought above all to raise the standard of living of the working class. Stressing the importance of immediate material goals, it paid scant heed to doctrinaires who sought to dampen the acquisitive spirit or to destroy the capitalistic system itself. European socialists often expressed amazement at the weakness of the socialist movement in the United States. "Indeed," remarked a European nonsocialist scholar, "I believe that the relation of the American laborer to capitalism is even more intimate than even these friendly declarations and testimonials of respect really express. I believe he enters into it with all his heart: I believe he loves it. . . . The greater intensity of American labor is nothing more than the expression of the laborer's fundamentally capitalist mental attitude." [105]

The American social structure also influenced the A.F. of L. in another and equally important manner. Unlike many European labor movements, the American labor movement's primary objective was to organize and stay organized. In a society lacking rigid class distinctions and marked by horizontal and vertical mobility, organizational stability along economic lines was difficult to achieve. Thus Gompers and other trade-union leaders had to contend with threats to the very existence of the movement. To meet these threats they proceeded to make full use of the economic power at their command. In so doing they abandoned the reform objectives of their predecessors with the astute observation that they were promising in theory but unattainable in practice.

The strength of the A.F. of L., therefore, lay in the fact that it not only had rank and file support, but that it harmonized with its environment. Lack of a rigid ideology and limited authority further had the effect of giving the Federation a high degree of pliability, enabling it to adapt to social change. In the end the A.F. of L. became a peculiarly American institution, with all of the virtues—as well as the vices—of its parent environment.

[104] Price Collier, *America and the Americans From a French Point of View* (New York, 1897), p. 139.

[105] Werner Sombart, "Study of the Historical Development and Evolution of the American Proletariat," *International Socialist Review*, VI (September, 1905), 135-36.

CHAPTER NINE

Trade Unionism, Politics, and Socialism, 1886–1896

I

ℰ FROM THE VERY BEGINNING of the A.F. of L. it was evident that the new leaders of American labor were determined that working-class energies should not be dissipated by too much concern with political action. This is not to say that the Federation was any more immune than its predecessors to the paradoxes and difficulties raised by the fact that it lived and operated in a political environment. As we will see subsequently, the leaders of the A.F. of L. could never avoid the implications of this fact. It is only to say that the answers that these leaders gave marked a radical new departure in American labor history—an explicit repudiation of the idea that politics was the primary vehicle of social and economic change, indeed, of the entire reformist tradition, and the espousal of the belief that direct economic action afforded the surest hope of achieving labor's goals. Since the leaders of the A.F. of L. held such convictions, it is almost needless to say that from the outset they were more interested in avoiding the pitfalls of politics than in capitalizing upon the advantages of direct political action. In the end they succeeded in laying the foundations for the limited political policy of the American labor movement, a policy that was to remain largely unchanged until recent times.

At the time of the founding of the A.F. of L. in 1886, however an unprecedented political uprising was sweeping through the ranks of workingmen throughout the nation.[1] Indeed, it is difficult to exaggerate the extent of labor's uprising at this time. Years of suppressed discontent and frustrations had ultimately reached a peak of intensity, resulting in numerous and widespread strikes, an eight-hour movement, a phenomenal growth of the Knights of Labor and the trade unions, and a desire to effect a change in the generally unfavorable attitude of government toward labor. Under these circumstances it was perhaps natural that a working class political movement would result, given the past heritage of similar endeavors.

[1] See Chapter Five.

Despite their growing antipathy toward political commitments, many trade unions were drawn into the vortex of the fierce political struggles of 1886 throughout the nation. The most famous of these conflicts, though by no means the sole one, occurred in New York City. There the Central Labor Union, representing perhaps 50,000 workers or more, had moved into the political arena after five of its members had been sentenced to jail terms. These five men, after conducting a successful boycott against an employer, had been brought to trial upon complaint of the employer, who asserted that his agreement with the union (including a payment of $1,000 to the union to cover costs) had constituted extortion. From this point on events moved rapidly, culminating in the formation of what later became known as the United Labor party and the nomination of Henry George for mayor of New York City.

The extent to which the political fervor had affected even the trade unions is demonstrated by the position taken by Samuel Gompers, soon to be elected as the new president of the A.F. of L. at its founding in December. Initially Gompers had expressed a singular lack of enthusiasm toward labor involvement in the New York campaign, remarking in a union journal that "Our friends John Swinton and Tom Armstrong and others we could name might give some reminiscences to our friends who are anxious for workingmen to rush into politics." [2] The enthusiasm of the rank and file, however, forced Gompers to modify his attitude. In his autobiography he recalled that while political action as such had no appeal to him, he nevertheless "appreciated the movement as a demonstration of protest." [3] During the ensuing campaign he took an active role, heading the Speakers' Bureau of the Henry George Clubs and making frequent public appearances.[4] In general, his actions coincided with the position taken by the trade unions and Knights in the New York area, as well as in other parts of the country.

Although George was defeated, the momentum of labor's political effort was to be carried well into 1887 and even beyond. Gompers, however, began to abandon his momentary absorption in politics, as did many other trade-union leaders. Several factors were responsible for Gompers' change of heart. In the first place, his participation in the campaign seems to have resulted from pressure by the rank and file rather than from any abiding faith in the efficacy of political action. Bowing to the popular demand, therefore, he had publicly supported George. But once the fervor of the election had subsided, he drew the same conclusions that he had drawn from his earlier experiences with political action in the Cigar Makers International Union, namely, that labor politics generally resulted in more harm than good. In many respects the campaign of 1886 simply confirmed Gompers' conversion to an outspoken opponent of partisan

---

[2] Gompers, *Seventy Years*, I, 312.
[3] *Ibid.*, p. 313.
[4] *Ibid.*, pp. 316–17.

political action. Reading the lessons of the election, and recognizing the inherent and almost insuperable difficulties of combining American workingmen into an efficient and coherent political phalanx, he was able to formulate a policy that avoided the pitfalls and divisions that previous political involvements had entailed, as well as one that would be acceptable to the rank and file of the trade unions. Months after the campaign, when asked for a statement on the nomination of George by the United Labor party for the governorship of New York State, Gompers replied that "The Federation of Labor as an organization is keeping its hands off this fight. The questions involved are purely political, not strictly affecting labor matters and call simply for individual expressions by men constituting the Federation. . . . Personally, I have nothing to say about the ticket." [5]

Secondly, during the campaign a new and potentially divisive element had been injected into the picture. The Catholic archbishop of New York, Michael Corrigan, was unfavorably disposed toward George's candidacy, largely because of the latter's allegedly radical character. The popular Catholic priest, Father Edward McGlynn, on the other hand, took a leading role in George's campaign, even though he was disobeying the wishes of the archbishop, and for this he was later suspended from the Church. The opposition by the Catholic hierarchy to George became an overt issue when the vicar-general, Monsignor Thomas S. Preston, issued a public statement prior to the election asserting that the Catholic clergy of New York were completely opposed to George. "They think his principles unsound and unsafe, and contrary to the teachings of the church," the vicar-general stated. "I have not met one among the priests of this archdiocese who would not deeply regret the election of Mr. George to any position of influence. His principles, logically carried out, would prove the ruin of the workingmen he professes to befriend. . . . And although we never interfere directly in elections, we would not wish now to be misunderstood at a time when the best interests of society may be in danger." [6] It is probable that many Catholics inclined toward George felt impelled to vote against him on election day.[7] The significance of this affair may not have been lost upon Gompers, who had supported George against the archbishop, but who also realized that a substantial proportion of the trade-union membership were sincere and devout Catholics. Thus his desire to avoid a split in the labor movement along religious lines probably reinforced his growing disillusionment with labor politics.[8]

[5] *Ibid.*, p. 322.

[6] Louis F. Post and Frederic C. Leubuscher, *An Account of the George-Hewitt Campaign in the New York Municipal Election of 1886* (New York, 1887), p. 133.

[7] Charles A. Barker, *Henry George* (New York, 1955), pp. 479–80; Howard H. Quint, *The Forging of American Socialism: Origins of the Modern Movement* (Columbia, South Carolina, 1953), p. 42.

[8] While there can be little doubt that the attitude of the Catholic Church has been opposed to any form of radical or socialist programs, it is still interesting to explore the

Finally, and perhaps most important, since Gompers and other union leaders were committed to a program that emphasized economic action as the primary weapon in the fight to raise the workers' standard of living, it followed that they would oppose partisan politics which detracted from the primary goal. Forced to modify their growing disillusionment and even hostility toward political action during 1886, they waited for a more opportune moment to return the labor movement to what they regarded

---

interaction of the Church's position and the development of the ideology of organized labor (as represented by the A.F. of L.) in the United States. As I have attempted to show in this chapter as well as in the others, the goals of the A.F. of L. were not particularly radical, and as a matter of fact they were possible of achievement only within the existing framework of American capitalistic society. Since Catholics have always constituted a substantial proportion of the leadership and rank and file of the trade unions (and hence the Federation), the question must ultimately be raised as to precisely what influence, if any, the Church has had over the development of the anti-socialist and antiradical ideology of American unionism.

Recently several investigations of this subject have appeared. Father Henry J. Browne in his excellent study *The Catholic Church and the Knights of Labor* (Washington, D. C., 1949), has asserted that the "influence of the Catholic Church . . . was exercised as a conserving force in American unionism, helping it to survive by at least the endorsement of silence, and aiding in the struggle which kept it an economic movement non-politicized by the socialists" (p. 357). The fullest and most detailed case for this point of view has been presented by Marc Karson in *American Labor Unions and Politics 1900–1918* (Carbondale, Illinois, 1958), who argues that "Aided by the predominantly Catholic officers of the international unions and by the large Catholic rank and file in the AF of L responsive to their Church's views on socialism, catholicism had helped to account for the moderate political philosophy and policies of the AF of L, for socialism's weakness in the AF of L, and, therefore, for the absence of a labor party in the United States" (p. 284). See also David J. Saposs, "The Catholic Church and the Labor Movement," *Modern Monthly*, VII (May, June, 1933), 225–30, 294–98, and Aaron I. Abell, "The Reception of Leo XIII's Labor Encyclical in America, 1891–1919," *Review of Politics*, VII (October, 1945), 464–95.

Yet the thesis that the position of the Catholic Church, especially as expressed in the papal encyclical *Rerum Novarum* (1891), which laid the foundation for a Catholic program of moderate social reform that maintained in a slightly modified version the institution of private property, was partially responsible for the antisocialism and conservatism of the American labor movement is not completely convincing. A more plausible explanation is that American labor ideology, including its political philosophy and program, developed out of the essentially middle-class psychology of the rank and file, a psychology that was characteristic of its societal environment. Since the typical worker, lacking a mature sense of class consciousness, was also an expectant capitalist or incipient entrepreneur, it is evident that he could not logically have propounded radical or socialist ideas without considerably modifying his own future aspirations. Thus the antisocialist position of American trade unionism and the antisocialism of the Catholic Church tended to parallel each other, although for somewhat different reasons. Trade unionists opposed socialism because they had become convinced that in the United States the obstacles to such an ideology were all but insurmountable. In developing a much more limited program based on economic action, they came to be the most bitter foe of the socialists. The Catholic Church, on the other hand, opposed socialism largely for religious doctrinal reasons. In actuality the antisocialism of the Catholic Church served to reinforce that which already existed within the framework of trade-union ideology.

as its rightful functions. And when the campaigns of 1886 had lost their forward momentum, Gompers and his colleagues were able to bring the trade unions back toward an economic program and transform overt political action into pressure group tactics. Thus at the first convention of the A.F. of L. in December, 1886, the delegates heard a report from the legislative committee endorsing the political uprising and urging a "most generous support to the independent political movement of the workingmen." [9] Because of the determination of the A.F. of L.'s leaders to avoid as far as possible political controversy and to concentrate upon establishing the Federation on a secure economic base, the convention took no action to implement the committee's report. Individual unions might do as they pleased, but the A.F. of L. remained uncommitted. Events seemed to justify this neutralist policy, for the political fervor had all but subsided by 1888. From a long range vantage point, it is evident that the political movements of 1886–1887 represented an historical divide. From that time on, the trade unions and the Federation renounced political panaceas, and although organized labor was frequently to take part in political campaigns after 1887, it did so on a very different basis and with different objectives in mind.

II

Nevertheless, the full consequences of the experiences of 1886–1887 were not immediately recognizable, and soon afterward the A.F. of L. was faced with a new challenge. Beginning in the late 1880's the Knights of Labor and various agrarian organizations began to make overtures to the Federation in the hope of sealing a farmer-labor coalition. As the Populist cause gained momentum, the pressures upon the A.F. of L. to abandon its new political policy increased in scope and intensity, and for a while it seemed as though it might be drawn back into politics.

Gompers, who exerted great influence over the development of A.F. of L. policy, and who also reflected accurately the direction in which the trade unions were moving, was highly dubious about the value of such an alliance, and he worked unceasingly to prevent his organization and its affiliates from being drawn into the vortex of political agitation between 1890 and 1896.

In the first place, Gompers argued, the Farmers' Alliance represented largely an employing class that often acted contrary to the interests of its employees. Hence an alliance between it and the A.F. of L. would not be consistent with the latter's hope of forming a union of farm laborers.[10]

---

[9] A.F. of L., *Proceedings*, 1886, pp. 8, 16.

[10] Gompers to Tom Mann, September 2, 1891; Gompers to O. P. Smith, February 10, 1892; Gompers to Alonzo Crouse, September 23, 1892; Gompers to John McBride, February 6, 1893, SGLB; Gompers, "Organized Labor in the Campaign," *North American Review*, CLV (July, 1892), 93.

Secondly and even more important was the fact that political entangle-
ments tended to sublimate the primary task of building the economic
power of the trade unions. Accepting economic strength as a prerequisite
for political success, Gompers and other leaders refused to place the cart
before the horse. Finally and most significant, the idea of an agrarian-
labor coalition was predicated on the assumption that both groups adhered to the Jacksonian antimonopolistic and equal-rights philosophy
that the workers and the farmers were the only bona fide producers.
Certainly this assumption applied to the Knights, which took the lead in
the movement to forge an alliance with the farmers. The trade unions,
on the other hand, had largely repudiated the older middle-class radicalism and had begun to accept their wage status as a permanent condition
and to develop a program of their own. In the end the farmer-labor alliance failed because the older radicalism and the new trade unionism
proved incompatible.

In the early 1890's, however, the unions had not as yet realized the full
implications of their new ideology, and many continued the traditional
efforts to reach a working agreement with the farmers on the basis of the
inherited antimonopolistic and reformist radicalism. In Illinois, labor and
agrarian groups made determined efforts to reach an accord. For a while
it seemed as though they had succeeded, but the embryonic alliance broke
down when the People's party turned to the free silver issue.[11] In Ohio,
John McBride and the United Mine Workers allied themselves with the
People's party, and pressure from local unions forced the national leadership of the International Association of Machinists to come out in support
of the Populists.[12] The *American Federationist,* official organ of the
A.F. of L., reported in 1894 that more than 300 unionists were running
for state and local offices,[13] most of them under the banner of the People's
party. Moreover, many unions favorably inclined toward socialism—
notably the Brewery Workers and Furniture Workers unions—opposed a
nonpartisan or neutralist political policy. Finally, many leading unionists,
including Thomas J. Morgan and J. Mahlon Barnes, fought to turn the
labor movement to an endorsement of independent political action based
on a socialist platform.

In response to pressure in favor of an agrarian alliance, Gompers and
other union leaders adopted the cautious policy of appearing to endorse
the Populist cause without taking any overt action. By resorting to legalis-
tic technicalities, Gompers avoided committing himself and the A.F. of L.
to any partisan position. When invited by agrarian representatives to attend political conferences, he refused on the grounds that he was not

[11] See Destler, *American Radicalism,* Chaps. VIII, IX, XI, for a perceptive treatment
of the labor-Populist movement in Illinois.
[12] John McBride to Jerre Dennis, July 28, 1895, SGLB; James Peterson, "The Trade
Unions and the Populist Party," *Science & Society,* VIII (Spring, 1944), 157.
[13] *American Federationist,* I (November, 1894), 205–06.

authorized to take such action.[14] During the presidential compaign of 1892 Gompers suggested that the A.F. of L. adopt a policy of "masterful inactivity," and he consistently resisted all efforts to pledge himself to any of the candidates.[15]

Gompers' neutralist policy, nevertheless, was undercut in 1893 by an economic depression that renewed the labor movement's dream of concluding the illusive farmer-labor alliance. Frick's victory over the Amalgamated Association of Iron and Steel Workers during the Homestead strike and the other disastrous defeats suffered by the Tennessee and Coeur d'Alene miners further disillusioned many workers with purely economic activity and turned them once more toward the political arena. Even the A.F. of L. wavered in its support of pure and simple trade unionism and in 1893 adopted a resolution instructing its Executive Council to do everything possible "to effect and perfect an alliance between the trade and labor unions and the farmers' organizations to the end that the best interests of all may be served." [16] The socialist delegates supported the proposed alliance because of the partial collectivism endorsed by the convention of the People's party at Omaha in 1892.

After the Omaha Populist meeting, however, the western rural Populists began to retreat from the radicalism of their platform. Expressing distrust of eastern urban radicals seeking to socialize the party, they turned to the free silver issue in the hope of attracting dissident Democrats and Republicans to the new party, as well as removing the stigma of extremism by supporting a historically-respectable program of monetary inflation. By placing more and more emphasis on the demand for the free and unlimited coinage of silver at a sixteen to one ratio with gold, the conservative faction within the People's party succeeded in playing down the more collectivistic planks of the Omaha platform.

Between 1893 and 1896 a fierce struggle ensued for control of the People's party. Socialists and unionists disillusioned with the apparent failure of trade unionism united on a semi-collectivist platform. Rural and western Populists, on the other hand, fought off left-wing attempts to socialize their organization, and in 1896 they succeeded in uniting with the silver Democrats behind Bryan on a free silver platform. Bitterly disillusioned with the fruits of their endeavors, the socialists either deserted or else gave only token support to the People's party during the campaign of 1896.

Meanwhile, the A.F. of L. had endorsed free silver in 1893,[17] but en-

[14] Gompers to J. F. Tillman, September 12, 1891, SGLB; A.F. of L., *Proceedings*, 1891, pp. 15, 40.
[15] Gompers, "Organized Labor in the Campaign," *loc. cit.*, pp. 93–94; Gompers to J. M. Smales, June 20, 1892; Gompers to Edward L. Daley, September 28, 1892; Gompers to F. U. Adams, November 4, 1892, SGLB.
[16] A.F. of L., *Proceedings*, 1893, pp. 38–39.
[17] A.F. of L., *Proceedings*, 1893, pp. 62–63.

suing developments were to demonstrate that the proposed farmer-labor alliance had again failed. As the Populists continued to place more and more emphasis on the silver issue to the exclusion of all others, Gompers and his associates became less and less friendly toward the People's party. To these unionists, free silver was an unrealistic panacea that hurt the labor movement by diverting attention from more important problems. "If asked in regard to the matter [of free silver]," Gompers remarked, "I simply place my index finger upon . . . [the resolution adopted by the A.F. of L.] and say not a word. . . . I believe that there are other and more important subjects which affect our wage earners more directly, more intensely, to which they should give their undivided attention. These middle class issues simply divert attention from their true interests." [18]

In the face of the mounting discontent resulting from the economic depression, however, the leaders of the A.F. of L. could do little except engage in a holding action and ward off attempts to commit their organization to a particular candidate or party. While accepting the convention's endorsement of free silver as official policy, they worked furiously to restrain the labor movement from becoming immersed in a single issue to the exclusion of bona fide trade-union activity. During the campaign of 1896, despite continued pressure, Gompers refused to come out in support of either Bryan or McKinley. "Since both of them are blessed with the same Christian name," he facetiously commented, "I cannot be charged with being partisan if I shout to you, 'Hurrah for William'!" [19] In a circular issued on June 27, 1896, Gompers warned affiliated organizations against the dangers of engaging in partisan politics, and he pointed to the disastrous experiences of the National Labor Union.[20] Consistently maintaining that the campaign, with its emphasis on the silver issue, was a dangerous digression, Gompers did everything within his power to prevent it from intruding on the legitimate work of the trade unions.

While Gompers succeeded in preventing the A.F. of L. from making any commitment during the campaign, many prominent labor leaders and not a few unions came out in open support of Bryan. Although he emphasized the silver issue, Bryan enjoyed strength in labor circles because of the other planks in his platform, notably the endorsement of an income tax and the expressed opposition to government by injunction.

[18] Gompers to Ben Tillett, November 4, 1896. See also Gompers to George L. Burr and Company, February 17, 1896; Gompers to L. Berliner, September 25, 1896, SGLB; Irving Bernstein, ed., "Samuel Gompers and Free Silver, 1896," *Mississippi Valley Historical Review*, XXIX (December, 1942), 394–400.

[19] Gompers to Ben Tillett, November 4, 1896. See also Gompers to John Turner, May 21, 1896; Gompers to J. D. Vaughn, June 2, 1896; Gompers to Douglas Wilson, June 16, 1896; Gompers to the New York *Herald*, July 27, 1896; Gompers to W. H. Montgomery, August 20, 1896; Gompers to A. G. Howland, October 27, 1896, SGLB.

[20] Gompers, "Trade Unions and Party Politics," *American Federationist*, III (August, 1896), 129–30.

In the end, however, Gompers' views prevailed. He recognized that the A.F. of L. could not affect the course of the election. This being the situation, much could be lost by pledging labor's support in advance of the election results. Moreover, the silver issue, Gompers argued, was an unrealistic panacea and a detraction; and after the election he expressed his hope that the workers would return to their legitimate business after sobering down "from the political inebriety." [21] Cognizant of the fact that the older antimonopolism and reformism had little in common with the new unionism, Gompers had clearly foreseen the incompatibility of a labor-farmer alliance based on the silver issue. After the campaign of 1896 had passed into history, the Federation resumed its efforts to strengthen the labor movement, and it succeeded in increasing its membership sixfold between 1897 and 1904.

III

The vision of an irresistible farmer-labor coalition, however, was not the only threat to the young trade-union movement during the 1890's. A much more serious challenge came from the socialists, who denied that trade unionism was an end in itself. While accepting unionism as historically correct and necessary, the socialists insisted that purely economic action was futile. Instead, they demanded the unification of economic and political action behind a socialist platform and the repudiation of established political parties as well as all reformist fads.

While socialist resolutions endorsing collectivism and independent political action were introduced regularly at the annual conventions of the A.F. of L., they were either defeated or else passed and almost as quickly forgotten (as in 1886). Nevertheless, the socialists played an important role in the Federation through their control of some unions and their representation in others. Adopting the policy of "boring from within," they sought to convert the labor movement to socialism by capturing control of the A.F. of L. and its affiliates.

Between 1886 and 1890 the socialists, although critical of some A.F. of L. policies, continued to view that organization as the best hope of uniting the workers behind a socialist program. The official organ of the Socialist Labor party, for example, while condemning the Federation's emphasis on the eight-hour movement and the lack of a radical political program, often commended it for its organizational work, and on occasion even spoke well of Gompers.[22] Thus the lack of complete unity and agreement between trade unionists and socialists did not appear to be a barrier to effective co-operation between the two groups.

Yet in reality there were unbridgeable differences between the economic

[21] Gompers to P. J. McGuire, November 19, 1896, SGLB.
[22] New Haven *Workmen's Advocate*, April 28, December 22, 1888, January 12, December 21, 28, 1889.

program of the trade unionists and the political emphasis of the socialists. But so long as the A.F. of L. did not come out in unequivocal opposition to collectivistic ideas, the socialists were content to bide their time and continue their efforts to seize control and convert the Federation to a radical program. Sooner or later, however, the fundamental differences between the two groups were bound to make themselves felt. What the final results would be few ventured to predict.

The first major clash between the trade unionists and socialists, which came at the Detroit convention of the A.F. of L. in 1890, grew out of a somewhat complicated situation in New York City. There the Central Labor Union had come under the domination of the Knights of Labor. A number of affiliated A.F. of L. unions withdrew in February, 1889, and organized the Central Labor Federation. When the new body applied to the A.F. of L. for a charter, the Executive Council voted in June, 1889, to grant the request.[23] In the interest of harmony, the Central Labor Federation attempted to effect a reconciliation with the Central Labor Union. Between December, 1889, and June, 1890, a temporary union was effected, and the Central Labor Federation returned its charter to Gompers. But in June, 1890, the *rapprochement* between the two New York organizations broke down, and Ernest Bohm, secretary of the Central Labor Federation, asked Gompers to return the charter. In refusing, Gompers replied that the Central Labor Federation had ceased to exist.[24]

Controversy developed when the Central Labor Federation re-applied for a charter. Noting that the American section of the Socialist Labor party held membership in Bohm's organization, Gompers refused to grant the request. "I cannot bring myself to understand," he wrote to Bohm, "how a political Party as such can be represented in a central trade organization. Of the merits or demerits of the 'Socialistic Labor Party' it is not within my province to discuss but the representation of that party or any other political party in a purely trade union central organization is to my mind not permissible." [25]

A bitter controversy followed, and partisans of the Socialist Labor party bitterly denounced the A.F. of L.'s president. "It seems to me," Gompers complained to Bohm, "that men in the labor movement can honestly differ with each other without finding it necessary to indulge in abuse and I cannot for the life of me understand why an expression of opinion should call forth the spleen manifested by you in your official journals, and which was given out officially by you for publication in the public

[23] Gompers to Ernest Bohm, March 14, June 14, 1889; Gompers to the A.F. of L. Executive Council, May 21, 1889, SGLB; A.F. of L., *Proceedings*, 1890, p. 12.
[24] Gompers to August Delebar, July 12, 1890; Gompers to Ernest Bohm, July 18, 1890, SGLB; A.F. of L., *Proceedings*, 1890, p. 12.
[25] Gompers to Ernest Bohm, September 11, 1890. See also Gompers to Bohm, August 6, 1890, SGLB.

press." [26] Gompers then decided to refer the matter to the A.F. of L. convention in December.

When the convention met in Detroit, Lucien Sanial was present to plead the socialist case. Denying that the Socialist Labor party was an ordinary political party in the accepted sense of the word, Sanial asserted that it was a working-class party whose unionizing activities predated the founding of the A.F. of L. "The Central Labor Federation," he continued, "has merely seen fit to declare—by the admission of the delegates of the American Section of the S.L.P., and by sending to this Convention, as its representative, one of those very delegates—its right to take independent political action with this economic labor party, which the members of its constituting organizations own and control; and in taking this step, deliberately and unflinchingly, it has at the same time virtually announced that the time is coming when Organized Labor in all parts of the country must and will recognize the absolute necessity of taking independent political action." [27]

In opposition to Sanial, Gompers expressed his hostility to having a political party represented in a purely trade-union organization. Denying that he was attempting to drive the socialists out of the labor movement, Gompers affirmed his willingness to surrender his post to further the cause of organized labor. "But I can not and will not," he proclaimed, "prove false to my convictions that the trade unions pure and simple are the natural organizations of the wage-workers to secure their present material and practical improvement and to achieve their final emancipation." [28]

For the better part of two days the delegates discussed the relative merits of the case.[29] The defenders of the socialist cause, while generally conceding that the Socialist Labor party had made a tactical error in trying to graft itself onto the A.F. of L., felt that the Federation would make an even greater error in excluding Sanial. The trade unionists, however, continued to reiterate their opposition to the Socialist Labor party. "We do not refuse to recognize the Socialist Labor party as an integral part of the labor movement," Frank K. Foster stated as he summed up the position of the unionists. "We simply decline to permit it, as a *political organization*, to engraft itself and its methods upon the organizations we represent upon this floor. We do not disdain the proffered hand of fraternity, or the propaganda of principles upon which we are mutually

[26] Gompers to Ernest Bohm, November 7, 1890, SGLB.

[27] *An Interesting Discussion at the Tenth Annual Convention of the American Federation of Labor Held at Detroit, Michigan, December 8–13, 1890* (New York, 1891), p. 6. See also *ibid.*, pp. 4–5.

[28] A.F. of L., *Proceedings*, 1890, p. 17.

[29] For a transcript of the various statements see *ibid.*, 1890, pp. 22–25, and *An Interesting Discussion at the Tenth Annual Convention of the American Federation of Labor, passim.*

agreed; but we do decline the admission of any organization or representation having for its object a political movement." [30]

In the end the convention, by the emphatic vote of 1,574 to 496, decided to exclude Sanial. While denying that the hopes and aspirations
of the trade unions and socialists differed markedly, the delegates refused
to permit partisan politics to intrude into a purely trade federation because they feared that the admission of the Socialist Labor party delegate
would inevitably open the gates to other political bodies, to the ultimate
detriment of the labor movement.[31]

Furious at its defeat, the Socialist Labor party renewed its attack upon
Gompers. "Gompers' 'policy'—if such may be called the intricate web of
an unprincipled and egotistic schemer, pandering to ignorance for the
sake of position—can deceive no one whose sense of right is not blunted
by corruption or obscured by prejudice," proclaimed the *Workmen's Advocate*.[32] Deciding to write off the A.F. of L., the Socialist Labor party
now embarked upon a campaign to win control of the dissension-ridden
Knights of Labor. Party leadership was quickly assumed by Daniel De-
Leon, a recent convert to orthodox Marxism. From a Columbia University
lectureship in Latin American Diplomacy, DeLeon had initially become a
devotee of Edward Bellamy's Nationalist movement and had then abandoned its utopianism for a more "scientific" socialism. More than any
other man, DeLeon succeeded in fragmentizing the American socialist
movement and completely alienating the young trade-union movement.

An individual of immense erudition, rare ability, and tremendous energy, DeLeon was fanatically devoted to the socialist cause. Morris Hillquit, an unfriendly but perceptive critic, commented that DeLeon "never
admitted a doubt about the soundness of his interpretation of the
Socialist philosophy or the infallibility of his methods and tactics. Those
who agreed with him were good Socialists. All who dissented from his
views were enemies of the movement. He never compromised or tem-
porized outside or inside the Socialist movement." DeLeon, concluded
Hillquit, "was the perfect American prototype of Russian Bolshevism." [33]

To DeLeon the only sound remedy was the overthrow of an incorrigible
capitalism by a revolutionary socialist movement. Attacking the trade
union's emphasis on "bread and butter" policies, he charged that labor
leaders had been bought off by the capitalists for the sake of small in-
creases in wages. The correct policy, DeLeon argued, was a labor movement organized along industrial lines and affiliated with the Socialist
Labor party. The test of any union policy was: "DOES THE CON-

[30] *An Interesting Discussion at the Tenth Annual Convention of the American
Federation of Labor*, p. 13.

[31] A.F. of L., *Proceedings*, 1890, pp. 21–22, 25.

[32] New Haven *Workmen's Advocate*, January 10, 1891. See also *The People*, November 15, 1891.

[33] Morris Hillquit, *Loose Leaves From a Busy Life* (New York, 1934), p. 46.

TEMPLATED STEP SQUARE WITH THE ULTIMATE AIM [of overthrowing capitalism]?" [34]

While DeLeon was emerging as the champion of a militant and dogmatic Socialist Labor party, Gompers was coming to the forefront of the trade-union movement and almost as quickly assumed the leadership in the struggle against the socialists. Gompers' conversion to an antisocialist position was a crucial event in the history of the American labor movement, and provides an excellent illustration of the process whereby many American labor leaders who began their careers as socialists could end up not only as staunch trade unionists, but also as vigorous opponents of socialism. Gompers, together with McGuire and other union leaders, played vital roles in isolating the socialists from the working class.

Familiar with the writings of socialist theoreticians, Gompers had taken part in the furious conflicts of the 1870's between Marxism, then identical with a class-conscious trade unionism, and Lassalleanism, with its emphasis on political action. Throughout the 1880's Gompers continued to express friendliness toward socialist goals, but his preoccupation with the daily problems of the unions tended to relegate ultimate objectives into the background. His initial disillusioning experience with socialism came in the early 1880's, when the socialists in the Cigar Makers International Union refused to support a member of the New York legislature who had led the fight for the abolition of tenement-house cigar manufacturing. In that episode, the socialists heaped vitriolic criticism upon Gompers and Strasser for abandoning ultimate reform for immediate advantages. In testifying before a Senate committee in 1883, Gompers showed the marks of the fight. "Whatever ideas we may have as to the future state of society," he remarked, "regardless of what the end of the labor movement as a movement between classes may be, they must remain in the background, and we must subordinate our convictions, and our views and our acts to the general good that the trades-union movement brings to the laborer." [35]

Gompers' study of history had convinced him that the labor movement's immersion in political and reform panaceas had proved its undoing, and he insisted upon concentrating on building the trade unions on a wider and more stable base. Yet he never advocated the exclusion of the socialists from the A.F. of L. and argued that the labor movement was broad enough to include men of all beliefs. The violent attacks of DeLeon and his followers, however, inevitably forced a subtle change in Gompers' moderate attitude. Convinced that the Socialist Labor party aimed at nothing less than control of the A.F. of L., Gompers' position began to harden. "After all," he wrote to a fellow unionist, "it is merely a difference of opinion as to the most practical methods to be employed in secur-

---

[34] Daniel DeLeon, *The Burning Question of Trades Unionism* (New York, 1904), p. 22.

[35] *Report of the Committee of the Senate Upon the Relations Between Labor and Capital*, I, 374.

ing to the laborer his just rights; and until the advent of Prof. De Leon in the Socialist movement we managed matters so that we could at least work together. This man's characteristics of intolerance to every one that does not adopt his policy, his venom and spite crop out at every opportunity [and] that makes it impossible for any one that has any self-respect to have any dealings with him or those for whom he speaks. He has simply widened the chasm between the different wings in the labor movement." [36]

Meanwhile, the conflict between the socialists and trade unionists in 1890 had also precipitated a crisis within the ranks of the former. The decision by the Socialist Labor party to abandon the A.F. of L. and work through the Knights of Labor had been resisted by a substantial proportion of socialists who, under the leadership of Thomas J. Morgan and J. Mahlon Barnes, decided to continue their efforts within the A.F. of L. to convert the labor movement to collectivism. But for a while it seemed as though DeLeon's prediction that the Federation was hopeless was justified, for in 1892 the convention, by a decisive vote of 1,615 to 559, rejected a proposition to endorse governmental ownership of the means of production, transportation, and communication. Instead, the delegates adopted a mild resolution calling for public ownership of the telephone, telegraph, railroad, and transportation systems.[37] To the socialists such a position was worse than futile.

The eclipse of the socialists within the A.F. of L., however, proved to be only temporary, and in 1893 they renewed their proselytizing activities. Circumstances augured well for the success of their efforts. The beginnings of an economic depression and the failure of a number of prominent strikes had given rise to widespread disillusionment in labor circles with the tactics and program of trade unionism. At the convention of the A.F. of L. in 1893 the socialists, led by Morgan, introduced an eleven-point "political programme." Praising the action of the British unionists who had endorsed the principle of independent political action, the socialist resolution called for: "1. Compulsory education. 2. Direct legislation. 3. A legal eight-hour workday. 4. Sanitary inspection of workshop, mine and home. 5. Liability of employers for injury to health, body or life. 6. The abolition of contract system in all public work. 7. The abolition of the sweating system. 8. The municipal ownership of street cars, and gas and electric plants for public distribution of light, heat and power. 9. The nationalization of telegraphs, telephones, railroad and mines. 10. *The collective ownership by the people of all means of production and distribution.*[38] 11. The principle of referendum in all legislation." The final section of the resolution called for the submission of the

---

[36] Gompers to Henry Lloyd, July 2, 1894. See also Gompers to P. J. McGuire, August 4, 1891; Gompers to Samuel Goldwater, December 1, 1893, SGLB.

[37] A.F. of L., *Proceedings*, 1892, p. 39.

[38] Italics mine.

programme to the affiliated unions for their "favorable consideration."
The unionists succeeded in deleting the word "favorable" by the narrow
margin of 1,253 to 1,182, but the amended version was adopted by the
overwhelming vote of 2,244 to 67.[39]

The crucial section of the resolution was the tenth plank. If adopted, it
would have unequivocally pledged the labor movement to the support of
a frankly socialist program. "The extent to which this radical sentiment
has permeated the Union labor movement of the United States," observed
Morgan, "will be shown by the instructions of the Unions to their delegates to the next annual convention of the A.F. of L., and in the vote
which will then be taken upon Section 10, of the programme, submitted
for their consideration. This alone will be the vital test. Every other section is common place, and from time to time can be safely sandwiched
into the political programmes of our masters, whenever the emergency
demands, but not so with number 10. In no capitalistic platform has or
will this section ever find a place; while in Europe, it is the foundation of
the whole political labor movement, *but it is socialism!*" [40]

Immediately following the convention of 1893 the affiliated unions began to consider the political programme. In a display of near-unanimity,
union after union voted to endorse the principles embodied in the resolution. The miners, iron and steel workers, lasters, tailors, wood workers,
cigarmakers, street-railway employees, waiters, shoe workers, textile workers, mule spinners, machinists, and the German-American Typographical
Union all voted their approval, as well as at least eleven state federations
and eight city centrals.[41] Only the bakers rejected it completely, while the
International Typographical Union and web-weavers union voted to
strike out plank ten, with the former substituting a land resolution in its
place.[42] The carpenters approved plank ten, but with the amendment, "as
the people elect to operate." [43] "We sincerely hope," summed up the
organ of the United Brewery Workers, "that plank 10 of the political
programme [will] be adopted and that the sound principles of scientific
Socialism will be officially recognized by the representative body of the
Trades and Labor Unions of America." [44]

But even while the socialists were joyously celebrating their coming tri-

[39] A.F. of L., *Proceedings*, 1893, pp. 37–38.

[40] Thomas J. Morgan, "The Programme," *American Federationist*, I (March, 1894),
7. All unionists, whether socialist or otherwise, agreed upon the crucial nature of
plank ten. See, for example, Frank K. Foster, "Labor Politics, Policies and Platforms,"
ibid., I (March, 1894), 5–6; Joseph R. Buchanan, "Political Action by Labor," *ibid.*, I
(May, 1894), 43–44; J. R. Flynn, "The Political Program," *ibid.*, I (July, 1894), 103.

[41] Commons, *History of Labour*, II, 511.

[42] *Ibid.*; International Typographical Union, *Proceedings*, 1896, p. 47 (these *Proceedings* were issued as a supplement to the *Typographical Journal*, IX [November 16,
1896]).

[43] Commons, *History of Labour*, II, 511.

[44] *Brauer-Zeitung*, IX (December 1, 1894), 1.

umph, events were transpiring that would conclude in the almost total emasculation of their programme. Gompers and McGuire, while publicly maintaining their silence, privately set to work to bring about the defeat of the resolution. "This is a time when it will require the exercise of our best judgment and the assertion that the trade unions shall not be made a plaything of nor diverted from their true sphere of action," Gompers wrote to a sympathetic McGuire.[45] Both leaders regarded the defeat of the socialists as an absolute necessity, and they agreed that almost any means would be justified. "The men who worship other gods and simply use the trade union house of worship are summoning their forces, and the trade union movement will indeed pass through its most crucial test at Denver," Gompers wrote to Foster. "There it will not be so much the question of a man or an officer as it will be the root and fundamental principles of the organization. If we successfully resist it this time I have little fear for the future. If those who do not understand the trade union movement together with those who are its enemies should divert our movement from its proper channel you may rest assured that it would mean a setback for our movement, and a deterioration in the condition of our fellow-workers for more than a decade." Therefore, concluded Gompers, "I propose to take a positive stand at the convention regardless of consequence to myself; at least I propose to do my duty as I see it and I can only hope that our earnest, intelligent trade unionists will view the danger as I know it to exist." [46]

At the beginning of December, 1894, Gompers, McGuire, and other A.F. of L. leaders met in Chicago and mapped out their strategy to wean delegates over to their side regardless of union instructions. Then at the Denver convention a few days later Gompers struck hard in his opening presidential address. Asserting that he favored nonpartisanship in politics, Gompers denounced the proposed platform and warned that a "political labor movement cannot and will not succeed upon the ruins of the trade unions." [47] On the fourth day of the convention the delegates took up the programme, and immediately voted to consider each plank separately. The unionists scored the initial victory when Strasser's motion to delete the first preamble (commending the English trade unionists for adopting independent political action) passed by a vote of 1,345 to 861. Thereafter the convention adopted all of the planks with the exception of the tenth one.[48]

When the tenth plank came up for discussion, the unionists made their move. First Strasser offered an amendment calling for the "collective own-

[45] Gompers to P. J. McGuire, November 1, 1894, SGLB.

[46] Gompers to Frank K. Foster, November 19, 1894, SGLB.

[47] A.F. of L., *Proceedings*, 1894, p. 14.

[48] *A Verbatim Report of the Discussion on the Political Programme, at the Denver Convention of the American Federation of Labor, December 14, 15, 1894* (New York, 1895), pp. 3, 13–25.

ership by the people of all means of production and distribution *by confiscation without compensation.*" This proposal was clearly intended to drive a wedge into the ranks of the socialists by making the article so obnoxious that many who favored the original would be forced to vote against the substitute. Other amendments emasculating the original intent of plank ten quickly followed. With Gompers keeping a firm hand over the convention proceedings, the socialists found that their entire programme was being amended to death. In the end the delegates voted 1,217 to 913 to accept a substitute for the original plank offered by the International Typographical Union calling for the "abolition of the monopoly system of land holding and the substituting therefor of a title of occupancy and use only." The culmination of the proceedings came with a motion to endorse the amended programme "as a whole," whereupon the convention defeated the move by a vote of 1,173 to 735.[49] As Gompers later admitted, the unionists had deliberately used ridicule to demolish the political programme.[50] In vengeance the socialists combined with the miners' delegation to elect John McBride as president of the A.F. of L.—the only time between 1886 and his death in 1924 that Gompers failed to be re-elected.

Thus the socialists had tasted the bitter fruits of defeat largely because of the tireless efforts of a small coterie of union leaders led by Gompers and McGuire. Undoubtedly preconvention sentiment had seemed to favor endorsement of the programme. Yet was this an accurate estimation of the true feelings of the working class? Obviously such a question cannot be answered with any degree of certainty. Yet if the labor movement had favored endorsement of socialism, we should expect to find a bitter uprising against those leaders who had been instrumental in defeating the programme. There was, in fact, no such revolt. Some unions, including McGuire's own organization, endorsed the actions of their representatives.[51] As a matter of fact, socialist strength at subsequent conventions declined drastically.

[49] *Ibid.,* pp. 25–26, 62. At the convention the following year the delegates declared that the A.F. of L. "has no political program," but they agreed to accept the amended planks as their "legislative demands." A.F. of L., *Proceedings,* 1895, pp. 66–67.

[50] Gompers, *Seventy Years,* I, 393–94.

[51] *The Carpenter,* XVI (October, 1896), 1. Edward L. Daley of the Lasters Protective Union offered the most common explanation for the actions of the trade unionists at Denver. "A number of amendments were offered to the programme as submitted and . . . my vote was against each and all of the amendments, my object being to prevent, if possible, any change in the programme, which I was instructed to vote for in its entirety. So many of these amendments were adopted as to completely change the structure and intent of the programme, and in the form in which it finally came to be voted upon, I voted against it, and did so fully believing that my course would meet with the full approval of our Union. This belief is based upon the fact that although this programme, including 'Plank Ten,' had been submitted to all our Local Branches in the call for our Convention last year, and had also been published in our official journal in the issues preceding the Convention, not a single delegate from any Branch

The final event in the isolation of the socialists from the main body of the trade-union movement came in 1895, when DeLeon, after failing to capture the near-moribund Knights of Labor, proceeded to organize his own union, the Socialist Trade and Labor Alliance. Designed to replace the A.F. of L. and Knights of Labor, it was nothing more or less than a dual union attached to and under the domination of the Socialist Labor party. While the party was the vanguard of the socialist movement in the political arena, the Socialist Trade and Labor Alliance would be its economic counterpart. Such a move was necessary because, according to one follower of DeLeon, "there was absolutely no hope from the old leaders." [52] Soon after its establishment, the Alliance embarked on a campaign to capture the national unions and force them to leave the A.F. of L..[53]

While it never became an important factor in the labor movement, the Socialist Trade and Labor Alliance did convince many trade unionists that socialism was utterly bankrupt.[54] Tolerant of ideological heterogeneity and differences over theory and tactics, these unionists could not forgive dual unionism, which in their minds was *the* unpardonable sin. Equating radicalism with schism, the trade unions became the socialists' most bitter foe.

DeLeon's disruptive tactics also completed Gompers' conversion to a militant antisocialist position. Heretofore Gompers had fought socialism on grounds of expediency; now he fought it solely on principle. Although always willing to work with individual socialists who remained faithful to their union, Gompers ceased to pay even lip-service to socialist ideals. After the socialists had failed in another of their proselytizing efforts soon after the turn of the century, Gompers, in perhaps the clearest and most incisive statement of his entire career, remarked:

> I want to tell you, Socialists, that I have studied your philosophy; read your works upon economics, and not the meanest of them; studied your standard works, both in English and German—have not only read, but studied them. I have heard your orators and watched the work of your movement the world over. I have kept close watch upon your doctrines for thirty years; have been closely associated with many of you, and know how you think and what you

had come instructed to vote for it, and, believing that our Union does not and never did wish to commit itself to an endorsement of socialism or any other political policy, it was plain to my mind that the disposal of the whole programme by the Denver Convention would be satisfactory to our Union; in fact, many of the members of different Branches of our Union have so stated to me." Lasters Protective Union, *Proceedings*, 1895, pp. 18–19.

[52] Socialist Labor Party, *Proceedings*, 1896, p. 28.

[53] See the *American Federationist*, IV (June, 1897), 79, (July, 1897), 93; United States Industrial Commission, *Report*, XVII, 209–10.

[54] For Gompers' harsh and unyielding attitude toward DeLeon and the Alliance see Gompers to A. von Elm, March 9, 1896; Gompers to A. McArthur, March 27, 1896; Gompers to Ben Tillett, May 2, 1896; Gompers to Fred S. Carter, March 1, 1897; Gompers to James Tole, September 2, 1897, SGLB.

propose. I know, too, what you have up your sleeve. And I want to say that I am entirely at variance with your philosophy. I declare it to you, I am not only at variance with your doctrines, but with your philosophy. Economically, you are unsound; socially, you are wrong; industrially, you are an impossibility.[55]

The failure of the socialists to capture the A.F. of L. was due to the interplay of several factors. It is clear that leaders like Gompers and McGuire proved themselves formidable opponents in the struggle with the socialists, but their efforts would probably not have succeeded without substantial support from other unionists and the rank and file. Above all, the fact remains that the American worker has been by tradition and by history inclined toward a capitalistic outlook, a phenomenon well recognized by such European scholars as Werner Sombart. This being the case, acceptance of a socialist ideology would have come into direct conflict with labor's outlook. It is true that on occasion socialists have enjoyed greater popularity, but such aberrations have generally proved to be short-lived. Thus at the Denver convention, as well as at other ones, the socialists were always unable to overcome the strength shown by the trade unionists, whose appeal to their followers was predicated largely, if not exclusively, on acceptance of industrial capitalism, within which labor could attain a higher standard of living. Leaders like Gompers were well aware of the capitalistic psychology of American workers, as well as the barriers imposed upon an organized socialist movement by the American environment. Like so many of his colleagues, he accepted what he felt he could not change. Undoubtedly such an attitude resulted in a political system that left the worker without any real choice, but this sacrifice, in the eyes of the trade unionists, was absolutely necessary if the labor movement were to survive. Perhaps Shaw was correct when he once remarked that trade unionism was not socialism, but rather the capitalism of the working class. In any event, the American labor movement, ironically enough, became one of the most bitter foes of socialism, a fact which played an important role in the failure of socialism to gain a foothold in the United States.

By the turn of the century, therefore, the socialists had been decisively defeated in their efforts to capture the A.F. of L. The high point of socialist hopes had come in 1894, and thereafter socialist strength within the Federation gradually diminished. While individual socialists like Max Hayes continued to play important roles within the Federation, and others left the fold to form the Industrial Workers of the World, the socialist movement as a whole was isolated from the main body of organized labor, and nothing that leaders like Eugene Debs or Victor Berger did could change this vital fact. Undoubtedly the failure of the socialists to play an important role in the United States was due to far more basic factors than

[55] A.F. of L., *Proceedings,* 1903, p. 198.

their inability to capture the A.F. of L.; [56] nevertheless, the influence of this fact should not be minimized, especially when we consider the history of trade unionism and socialism in England, where events finally culminated in the establishment of the Labour party in 1906.

IV

Although eschewing socialism and Populism, the A.F. of L. never claimed that it had no political interests or goals. But its leaders, cognizant of the disruptive influence of politics upon previous labor organizations, attempted to formulate a political program that would be compatible with trade-union aspirations at the same time that it avoided issues that excited partisan emotions. In the decade following 1886 they succeeded in laying the foundation for what ultimately proved to be, with some significant exceptions, the accepted political policy of American labor for a large part of the twentieth century.

Basically two factors were responsible for the Federation's approach to politics. In the first place, a crude economic determinism based on an acquaintance with socialist theories led union leaders to emphasize the primacy of economics over politics. "It is a mistake," Gompers frequently asserted, "to imagine that political action without the organizations of the trade unions will bring either amelioration or emancipation, or in fact the wage-workers will be able to defend their position either economically-politically or in any field unless they are organized in the Unions of their respective trades and callings." [57] Thus trade-union rather than political action would best serve the interests of the working class. "You may rest assured," Gompers concluded, "that when all the fighting of the campaign is over and the votes have been counted, you who have continued in the straight course of organization will find a larger constituency than all others combined." [58]

Secondly and equally important was the disillusionment of the trade unions with partisan political action. Since the Jacksonian era workingmen had rushed headlong into politics. In so doing they had often become inextricably entangled with nonlabor elements. As a result, the economic functions of unions had been subordinated to political activity. Ultimately the union had disintegrated, partly because of internal tensions, and partly because of the lack of concrete results. Consequently, the political policy of the A.F. of L. represented a reaction against the experiences of its more politically-minded predecessors.

The implications of the Federation's insistence upon the primacy of

[56] For a good discussion about the weaknesses of socialism in the United States see David A. Shannon, *The Socialist Party of America: A History* (New York, 1955), pp. 258–67.

[57] Gompers to James G. Bacon, August 11, 1893, SGLB.

[58] Gompers to L. E. Tossey, August 31, 1894, SGLB.

economic power were indeed significant. Earlier labor organizations, including the National Labor Union and the Knights of Labor, had emphasized the reform of society through political action, and this had led to unending controversy. In contrast, the A.F. of L. averted disputes by emphasizing only methods and objectives that were acceptable to a large proportion of workingmen. While such a position often led to an ambiguous political policy, the Federation argued that in the long run it was trade-union rather than governmental action that would best serve the interests of the working class. "There can scarcely be a division of opinion," Gompers observed, "that when the economic movement has sufficiently developed so as to produce a unity of thought on all essentials, that a Political Labor Movement will be the result. In fact, there is, and cannot be any economic action taken by organized labor unless it has its political and social influence. We in America who enjoy absolute political liberty, have long ago recognized that without economic freedom, accomplished by economic organization, political liberty is but a phantasy and a delusion." [59]

Since the leaders of the Federation placed more faith in economic than in political action, they frequently refused to support programs advanced by reformers and progressives that were designed to abolish monopoly or fragmentize concentrated industrial holdings. Recognizing that the ideal of self-employment had been rendered obsolete by technological and industrial evolution, the trade unions accepted bigness in economic life as a natural and logical consequence. "In fact," Gompers argued, "the trust may be said to have successfully solved the problem of the greatest economy in production." [60] Since large industrial concentrations allegedly had certain inherent advantages, the unions as a rule opposed any "trust-busting" plans.[61] "We are convinced," Gompers asserted, "that the state is not capable of preventing the legitimate development or natural concentration of industry." [62] Even more important, however, was the fact that government antitrust action had in the past worked to the detriment of organized labor, as during the Pullman strike of 1894.[63]

[59] Gompers to the Delegates to the International Labor Congress (Brussels, Belgium), August 4, 1891, SGLB.

[60] Gompers, "Labor and its Attitude Toward Trusts," *American Federationist*, XIV (November, 1907), 881. See also *idem.*, "Attacking the Trusts," *ibid.*, III (December, 1896), 217, and *ibid.*, VI (August, 1899), 130–31.

[61] See, for example, A.F. of L., *Proceedings*, 1891, pp. 26, 33; 1892, p. 46.

[62] Gompers, "A Word on Trusts," *American Federationist*, VI (October, 1899), 195.

[63] See Gompers to Ernst A. Weier, November 27, 1899, SGLB; Frank Valesh, "Labor Legislation (?)," *American Federationist*, II (April, 1895), 26–27. During the Pullman strike of 1894 Attorney-General Richard Olney had obtained a sweeping injunction against the officers and members of the American Railway Union, prohibiting them from interfering with the mails, with interstate commerce, with the conduct of the business of twenty-three railroads specifically named, and from attempting to persuade other employees to quit work.

The Federation, therefore, advocated a strong trade-union movement capable of acting as a countervailing force to the power of organized capital. "I have insisted, and do now insist," Gompers proclaimed, "that the only power capable of coping with and, (if necessary) smashing the trusts, is that much abused and often ridiculed force known under the euphonious title of 'The Trades Union Movement' as understood and practiced by the A.F. of L." [64]

Not only was the A.F. of L. wary of governmental regulation of business, but it was also suspicious of many social reform measures. While favoring a minimum living wage, Gompers opposed any governmental action for its establishment, for the "minimum would become the maximum." [65] Similarly, he fought against federal or state enactment of general eight-hour laws for workers in private industry and opposed any compulsory insurance system similar to the one adopted in Germany.[66] Occasionally, especially during a period of depression, the A.F. of L. would momentarily abandon its antigovernment bias. In 1893, for example, it went on record as favoring an expanded program of public works to meet the problem of unemployment.[67] On the whole, however, the A.F. of L., because of labor's past disillusioning experiences with government, was very reluctant to approve regulatory legislation.

The primary political objective of the A.F. of L., therefore, was to ensure, if not a government favorably disposed toward organized labor, then at least a neutral one. Confident of the ability of their organizations to cope with the power and influence of organized capital, union leaders worked to eliminate governmental intervention, either by military force or by court injunctions, in labor disputes. Following a Pennsylvania court decision in 1891 restraining striking printers from picketing, and Attorney-General Richard Olney's actions three years later during the Pullman strike, the A.F. of L. embarked on a campaign to limit the use of injunctions against unions. Similarly, it fought vigorously against the utilization of federal and state troops, especially when such forces worked as strikebreakers.[68]

In addition, the A.F. of L. also supported a limited legislative program to benefit the working class. It pioneered in the movement to abolish child labor and actively endorsed the passage of liability acts making employers liable for damages for accidents resulting in either death or

[64] Gompers to W. B. Mahon, November 8, 1899. See also Gompers to D. L. Alexander, February 14, 1890, SGLB.

[65] Gompers, "A Minimum Living Wage," American Federationist, V (April, 1898), 25.

[66] Gompers to Senator George P. Edmunds, August 14, 1889; Gompers to Ralph H. Shephard, January 15, 1891; Gompers to E. M. Sharon, May 31, 1893, SGLB.

[67] A.F. of L., Proceedings, 1893, pp. 37, 47–48.

[68] Ibid., 1891, pp. 24–25, 27–28; 1892, pp. 9, 12, 32–33; 1893, pp. 14, 42; 1894, pp. 48, 50–51; 1896, p. 50; United States Congress, House Judiciary Committee, Hearing on Conspiracies and Injunctions (Washington, D. C., 1900), pp. 19–20.

injury to their employees. Unable to resist the traditional slogans of American radicalism, the Federation also supported such measures as land reform, government ownership of the telegraph and telephone systems, income tax legislation, the direct election of senators, and the initiative and referendum.[69] In lending its support to such measures, however, the A.F. of L. did so only half-heartedly, and never really exerted any substantial amount of pressure to secure their passage. On a more controversial issue like the tariff it avoided taking any position.[70]

Finally, the A.F. of L. labored to secure the passage of legislation limiting immigration to the United States. It vigorously supported the total exclusion of Chinese immigration, using racial as well as economic arguments to buttress its position.[71] But since a large proportion of its members were of foreign origin, the Federation adopted a much milder position when it came to excluding other than Asiatic immigration, and generally it lagged behind the more vociferous elements in the United States demanding an end to all immigration. In 1888 the convention of the A.F. of L. refused to support a per capita tax on foreigners arriving on American shores. Three years later, however, the delegates agreed to endorse restriction of all "artificially stimulated immigration . . . contract and assisted emigrants." Obviously aiming at strengthening the bargaining hand of the labor movement through cutting off of an additional supply of manpower, the Federation at this time never argued against immigration per se, and in 1894 it affirmed that "further restriction of immigration is unnecessary except in keeping out contract laborers, criminal other than political, and those who are apt to become a public charge." In 1897, nevertheless, the Federation voted to support the literacy test of the Lodge bill to restrict immigration.[72]

The legislative demands of the A.F. of L. during the first ten years of its existence, therefore, clearly represented a minimum program. Eschewing partisanship in politics, the Federation's convention in 1895 adopted by an overwhelming margin a resolution declaring "that party politics whether they be democratic, republican, socialistic, populistic, prohibition or any other, should have no place in the conventions of the A.F.

[69] A.F. of L., *Proceedings*, 1889, p. 23; 1890, p. 40; 1892, pp. 39, 45; 1893, pp. 36, 47; 1894, pp. 28, 46; 1895, p. 81; 1898, pp. 63, 82–83; 1899, pp. 61, 105–06; Gompers, "Trade Unions the Precursors of Progressive Thought," *American Federationist*, III (September, 1896), 142.

[70] A.F. of L., *Proceedings*, 1895, p. 59. Gompers generally took the position that there were more important issues facing the working class than the tariff. See Gompers to W. S. Gammon, December 28, 1894; Gompers to L. Berliner, September 25, 1896, SGLB.

[71] See A.F. of L., *Proceedings*, 1886, p. 17; 1887, pp. 23, 30; 1889, pp. 15, 19–20; 1894, p. 12; Gompers to Adlai E. Stevenson, April 4, 1894, SGLB; A.F. of L., *Some Reasons for Chinese Exclusion* (Washington, D. C., n.d.).

[72] A.F. of L., *Proceedings*, 1888, p. 26; 1891, p. 51; 1894, p. 47; 1897, pp. 88–91. Behind the scenes Gompers worked hard to convert the Federation to an outright exclusionist position. See Gompers to P. J. McGuire, January 9, 1893; Gompers to the A.F. of L. Executive Council, January 16, 1893, SGLB.

of L." [73] Thus the Federation's tradition of nonpartisanship, coupled with its rejection of socialism and independent political action, were indeed significant for American history. In England and on the continent the labor movement turned to socialism and ultimately to independent political action through new political alignments. In the United States, however, the labor movement (as embodied in the A.F. of L.) elected to function as a pressure group within the institutional framework of the existing political system. The Federation's dismissal of collectivism and independent political action in the 1890's played an important role in virtually destroying whatever future the socialist movement might have had in the United States. In the final analysis, the political program of the A.F. of L. was nothing more or less than a reflection of its pragmatic policy of emphasizing higher wages, shorter hours, and work rules, to the exclusion of proposals for fundamental changes in the fabric of society.

[73] A.F. of L., *Proceedings*, 1895, pp. 79–80.

CHAPTER TEN

Conclusion

❦ THE YEARS BETWEEN the Civil War and the turn of the century were indeed crucial ones for the American labor movement. By this time the industrial worker had found that his bargaining strength as an individual had declined markedly, and that he simply constituted the nucleus of a permanent wage-earning class. During the colonial period, on the other hand, the skilled artisan had occupied a highly respected status in society, and frequently had performed the functions not only of a worker, but also of a manager, salesman, and entrepreneur. As an important member of the community his economic position was relatively strong. But in the new industrialized economy, with its national market, its emphasis on large scale productive units, specialization, and mechanization, the artisan found that all he had left to sell was his labor. In such a dehumanized society the end result was a drastic decline in the status of workers, especially since mechanization had made skill acquired over a long period of time less essential. By the middle and late nineteenth century the transition from the skilled artisan to the industrial worker was nearing completion.

Faced by the erosion of its traditional position, labor attempted to develop a *modus vivendi* that would once again restore its status in the community. Initially it endeavored to revive the ideal of an older society, where the distinction between employer and employee did not seem to exist, and where the functions of both were united in the same person. Thus during the first half of the nineteenth century the foundation was laid for a labor tradition which emphasized that only the basic reform of society could arrest the ever-declining position of the working class. Asserting that such things as higher wages, shorter hours, and other benefits were simply amelioratives that avoided the root of the problem, the spokesmen for reform unionism attempted to meet the challenge of industrialism and a nationalized economy by returning to an earlier epoch in which the individual entrepreneur rather than the giant corporation was the characteristic unit of production. Both the National Labor Union and the Knights of Labor were in the reform tradition of American unionism. Both emphasized co-operation and reform politics in place of collective bargaining and economic action. Refusing to accept the permanency of an impersonal system that was transforming the worker from a skilled craftsman into an unskilled or semiskilled robot, its leaders

187

fought bitterly against a way of life that appeared alien to American traditions. Idealizing the America of Jefferson and Jackson, they sought their inspiration in an earlier society that probably in fact never existed. Reform unionism, therefore, was nothing more or less than a protest against a system that made the laborer an economic entity rather than an active and responsible individual who regarded his occupation as a means of fulfilment and who enjoyed an important and respected position in the community.

The solutions advanced by the National Labor Union and Knights of Labor were, however, at variance with technological and industrial developments. Production by small units, antimonopolism, and land reform, were objectives that were no longer meaningful within the context of the changing environment. The co-operative or individually owned workshop had become an anachronism, while the small producer had been rendered technologically obsolete. Thus the program of reform unionism proved to be ineffective in an industrialized society featuring a market economy.

While the National Labor Union and the Knights of Labor were vainly struggling to hold back the onrushing tide by advocating the restoration and preservation of older values, the trade unions commenced their rise to power. Recognizing that the hitherto close and friendly relations between employer and employee no longer existed, they set out to restore a measure of equality between the two. Conservative rather than radical, the trade unions accepted the basic framework of the capitalistic system with its large-scale productive units. Reflecting the acquisitive and expanding society in which they operated, they worked to achieve a higher standard of living and greater security for their members, as well as social and industrial rights that recognized the workers' legitimate claim of interest in their jobs and the means of safeguarding this claim.

To translate their program into reality, the unions proceeded to develop and elaborate a new set of techniques and institutions. The concept of the trade agreement and collective bargaining became their foremost contribution, and hand in hand with them also went such peculiarly union institutions as the business agent and, in a later period, industry-wide bargaining. Emphasizing immediate conditions, job-control, and industrial democracy, the unions slowly began to challenge the unilateral and arbitrary control of the managers of industry. By concentrating on developing their economic power, they began to act as a countervailing force to capital's unbridled authority.

The trade unions succeeded where their predecessors had failed because they were better adapted to their surroundings. In an environment of abundance the labor movement came to aim at achieving greater material benefits for their members to the exclusion of institutional reform panaceas. In essence, the American workingmen adapted themselves to an acquisitive society that interpreted success largely in terms of material advances. Labor leaders, recognizing that the rank and file had not developed a mature sense of class consciousness and that most workers still thought of themselves as expectant capitalists, built their organizations in such a way as to bring them into harmony with the larger societal environment. By the time of the Civil War business values had permeated American culture, and thus the labor movement, which equated organizational success with material gains, spoke in terms easily recognizable by its members. American trade unionism, therefore, was simply a response to the values and goals that characterized society at large.

The objectives of the trade unions were also compatible with the middle-class psychology of American laborers. Generally speaking, workingmen in the United States have never fully accepted their position in life as fixed or permanent. Instead they have frequently looked upon their working-class affiliation as a temporary one, serving only until that moment when they could rise to membership in the middle class. Abraham Lincoln expressed very well the historic hopes and aspirations of the American worker when he remarked that "there is not, of necessity, any such thing as the free hired laborer being fixed to that condition for life. Many independent men everywhere in these States, a few years back in their lives, were hired laborers. The prudent, penniless beginner in the world, labors for wages awhile, saves a surplus with which to buy tools or land for himself; then labors on his own account another while, and at length hires another new beginner to help him. This is the just, and generous, and prosperous system, which opens the way to all—gives hope to all, and consequent energy, and progress, and improvement of condition to all." [1] Since workingmen had adopted a middle-class value system and psychology that depicted a harmonious society unmarked by a class struggle and emphasizing equal opportunity for all, it would have been difficult for trade-union leaders to appeal to their followers on a class basis (even though an individual like Samuel Gompers *privately* expressed his belief in the existence of a permanent wage-earning class). Instead the unions appealed to the membership in terms of material gains and advantages, and thus never came into overt conflict with the workers' dreams of rising to a middle-class status. Indeed, the goals of the labor movement in the United States have simply been an adaptation on a smaller scale of those the middle class had historically oriented itself toward.

The structural evolution of trade unionism followed directly from the values that it had derived from the context of the larger environment. Since it aimed at attaining a higher standard of living for its members, it developed a framework that would facilitate the achievement of its ends. The national union as an economic institution represented a direct response to the national market and the geographical mobility of work-

[1] Roy P. Basler, ed., *The Collected Works of Abraham Lincoln* (9 vols: New Brunswick, New Jersey, 1953–1955), V, 52.

ers. A rapidly expanding economy, a relative scarcity of labor, and the absence of feudal restrictions that in Europe played such an important role in economic life, provided favorable conditions within which the unions could successfully function. In harmony with industrial developments, the unions ultimately developed their inherent economic power in order to equalize the unbalance in the positions of the corporation and the worker.

There were also other reasons for the success of the unions. To regard the labor movement as simply an economic movement is to misunderstand partially its basic nature as well as its functions. The modern trade union, in addition to performing certain economic functions, also filled a psychological and a social need. In pre-industrial society the worker, as a skilled craftsman, had maintained a highly-respected position in the community. The complex forces that had brought modern industry into being, however, destroyed the earlier habits and customs that had held the community together. Each individual was thrown upon his own resources, and the rise of the wage payment completed the isolation of the individual from the group.

The workers' loss of identity and status prepared the ground for the rise of trade unionism. While accepting industrial society, the unions set to work to replace the community that had disintegrated. Thus the workers again became members of a social group having common interests.[2] Although trade unions were at first bitterly resisted because of America's frontier heritage, its cult of individualism, and its lack of class consciousness, they succeeded in the end in overcoming the obstacles in their path and gaining a significant voice in all matters affecting their members.

In attempting to meet the economic, social, and psychological needs of its members, the labor movement never developed any specific formula, ideology, or structural organization. If pragmatism and practicality are some of the major forces at work in the intellectual and cultural sphere in the United States, so too have they permeated trade-union ideology. As a matter of fact, union leaders since the 1880's have generally opposed any attempt to develop an articulate theory of unionism, and have frequently expressed contempt for so-called intellectuals who did not understand the nature and functions of organized labor.[3] This anti-intellectual strain, with its emphasis on action rather than thought, has exerted an important influence on the labor movement, as it has on American society. Like most of their fellow citizens, union leaders have resisted efforts

[2] The social, psychological, and moral roles of trade unionism are explored and elaborated in Frank Tannenbaum, *A Philosophy of Labor* (New York, 1951).

[3] See the testimony by Samuel Gompers before the Commission on Industrial Relations in 1914, in U. S. Commission on Industrial Relations, *Final Report and Testimony*, 64th Congress, 1st Session, *Senate Document 415* (11 vols: Washington, D. C., 1916), II, 1534.

to explore the assumptions and presuppositions upon which their ideology rested and the final goals toward which they are moving. The typical American, including most workers, measures his success by the distance he has covered from his initial starting point rather than by his current position. Thus the quest for success becomes in effect a goal that always remains in the future and is never achieved in the present. The labor movement, as an institution functioning within its culture, has also come to reflect the materialistic and acquisitive strivings of that culture. The debate between Samuel Gompers and Morris Hillquit, the socialist leader, before the Commission on Industrial Relations in 1914, is particularly revealing in this respect:

> Mr. Hillquit. Then, inform me upon this matter: In your political work of the labor movement is the American Federation of Labor guided by a general social philosophy, or is it not?
>
> Mr. Gompers. It is guided by the history of the past, drawing its lessons from history, to know of the conditions by which the working people are surrounded and confronted; to work along the lines of least resistance; to accomplish the best results in improving the condition of the working people, men and women and children, to-day and to-morrow and to-morrow—and to-morrow's to-morrow; and each day making it a better day than the one that had gone before. That is the guiding principle and philosophy and aim of the labor movement—in order to secure a better life for all. . . .
>
> Mr. Hillquit. Now, my question is, Will this effort on the part of organized labor ever stop until it has the full reward for its labor?
>
> Mr. Gompers. It won't stop at all.
>
> Mr. Hillquit. That is a question—
>
> Mr. Gompers (interrupting). Not when any particular point is reached, whether it be that toward which you have just declared or anything else. The working people will never stop—
>
> Mr. Hillquit. Exactly.
>
> Mr. Gompers (continuing). In their effort to obtain a better life for themselves and for their wives and for their children and for humanity.
>
> Mr. Hillquit. Then, the object of the labor union is to obtain complete social justice for themselves and for their wives and for their children?
>
> Mr. Gompers. It is the effort to obtain a better life every day.
>
> Mr. Hillquit. Every day and always—
>
> Mr. Gompers. Every day. That does not limit it.
>
> Mr. Hillquit. Until such time—
>
> Mr. Gompers. Not until any time.
>
> Mr. Hillquit. In other words—
>
> Mr. Gompers (interrupting). In other words, we go further than you. [Laughter and applause in the audience.] You have an end; we have not.[4]

Later in the hearings Gompers added:

> The . . . point of difference particularly is, and I want to emphasize it, that the attempt, and the constant attempt, of Socialist speakers and writers to

[4] *Ibid.*, pp. 1528–29.

belittle the achievements of the organized labor movement of America. The other is that, even after you increase wages, it does you no material good; it does not do any material good; it is simply so much effort wasted. It is the effort of the Socialist Party to divert the attention of the American working people from the immediate need and from the immediate struggle to something remote. If the working people of America can be made to believe that they can secure the relief that they need, the improvement which is justly theirs, the freedom which they ought to have, by casting a vote once every year, wherefore join in the unions engaged in the everyday struggle to improve material conditions now? It is the difference between the man who preaches from the pulpit that the working people are in the positions God ordained and that they will have a better time in the sweet by-and-by. And on the same hand the Socialists who paint a beautiful picture of a future, alluring the workmen from the immediate struggles to the hopes for the future. It is the idea of men being diverted from the immediate struggle and immediate needs for the natural, rational development of the human race; and securing day by day and week by week and month by month and year by year, a little to-day, a little to-morrow, adding, adding, gaining, gaining, moving forward, every step in advance, and never taking one receding step except it be to plant the foot forward firmer than ever before.

I would not want any man to believe nor to so place our movement as if we were satisfied. There is not anything satisfying in what we have accomplished. It is gratifying, but simply whets our appetite and desires and the aims and aspirations for still better and better and still better things.[5]

Lacking any final commitment to a particular ideology or structural form, the American labor movement has proven sufficiently flexible to change whenever the need arose. Thus the simple unions of the 1880's and 1890's, with their monolithic preoccupation with economic power, ultimately evolved into the modern organizations of the middle twentieth century with their bureaucracy and complicated welfare and pension programs that reaches into almost every corner of their members' lives. The labor movement obviously lacks the roundness and symmetry of a complicated philosophical system but, as Philip Taft has astutely observed, the lack of this quality has helped to make it "more democratic, tolerant, and flexible." American unionism, he concludes, "is a means of protecting the individual against arbitrary rule and raising his standard of living. While it may not rank high for philosophy, it deserves high score on the latter count." [6] Only time, however, will reveal whether or not the labor movement can continue to function in this manner without defining its final aims. So long as the economy continues to prosper and expand, the question will probably remain an academic one. Nevertheless, a change in either of these factors would immediately cause at-

[5] *Ibid.*, pp. 1576–77.
[6] Philip Taft, "Theories of the Labor Movement," in Industrial Relations Research Association, *Interpreting the Labor Movement* (Champaign, Illinois, 1952) , p. 38.

tention to shift to fundamental ideology and goals, not only in regard to the labor movement, but American society in general.

In adjusting itself to the American environment, the modern labor movement ignored certain factors that had played an important role in the ideology of reform unionism. While the trade unions endeavored to give the workers a sense of belonging and an identity within a group, they paid little or no attention to the work process itself. After the Civil War the subdivision of labor approached a degree of specialization never before dreamed possible, and the automation of work in the twentieth century has made the individual little more than a human machine deriving practically no satisfaction from the finished product. Originally the trade unions were established by the skilled laborers to protect themselves against the inroads that advancing technology was making upon their craft, but this aspect of unionism became less and less important as time went on. At present the overwhelming majority of workers sell their physical and mental labor to an employer, to be utilized for purposes from which they derive little or no satisfaction and pride. When we compare the concept of work in modern industrial society with the past, the extent of its dehumanization becomes quite striking. To the modern laborer work is simply a means for fulfilling his desires and greed as a consumer. As a matter of fact, as Hannah Arendt has pointed out, "laboring" is much too ambitious a word for what modern man is doing. "The last stage of the laboring society, the society of jobholders, demands of its members a sheer automatic functioning, as though individual life had actually been submerged in the over-all life process of the species and the only active decision still required of the individual were to let go, so to speak, to abandon his individuality, the still individually sensed pain and trouble of living, and acquiesce in a dazed, 'tranquilized,' functional type of behavior." [7]

Recently some proposals have been suggested to mitigate the impact of automation and the loss of what is sometimes referred to as the "instinct of workmanship." A number of prominent unions, including the United Steelworkers of America and the International Ladies Garment Workers Union, have undertaken programs intended to educate their members not only in union and labor matters, but also in cultural and aesthetic values. While intended to develop a well-rounded individual, as well as to enable the worker to put leisure time to creative and constructive use, such programs again avoid implicating the actual work process in any significant way. Similarly, company schemes, including profit-sharing, incentive plans, coffee breaks, intra- and inter-factory athletics, and on-the-job music, are also intended to make working conditions more pleasant (and thus to increase productivity) rather than to make the job more meaningful to the individual laborer.

[7] Hannah Arendt, *The Human Condition* (Chicago, 1958), p. 322. For a similar point of view see Erich Fromm, *The Sane Society* (New York, 1955), *passim*.

The National Labor Union and the Knights of Labor, on the other hand, were greatly concerned about the nature of the work process. In attempting to re-establish a society characterized by the small productive unit, they implicitly hoped to retain the sense of pride and achievement that the craftsman could derive from the finished product. Work, in other words, would not be an end in itself, but rather a means to an end. That end was the development of each individual to the fullest extent possible, and the job was simply a way of achieving this goal. Because the methods advocated by the National Labor Union and the Knights of Labor conflicted with the direction of economic evolution, these two organizations were superseded by the trade unions.

The ultimate triumph of trade unionism in the 1880's and 1890's was indeed significant for the future of American labor. Although, because of their weakness, the unions played a relatively minor role in helping to raise their constituents' standard of living during the period under discussion,[8] their basic ideology (or lack of ideology), and to a lesser extent, their basic structure, had been institutionalized by 1900.

For the first part of the twentieth century both the trade unions and the A.F. of L. continued to follow the general principles and patterns that had been established in the decades following the Civil War. Established at a time when the mass production industries had not as yet become dominant in the economy, the trade unions found that organization along craft or semi-industrial lines was sufficiently broad and flexible. As time wore on, however, it gradually became clear that the basis of the labor movement would have to be broadened because of the increasing predominance of the heavy mass production industries, a development that had further diminished the required degree of skill and blurred craft and jurisdictional lines until barely discernible. Many of the national unions, however, having achieved a certain degree of success and stability with a relatively small membership (small in terms of the total size of the working class), were reluctant to undertake any large organizational campaigns to bring together workers in large industrial unions. These older unions, led by men who had fought desperately to surmount government and employer resistance since the latter half of the nineteenth century, had been conditioned by the intensity of the struggle and their many defeats, and their psychology was one of defense rather than offense.

While the A.F. of L. and its affiliates were following traditional and tested policies, there arose within the labor movement a younger and more aggressive group of leaders. Impatient with the seemingly short-sighted and narrow vision of the older leaders, they commenced a struggle to widen the base of the labor movement. Thus there developed an internecine struggle within organized labor that culminated in open

[8] See Paul H. Douglas, *Real Wages in the United States 1890–1926* (Boston, 1930), pp. 557–64.

civil war with the rise of the C.I.O. in the 1930's. This conflict, although in some aspects a power struggle involving unions and personalities, was in reality one between industrial unionism and craft unionism, the less skilled and the higher skilled, the more politically-minded unionists and those who eschewed partisan politics and thought almost exclusively in terms of economic action and collective bargaining, those younger leaders who argued that the labor movement had to concern itself even with the great mass of unorganized workers and those older unionists who were committed to advancing their particular organizations, in short, between "idealists who took in all society at a glance and business unionists who specialized in advancing the interests of a craft at a time." [9]

In a broader sense, however, the divided house of labor that came into being in the 1930's was less a struggle over basic ideology than it was over means. It is true that the positions of the A.F. of L. and C.I.O. were far apart on such issues as industrial unionism, political action, greater governmental responsibility in the social welfare realm, and the like. Yet in their acceptance of American society and its culture, collective bargaining techniques, opposition to radical ideologies, and visions of an ever-rising standard of living, the A.F. of L. and C.I.O. stood as one despite their quarrels. Eventually the former was to adopt practically all the goals of the latter, a development that prepared the ground for the unification of the labor movement in 1955. Although the conflict between them had been a bitter and acrimonious one, agreement on basic principles had always remained intact, and in due course it was possible to adjust their differences over means to meet changing conditions.

The trade-union leaders of the 1880's and 1890's were for the most part no longer alive to witness the changes that occurred in their creation since the New Deal, but their dreams, their hopes, and their aspirations had seemingly been realized through a labor movement which they had been instrumental in establishing. These older leaders, had they lived to see the events of the 1930's and beyond, might for a brief moment have felt themselves to be aliens in their own house. In time, however, they would have grown accustomed to their now mature offspring, recognizing its basic affinity and closeness to their own principles and ideals. Certainly their monument can hardly be more imposing than their creation.

[9] James O. Morris, *Conflict Within the AFL: A Study of Craft Versus Industrial Unionism, 1901–1938* (Ithaca, New York, 1958) , pp. 288–89.

Bibliographical Essay

I. MANUSCRIPTS

Of greatest importance to the student of American labor history are the collection of Powderly manuscripts at the Department of Archives and Manuscripts, Catholic University of America, Washington, D. C., the John W. Hayes collection at the same repository, and the Samuel Gompers Letter Books at the A.F. of L.-C.I.O. Building, Washington, D. C. The A.F. of L.-C.I.O. is also in the process of microfilming many other documents pertaining to its affiliated unions, but it has unfortunately destroyed much of the incoming correspondence. The John Samuel Papers, Wisconsin State Historical Society, Madison, Wisconsin, and the Joseph Labadie Collection, University of Michigan, Ann Arbor, Michigan, are also revealing. Vaughn D. Bornet, "The New Labor History: A Challenge for American Historians," *The Historian*, XVIII (Autumn, 1955), 1–24, discusses the importance of manuscript materials for labor historians and also describes the holdings of the A.F. of L., but the author's description of the documents available is not always accurate.

II. THE LABOR PRESS *

A. *General*

For the labor movement of the 1860's *Fincher's Trades' Review* (Philadelphia, 1863–1866), the *Workingman's Advocate* (Chicago, 1864–1877), and the *Daily Evening Voice* (Boston, 1865–1867), are indispensable. *The Revolution* (New York, 1868–1872), and *Woodhull & Claflin's Weekly* (New York, 1870–1876) provides information about the relationship of women to the young labor movement. The *Labor Standard* (New York, 1876–1881) is useful for the depression of the 1870's and the attempts by labor to reorganize its broken forces. *John Swinton's Paper* (New York, 1883–1887) is undoubtedly one of the finest examples of labor journalism, as well as one of the most important sources of information for the mid-1880's. The *Workmen's Advocate* (New Haven, Con-

---

* All dates given for the periodicals and proceedings cited in this section include only the issues consulted by the author (although in most cases complete files for the period were examined). More complete dates and places of publication can be found in Lloyd G. Reynolds and Charles C. Killingsworth, *Trade Union Publications* (3 vols: Baltimore, 1944–1945); Bernard G. Naas and Carmelita S. Sakr, *American Labor Union Periodicals: A Guide to Their Location* (Ithaca, New York, 1956); Winifred Gregory, *Union List of Serials* (2nd ed: New York, 1943).

necticut, 1885–1891) , and *The People* (New York, 1891–1900) gives the viewpoint of the Socialist Labor party during this period.

B. *Labor Periodicals*

The labor periodicals published during the period covered by this study constitute a major source. These journals, although avowedly partisan, generally included anything of significance concerning their organizations, as well as much of the correspondence of their officials. Unlike many present-day labor periodicals, which reveal little of importance about the contemporary movement, they are invaluable for an understanding of the labor movement in the last half of the nineteenth century. Among the most important of these journals are:

American Federationist, 1894–1910 (A.F. of L.) .

Bakers' Journal, 1888–1895 (Journeymen Bakers and Confectioners International Union) .

Brauer-Zeitung, 1886–1900 (United Brewery Workers) .

The Carpenter, 1881–1906 (United Brotherhood of Carpenters and Joiners) .

Carriage and Wagon Workers Journal, 1899–1901 (Carriage and Wagon Workers International Union) .

Cigar Makers' Official Journal, 1876–1900 (Cigar Makers International Union) .

Coopers' Journal, 1870–1873 (Coopers International Union) .

Garment Worker, 1896–1900 (United Garment Workers) .

Granite Cutters' Journal, 1877–1900 (Granite Cutters National Union) .

Iron Molders' Journal, 1866–1900 (Iron Molders International Union) .

The Laster, 1888–1892 (New England Lasters Protective Union) .

Machine and Forge, 1893 (International Machinists Union) .

Monthly Journal of the International Association of Machinists, 1893–1900 (International Association of Machinists) .

National Labor Tribune, 1875–1900 (Amalgamated Association of Iron and Steel Workers) .

Locomotive Engineer's Journal, 1888–1900 (Brotherhood of Locomotive Engineers) .

Locomotive Firemen's Magazine, 1882–1900 (Brotherhood of Locomotive Firemen) .

Journal of the International Brotherhood of Machinery Molders, 1888–1892 (International Brotherhood of Machinery Molders) .

Journal of United Labor, 1880–1889, *Journal of the Knights of Labor,* 1889–1900 (Knights of Labor) .

Machinists and Blacksmiths International Journal, 1870–1875 (International Union of Machinists and Blacksmiths) .

The Painter, 1887–1889, *Painters Journal,* 1890–1900 (Brotherhood of Painters and Decorators) .

Monthly Trade Journal of Pattern Makers, 1893–1896 (Pattern Makers National League) .

Printers' Circular, 1868–1888 (an independent journal published in Philadelphia, but containing much information concerning the International Typographical Union) .

Railroad Brakemen's Journal, 1887–1895 (Brotherhood of Railroad Brakemen) .

Railway Telegrapher, 1889–1895 (Order of Railway Telegraphers) .

Stone Cutters Journal, 1887–1900 (Journeymen Stone Cutters Association) .

The Tailor, 1888–1900 (Journeymen Tailors National Union).

The Craftsman, 1884–1888 (International Typographical Union).

Typographical Journal, 1889–1900 (International Typographical Union).

United Mine Workers Journal, 1891–1900 (United Mine Workers).

C. *Union Proceedings*

No less valuable than the labor journals are the proceedings of the conventions of the various labor organizations. Among the most important are:

Amalgamated Association of Iron and Steel Workers, *Proceedings,* 1876–1900.

American Federation of Labor, *Proceedings,* 1886–1903 (reprinted in 1905 and 1906).

American Flint Glass Workers Union, *Proceedings,* 1887–1895.

Bricklayers and Masons International Union, *Proceedings,* 1865–1900.

Brotherhood of Railroad Brakemen, *Proceedings,* 1884–1895.

Carpenters and Joiners National Union, *Proceedings,* 1865–1867.

Cigar Makers International Union, *Proceedings,* 1867–1899 (many of these *Proceedings* were either printed in the Chicago *Workingman's Advocate* or the *Cigar Makers' Official Journal*).

Federation of Organized Trades and Labor Unions of the United States and Canada, *Proceedings,* 1881–1886 (reprinted in 1905).

International Typographical Union, *Proceedings,* 1865–1900.

International Working Men's Association, *Report of the Fourth Annual Congress of the International Working Men's Association, Held at Basle, in Switzerland. . . . 1869* (London, n.d.).

Iron Molders International Union, *Proceedings,* 1876–1899.

Journeymen Barbers International Union, *Proceedings,* 1893–1896.

Knights of Labor, *Proceedings of the General Assembly,* 1878–1900.

Knights of Labor, *Proceedings of the Ninth Annual Session of the Knights of Labor New York State . . . 1898* (n.p., n.d.).

Knights of Labor, *Quarterly Report of District Assembly No. 30, K. of L. . . . 1886* (Boston, 1886).

Knights of Labor, *Thirteenth Annual Convention of the New York Protective Associations Affiliated with District Assembly 49, K. of L. on Labor Day . . . 1895* (n.p., 1895).

Knights of Labor, *Fourteenth Annual Convention of the New York Protective Associations Affiliated with D.A. 49 on Labor Day . . . 1896* (n.p., 1896).

New England Lasters Protective Union, *Proceedings,* 1888–1895.

National Civic Federation, *Industrial Conference Under the Auspices of the National Civic Federation . . . 1902* (New York, 1903).

National Federation of Miners and Mine Laborers, *Proceedings,* 1886–1888.

National Labor Union, *Second Annual Session of the National Labor Union, Assembled in New York City, September 21, 1868* (Philadelphia, 1868).

National League of Musicians, *Proceedings,* 1888–1895.

New York State Workingmen's Assembly, *Proceedings,* 1869–1871.

Pattern Makers National League, *Proceedings,* 1888–1896.

Socialist Labor party, *Proceedings,* 1885, 1896, 1900.

United Brewery Workers, *Proceedings,* 1886–1900.

United Brotherhood of Carpenters and Joiners, *Proceedings,* 1888–1900.

United Mine Workers, *Proceedings,* 1911.

United Sons of Vulcan, *Vulcan Record,* 1868–1875.
Window Glass Workers Assembly No. 300 (Knights of Labor), *Proceedings,*
1884–1899.

III. GOVERNMENT PUBLICATIONS

A. *Federal Government Publications*

The *Annual Reports* of the United States Commissioner of Labor, which
commenced publication in 1886, contain much information. The following
Annual Reports were found to be especially useful: I (March, 1886), *Industrial
Depressions;* III (1887), *Strikes and Lockouts;* X (1894), *Strikes and Lockouts;*
XI (1895–1896), *Work and Wages of Men, Women, and Children;* XIII (1898),
Hand and Machine Labor.

The *Report of the Committee of the Senate Upon the Relations Between
Labor and Capital, and Testimony Taken by the Committee* (4 vols: Washington, D. C., 1885), contains the testimony of leading industrial figures and labor
leaders. The final report of the committee was never published, having perhaps
been suppressed. The United States Industrial Commission, *Report of the Industrial Commission* (19 vols: Washington, D. C., 1900–1902), and the United
States Commission on Industrial Relations, *Final Report and Testimony* (11
vols: Washington, D. C., 1916), are both replete with information about the
labor and industrial scene.

B. *State Government Publications*

During this period many of the states established labor and industrial bu-
reaus, and the reports of these agencies contain material about working conditions, wages, labor organizations, plus many other aspects of economic life. The
following were consulted in the preparation of this study:

California Bureau of Labor Statistics, *Biennial Report,* I–IV (1884–1890).
Colorado Bureau of Labor Statistics, *Biennial Report,* I–II (1888–1890).
Connecticut Bureau of Labor Statistics, *Annual Report,* I–VI (1885–1890).
Illinois Bureau of Labor Statistics, *Biennial Report,* I–VI (1881–1890).
Indiana Department of Statistics, *Annual Report,* II–IX (1880–1890).
Iowa Bureau of Labor Statistics, *Biennial Report,* I–IV (1884/5–1890/1).
Kansas Bureau of Labor and Industrial Statistics, *Annual Report,* I–VI (1885–
1890).
Kentucky Bureau of Agriculture, Horticulture, and Statistics, *Annual Report,*
III–VIII (1880–1889).
Maine Bureau of Industrial and Labor Statistics, *Annual Report,* I–IV (1887–
1890).
Maryland Bureau of Industrial Statistics and Information, *Biennial Report,*
I–IV (1885–1891).
Massachusetts Bureau of Statistics of Labor, *Annual Report,* XI–XXI (1880–
1891).
Michigan Bureau of Labor and Industrial Statistics, *Annual Report,* I–VIII
(1884–1890).
Minnesota Bureau of Labor Statistics, *Biennial Report,* I–II (1888–1890).
Missouri Bureau of Labor Statistics, *Annual Report,* I–XII (1879–1890).
Nebraska Bureau of Labor and Industrial Statistics, *Biennial Report,* I–II (1887–
1890).

New Jersey Bureau of Statistics of Labor and Industries, *Annual Report*, I–XIII (1878–1890).
New York Bureau of Statistics of Labor, *Annual Report*, I–VIII (1883–1890).
North Carolina Bureau of Labor Statistics, *Annual Report*, I–IV (1887–1890).
North Dakota Commissioner of Agriculture and Labor, *Report*, I (1890).
Ohio Bureau of Labor Statistics, *Annual Report*, IV–XIV (1880–1890).
Pennsylvania Secretary of Internal Affairs, *Annual Report*, Pt. III, *Industrial Statistics*, VIII–XVIII (1879–1890).
Rhode Island Bureau of Industrial Statistics, *Annual Report*, I–IV (1887–1890).
West Virginia Bureau of Labor, *Report*, I (1890).
Wisconsin Bureau of Labor and Industrial Statistics, *Biennial Report*, I–IV (1884–1890).

IV. GENERAL WORKS

A. *General Labor Histories*

Richard T. Ely's *The Labor Movement in America* (New York, 1886), was one of the earliest general accounts by a professional scholar. Almost simultaneously with Ely's work came George E. McNeill, ed., *The Labor Movement: The Problem of To-day* (Boston, 1887), which is a primary source containing much information not available elsewhere. Some other useful contemporary accounts include Richard F. Hinton, "American Labor Organizations," *North American Review*, CXL (January, 1885), 48–62; William E. Barns, ed., *The Labor Problem: Plain Questions and Practical Answers* (New York, 1886); S. M. Jelley, *The Voice of Labor* (Philadelphia, 1888); John Swinton, *Striking for Life: Labor's Side of the Labor Question* (n.p., 1894), and *A Momentous Question: The Respective Attitudes of Labor and Capital* (Philadelphia, 1895); John Mitchell, *Organized Labor* (Philadelphia, 1903).

At the beginning of the twentieth century the study of American labor was stimulated by the work of Jacob H. Hollander and George E. Barnett of Johns Hopkins University. While their own writings were relatively modest, they sponsored numerous studies on various aspects of the labor movements by their graduate students. See especially Hollander and Barnett, *Studies in American Trade Unionism* (New York, 1906). A different but equally important approach to the study of American labor, emphasizing the various types of unions, was set forth by Robert F. Hoxie in his influential *Trade Unionism in the United States* (New York, 1917).

By far the most authoritative and important work in American labor history was the John R. Commons and associates monumental *History of Labour in the United States* (4 vols: New York, 1918–1935). Adopting a pragmatic theory of the labor movement, this work instantly became the starting point for all later studies of the labor movement. Exhaustive in research, provocative in interpretation, and invaluable to the serious scholar, the *History of Labour* is nevertheless weakened by its divorce of labor from the mainstream of American thought and its preoccupation with the economic aspects of organized labor. The theoretical aspects of the Commons school approach to labor is brilliantly elaborated in Selig Perlman's *A Theory of the Labor Movement* (New York, 1928), and "The Basic Philosophy of the American Labor Movement," American Academy of Political and Social Science, *Annals*, CCLXXIV (March, 1951),

57–63. For comments on the Perlman hypothesis see Charles A. Gulick and Melvin K. Bers, "Insight and Illusion in Perlman's Theory of the Labor Movement," *Industrial and Labor Relations Review,* VI (July, 1953) , 510–31; Adolph Sturmthal, "Comments on Selig Perlman's *A Theory of the Labor Movement,*" *Industrial and Labor Relations Review,* IV (July, 1951) , 483–96; Philip Taft, "*A Rereading of Selig Perlman's* A Theory of the Labor Movement," *Industrial and Labor Relations Review,* IV (October, 1950) , 70–77.

The synthesis by the Commons school was followed by Norman J. Ware's *The Labor Movement in the United States 1860–1895* (New York, 1929), which emphasized conflicting personalities and reflected the disillusionment of the 1920's with American trade unionism. Philip S. Foner, *History of the Labor Movement in the United States* (2 vols: New York, 1947–1955), while based on extensive research in the primary sources, interprets the evolution of organized labor through a rigid Marxian framework. John Herman Randall, Jr., *The Problem of Group Responsibility to Society: An Interpretation of the History of American Labor* (New York, 1922), is a provocative though completely neglected interpretation. Lloyd Ulman, *The Rise of the National Trade Union* (Cambridge, Massachusetts, 1955), emphasizes the economic aspects of trade unionism in the last quarter of the nineteenth century while generally minimizing the historical setting of the period. The philosophical aspects of trade unionism are explored by Paul Crosser, *Ideologies and American Labor* (New York, 1941), and Frank Tannenbaum, *A Philosophy of Labor* (New York, 1951). Also useful were Industrial Relations Research Association, *Interpreting the Labor Movement* (Champaign, Illinois, 1952), and Jack Barbash, *The Practice of Unionism* (New York, 1956). Charles A. Madison, *American Labor Leaders* (New York, 1950), contains short biographies of prominent labor leaders. There are also valuable insights by foreigners viewing the American labor movement. See especially E. Levasseur, *The American Workman* (Baltimore, 1900), and Robert W. Smuts, *European Impressions of the American Worker* (New York, 1953). The influence of British men and ideas on the American labor movement is discussed by Clifton K. Yearley, Jr., *Britons in American Labor: A History of the Influence of the United Kingdom Immigrants on American Labor, 1820–1914* (Baltimore, 1957), and Rowland T. Berthoff, *British Immigrants in Industrial America 1790–1950* (Cambridge, Massachusetts, 1953).

Some useful guides to the historiography of the labor movement are Maurice F. Neufeld, *A Bibliography of American Labor Union History* (Ithaca, New York, 1958), Mark Perlman, *Labor Union Theories in America: Background and Development* (Evanston, Illinois, 1958), and Walter Galenson, "Reflections on the Writing of Labor History," *Industrial and Labor Relations Review,* XI (October, 1957) , 85–95.

B. *The Ante-Bellum Labor Movement*

Richard B. Morris, *Government and Labor in Early America* (New York, 1946), and Marcus W. Jernegan, *Laboring and Dependent Classes in Colonial America 1607–1783* (Chicago, 1931), are valuable for the colonial background. Norman J. Ware's *The Industrial Worker 1840–1860* (Boston, 1924) is the best work on the labor movement prior to the Civil War. A provocative interpretation of the Jacksonian labor movement has been advanced by Arthur M. Schlesinger, Jr., *The Age of Jackson* (Boston, 1945). His interpretation, however, has come under strong attack by some historians. See especially Joseph Dorfman, "The Jackson Wage-Earner Thesis," *American Historical Review,* LIV (January, 1949), 293–306; Edward Pessen, "The Workingmen's Movement of the Jackson Era," *Mississippi Valley Historical Review,* XLIII (December, 1956), 428–43; William A. Sullivan, *The Industrial Worker in Pennsylvania 1800–1840* (Harrisburg, Pennsylvania, 1955); Louis Arky, "The Mechanics' Union of Trade Associations and the Formation of the Philadelphia Workingmen's Movement," *Pennsylvania Magazine of History and Biography,* LXXVI (April, 1952), 142–76. Marvin Meyers, *The Jacksonian Persuasion: Politics and Belief* (Stanford, California, 1957), is a brilliant interpretive essay on the intellectual milieu of the Jackson period that offers insight to the student of labor history. Helene S. Zahler, *Eastern Workingmen and National Land Policy, 1829–1862* (New York, 1941), is an important contribution to an understanding of the origins of labor reformism. Louis Hartz, *Economic Policy and Democratic Thought: Pennsylvania, 1776–1860* (Cambridge, Massachusetts, 1948), and Oscar and Mary F. Handlin, *Commonwealth: A Study of the Role of Government in the American Economy: Massachusetts, 1774–1861* (New York, 1947), are also important studies containing much background material on the ante-bellum labor scene.

C. Trade Unionism: Organizations and Institutions

For the growth of trade unions consult Leo Wolman, *The Growth of American Trade Unions 1880–1923* (New York, 1924), and *Ebb and Flow in Trade Unionism* (New York, 1936). Facts concerning wages are to be found in *History of Wages in the United States From Colonial Times to 1928,* U. S. Bureau of Labor Statistics, *Bulletin No. 499* (Washington, D. C., 1929), and Paul H. Douglas, *Real Wages in the United States 1890–1926* (Boston, 1930).

The dominance of the national union is treated in Ulman, previously cited, and George E. Barnett, "The Dominance of the National Union in American Labor Organization," *Quarterly Journal of Economics,* XXVII (May, 1913), 455–81. Some important studies inspired by Hollander and Barnett at the Johns Hopkins University include John H. Ashworth, *The Helper and American Trade Unions* (Baltimore, 1915); Theodore W. Glocker, *The Government of American Trade Unions* (Baltimore, 1913); George M. Janes, *The Control of Strikes in American Trade Unions* (Baltimore, 1916); William Kirk, *National Labor Federations in the United States* (Baltimore, 1906); Leo Wolman, *The Boycott in American Trade Unions* (Baltimore, 1916); Aaron M. Sakolski, *The Finances of American Trade Unions* (Baltimore, 1906); Ernest R. Spedden, *The Trade Union Label* (Baltimore, 1910). The following also proved to be informative: Theodore W. Glocker, "Amalgamation of Related Trades in American Unions," *American Economic Review,* V (September, 1915), 554–75; Edward W. Bemis, "Benefit Features of American Trade Unions," U. S. Department of Labor, *Bulletin,* IV (May, 1899), 361–400; John G. Brooks, "The Trade-Union Label," U. S. Department of Labor, *Bulletin,* III (March, 1898), 197–219; Solomon Blum, "Jurisdictional Disputes Resulting From Structural Differences in American Trade Unions," University of California, *Publications in Economics,* III (September 27, 1913), 409–47.

Unfortunately, few first-rate studies of individual unions have been written. One exception is Robert A. Christie, *Empire in Wood: A History of the Car-*

penters' Union (Ithaca, New York, 1956), which is a model of its kind. Also useful, but emphasizing the twentieth century, is Vernon H. Jensen, *Heritage of Conflict: Labor Relations in the Nonferrous Metals Industry Up to 1930* (Ithaca, New York, 1950). See also the following studies: W. Scott Hall, *The Journeymen Barbers' International Union of America* (Baltimore, 1936); Hermann Schlüter, *The Brewing Industry and the Brewery Workers' Movement in America* (Cincinnati, 1910); Harry C. Bates, *Bricklayers' Century of Craftsmanship: A History of the Bricklayers, Masons and Plasterers' International Union of America* (Washington, D. C., 1955); E. E. Cummins, "Political and Social Philosophy of the Carpenters' Union," *Political Science Quarterly,* XLII (September, 1927), 397–418; Philip S. Foner, *The Fur and Leather Workers Union* (Newark, New Jersey, 1950); "The Passing of the National Glass Window Workers," U. S. Bureau of Labor Statistics, *Monthly Labor Review,* XXIX (October, 1929), 1–16; James Campbell, "The Window-Glass Blowers' Association," Pennsylvania Secretary of Internal Affairs, *Annual Report,* XVI (1888), Pt. III, *Industrial Statistics,* Section F, pp. 30–37; Charles H. Green, *The Headwear Workers: A Century of Trade Unionism* (New York, 1944); Donald B. Robinson, *Spotlight on a Union: The Story of the United Hatters, Cap and Millinery Workers International Union* (New York, 1948); Carroll D. Wright, "The Amalgamated Association of Iron and Steel Workers," *Quarterly Journal of Economics,* VII (July, 1893), 400–32; Jesse S. Robinson, *The Amalgamated Association of Iron, Steel and Tin Workers* (Baltimore, 1920); John A. Fitch, *The Steel Workers* (New York, 1910), and "Unionism in the Iron and Steel Industry," *Political Science Quarterly,* XXIV (March, 1909), 57–79; Edward A. Wieck, *The American Miners' Association* (New York, 1940); Chris Evans, *History of United Mine Workers of America* (2 vols: n.p., 1918–1920); Andrew Roy, *A History of the Coal Miners of the United States* (3rd ed: Columbus, Ohio, 1907); William J. Walsh, *The United Mine Workers of America as an Economic and Social Force in the Anthracite Territory* (Washington, D. C., 1931); Arthur E. Suffern, *The Coal Miners' Struggle for Industrial Status* (New York, 1926); David J. McDonald and Edward A. Lynch, *Coal and Unionism: A History of the American Coal Miners' Unions* (Silver Spring, Maryland, 1939); Frank T. Stockton, *The International Molders Union of North America* (Baltimore, 1921); H. E. Hoagland, "The Rise of the Iron Molders' International Union," *American Economic Review,* III (June, 1913), 296–313; John R. Commons, "American Shoemakers, 1648–1895: A Sketch of Industrial Evolution," *Quarterly Journal of Economics,* XXIV (November, 1909), 39–84; Don D. Lescohier, *The Knights of St. Crispin, 1867–1874* (Madison, Wisconsin, 1910); George E. McNeill, "Questions for Boot and Shoe Workers to Answer," *Union Boot and Shoe Worker,* I (February, 1900), 5–7, (March, 1900), 6–8, (April, 1900), 8–9, (May, 1900), 7–8; "A Review of the Unions in the Shoe Trade of America," *Shoe Workers' Journal,* XI (May, 1910), 5–9, (June, 1910), 5–11, (July, 1910), 5–14, (August, 1910), 5–11, (September, 1910), 5–8, (November, 1910), 5–8; Augusta E. Galster, *The Labor Movement in the Shoe Industry With Special Reference to Philadelphia* (New York, 1924); Charles J. Stowell, *Studies in Trade Unionism in the Custom Tailoring Trade* (Bloomington, Illinois, 1913), and *The Journeymen Tailors' Union of America* (Urbana, Illinois, 1918); Benjamin Stolberg, *Tailor's Progress: The Story of a Famous Union and the Men Who Made It* (New York, 1944); Louis Levine (Lorwin), *The*

Women's Garment Workers: A History of the International Ladies' Garment Workers' Union (New York, 1924); Vidkunn Ulriksson, *The Telegraphers: Their Craft and Their Unions* (Washington, D. C., 1953); George A. Tracy, *History of the Typographical Union* (Indianapolis, Indiana, 1913): George E. Barnett, *The Printers: A Study in American Trade Unionism* (Cambridge, Massachusetts, 1909); John McVicar, *Origin and Progress of the Typographical Union: Its Proceedings as a National and International Organization, 1850–1891* (Lansing, Michigan, 1891); George A. Stevens, *New York Typographical Union No. 6* (Albany, New York, 1913); W. L. Mackenzie King, "The International Typographical Union," *Journal of Political Economy*, V (September, 1897), 458–84; Frederick S. Deibler, *The Amalgamated Wood Workers' International Union of America* (Madison, Wisconsin, 1912).

One of the greatest gaps in the history of organized labor is the lack of monographic studies emphasizing local developments, especially on the city and state levels. Grace H. Stimson, *Rise of the Labor Movement in Los Angeles* (Berkeley, California, 1955), is an example of the possibilities inherent in this approach. Other suggestive local studies include Eugene Staley, *History of the Illinois State Federation of Labor* (Chicago, 1930); Ira B. Cross, *A History of the Labor Movement in California* (Berkeley, California, 1935); Ruth Allen, *Chapters in the History of Organized Labor in Texas* (Austin, Texas, 1941); John P. Hall, "The Knights of St. Crispin in Massachusetts, 1869–1878," *Journal of Economic History*, XVIII (June, 1958), 161–75; Ralph W. Van Valer, "The Indiana State Federation of Labor," *Indiana Magazine of History*, XI (March, 1915), 40–58; H. M. Douty, "Early Labor Organization in North Carolina, 1880–1900," *South Atlantic Quarterly*, XXXIV (July, 1935), 260–68; Sidney Glazer, "The Michigan Labor Movement," *Michigan History*, XXIX (January–March, 1945), 73–82; Russell M. Nolen, "The Labor Movement in St. Louis From 1860 to 1890," *Missouri Historical Review*, XXXIV (January, 1940), 157–81.

D. *The National Labor Union*

John R. Commons et. al., eds., *A Documentary History of American Industrial Society* (10 vols: Cleveland, 1910–1911), reprints many of the important documents pertaining to the National Labor Union. James C. Sylvis, *The Life, Speeches, Labors and Essays of William H. Sylvis* (Philadelphia, 1872), is an invaluable source for the career of Sylvis. The *Address of the National Labor Union, to the People of the United States, on Money, Land, and Other Subjects of National Importance* (Washington, D. C., 1870), and the *Address of the Executive Committee of the National Labor Union of the State of California, June 15th, 1871* (San Francisco, 1871), sheds light on the reform orientation of the National Labor Union. There are some pertinent observations in Richard F. Hinton, "Organization of Labor: Its Aggressive Phases," *Atlantic Monthly*, XXVII (May, 1871), 544–59.

Gerald N. Grob, "Reform Unionism: The National Labor Union," *Journal of Economic History*, XIV (Spring, 1954), 126–42, attempts to place that organization in its proper historical perspective. Jonathan Grossman, *William Sylvis, Pioneer of American Labor* (New York, 1945), is the best biography of Sylvis and is indispensable for an understanding of the labor movement of the 1860's. See also the same author's "William Sylvis and the Labor Press," *Iron Molders Journal*, LXXIX (April–June, 1943), 204–08, 274–75, 334–35, and "The Molders' Struggle Against Contract Prison Labor," *New York History*, XXIII (October, 1942), 449–57. Charlotte Todes, *William H. Sylvis and the National Labor Union* (New York, 1942), is a Marxian interpretation. The career of Sylvis' successor can be followed in Clifton K. Yearley, Jr., "Richard Trevellick: Labor Agitator," *Michigan History*, XXXIX (December, 1955), 423–44, and Obadiah Hicks, *Life of Richard F. Trevellick* (Joliet, Illinois, 1896).

The influence of Edward Kellogg upon the monetary theories of the National Labor Union is elaborated in detail by Chester M. Destler, "The Influence of Edward Kellogg Upon American Radicalism, 1865–1896," *Journal of Political Economy*, XL (June, 1932), 338–65. See also Kellogg's own work, *Labor and Other Capital: the Rights of Each Secured and the Wrongs of Both Eradicated* (New York, 1849), later reprinted as *A New Monetary System* (New York, 1861). Kellogg's views were publicized during the 1860's by Alexander Campbell, *The True American System of Finance* (Chicago, 1864). There is a useful discussion of the monetary controversy after the Civil War in Robert P. Sharkey, *Money, Class, and Party: An Economic Study of Civil War and Reconstruction* (Baltimore, 1959). Information on the co-operative movement in the 1860's can be found in Jonathan Grossman, "Co-operative Foundries," *New York History*, XXIV (April, 1943), 196–210; Edwin L. Godkin, "Co-operation," *North American Review*, CVI (January, 1868), 150–75; Horace Greeley, *Recollections of a Busy Life* (New York, 1868).

E. *The Knights of Labor*

The condition of the working class in the 1870's and background material on the period in which the Order was established is provided in Samuel Bernstein's "American Labor in the Long Depression, 1873–1878," *Science & Society*, XX (Winter, 1956), 59–83. Contemporary accounts of the Knights that are revealing include Carroll D. Wright, "An Historical Sketch of the Knights of Labor," *Quarterly Journal of Economics*, I (January, 1887), 137–68; Francis A. Walker, "The Knights of Labor," *New Princeton Review*, VI (September, 1888), 196–209; A. C. Dunham, "The Knights of Labor," *New Englander and Yale Review*, XLV (June, 1886), 490–97. John W. Hayes, a prominent official of the Order, began a history of the Knights that appeared serially in his magazine, the *National Digest*, between 1921 and 1923 (volumes III–V). The glowing claims made by the leaders of the Knights concerning the principles and potentialities of their organization can be followed in H. F. Hover, *Light on the Labor Question, or the Aims and Objects of the Knights of Labor* (n.p., n.d.); R. R. Jackaway, *The Great Labor Question or the Noble Mission of the Knights of Labor* (Savannah, Georgia, 1886); Ralph Beaumont, *A Lecture on the Declaration of Principles of the Knights of Labor* (Cincinnati, 1887).

Aside from the *Proceedings of the General Assembly* and the official journal, the following primary sources have contributed much toward an understanding of the Knights of Labor: Knights of Labor, *Decisions of the General Master Workman* (Philadelphia, 1887, 1890); Knights of Labor, *Constitution* (editions of 1878, 1879, 1883, 1887, 1890, 1892, 1895, 1899, 1900); Knights of Labor, *Adelphon Kruptos* (editions of 1879, 1886, 1891). The *Fifteenth Annual Official Hand-Book District Assembly 49 Knights of Labor and Affiliated Trades* (New York, n.d.), contains information on the difficulties in New York City during the mid-1890's.

William C. Birdsall, "The Problem of Structure in the Knights of Labor," *Industrial and Labor Relations Review*, VI (July, 1953), 532–46, is a clear discussion of the structure of the Knights, while Fred Landon, "The Knights of Labor: Predecessor of the C.I.O.," *Quarterly Review of Commerce*, IV–V (Summer–Autumn, 1937), 133–39, gives the popular though distorted view of the subject. The growth of the Order in 1885–1886 is analyzed in Donald L. Kemmerer and Edward D. Wickersham, "Reasons for the Growth of the Knights of Labor in 1885–1886," *Industrial and Labor Relations Review*, III (January, 1950), 213–20. Gerald N. Grob, "The Knights of Labor and the Trade Unions, 1878–1886," *Journal of Economic History*, XVIII (June, 1958), 176–92, traces the origins of the internecine struggle in the labor movement culminating with the organization of the A.F. of L. in 1886. Some material on local and area activities of the Knights is provided in R. T. Crane, "The Knights of Labor Movement in Baltimore," *Johns Hopkins University Circulars*, XXII (April, 1903), 39; Frederic Meyers, "The Knights of Labor in the South," *Southern Economic Journal*, VI (April, 1940), 479–87; George B. Engberg, "The Knights of Labor in Minnesota," *Minnesota History*, XXII (December, 1941), 367–90. Henry J. Browne, "Terence V. Powderly and Church-Labor Difficulties of the Early 1880's" *Catholic Historical Review*, XXXII (April, 1946), 1–27, and *The Catholic Church and the Knights of Labor* (Washington, D. C., 1949), treats the relationship between the Order and the Catholic Church. Some of the cooperative activities of the Knights are covered in *History of Coöperation in the United States* (Baltimore, 1888). The Knights in Canada is covered in Douglas R. Kennedy, *The Knights of Labor in Canada* (London, Canada, 1956).

No treatment of the Knights would be complete without an understanding of its leader during its period of national importance—Terence Vincent Powderly. Powderly's own volume, *Thirty Years of Labor. 1859 to 1889* (Columbus, Ohio, 1889), is valuable for its treatment of the early history of the Knights. His autobiography, *The Path I Trod* (New York, 1940), is disappointing as well as unreliable, since it was written nearly thirty years after the events had happened. Gerald N. Grob, "Terence V. Powderly and the Knights of Labor," *Mid-America*, XXXIX (January, 1957), 39–55, is based on the Powderly manuscripts and attempts to reassess Powderly's career. Less useful are Harry J. Carman, "Terence Vincent Powderly—An Appraisal," *Journal of Economic History*, I (May, 1941), 83–87, and J. C. Walsh, "Powderly of the Knights of Labor," *American Irish Historical Society, Journal*, XXXII (1941), 85–91. Some informative articles written by Powderly include: "The Organization of Labor," *North American Review*, CXXXV (August, 1882), 118–26; "The Army of the Discontented," *North American Review*, CXL (April, 1885), 369–77; "The Federal Election Bill," *North American Review*, CLI (September, 1890), 266–73; *Trusts. Arguments Pro and Con by S. C. T. Dodd, Solicitor of the Standard Oil Co. and Terrence V. Powderly, Grand Master Workman, K. of L.* (n.p., 1892). Joseph R. Buchanan's autobiography, *The Story of a Labor Agitator* (New York, 1903), gives the views of the opposition to Powderly.

The Southwest strike of 1886 can be followed from the following sources: Ruth A. Allen, *The Great Southwest Strike* (Austin, Texas, 1942); Harry Frumerman, "The Railroad Strikes of 1885–86," *Marxist Quarterly*, I (October–December, 1937), 394–405; Frank W. Taussig, "The South-western Strike of 1886," *Quarterly Journal of Economics*, I (January, 1887), 184–222; Edith

Walker, "Labor Problems During the First Year of Governor Martin's Administration," *Kansas Historical Quarterly*, V (February, 1936), 33–53; Dorothy Leibengood, "Labor Problems in the Second Year of Governor Martin's Administration," *Kansas Historical Quarterly*, V (May, 1936), 191–207. Three indispensable contemporary sources include: *Investigation of Labor Troubles in Missouri, Arkansas, Kansas, Texas, and Illinois*, 49th Congress, 2d Session, *House Report No. 4174* (Washington, D. C., 1887); Missouri Bureau of Labor Statistics and Inspection, *The Official History of the Great Strike of 1886 on the Southwestern Railway System* (Jefferson City, Missouri, 1887); Martin Irons, "My Experiences in the Labor Movement," *Lippincott's Magazine*, XXXVII (June, 1886), 618–27.

F. *The American Federation of Labor*

Philip Taft, *The A.F. of L. in the Time of Gompers* (New York, 1957), and *The A.F. of L. From the Death of Gompers to the Merger* (New York, 1959), are the best available accounts. Based on extensive research in the archives of the A.F. of L., the two volumes are more descriptive than analytic, emphasizing primarily the attitude of the Federation on different subjects. Louis L. Lorwin, *The American Federation of Labor: History, Policies, and Prospects* (Washington, D. C., 1933), is an illuminating though unfriendly treatment that reflects the disillusionment of the early 1930's with the Federation. James O. Morris, *Conflict Within the AFL: A Study of Craft Versus Industrial Unionism, 1901–1938* (Ithaca, New York, 1958), is useful for the twentieth-century development of the Federation. See also Albert T. Helbing, *The Departments of the American Federation of Labor* (Baltimore, 1931); Morton A. Aldrich, *The American Federation of Labor* (New York, 1898); A.F. of L., *History, Encyclopedia Reference Book* (2 vols: Washington, D. C., 1919–1924). Marguerite Green, *The National Civic Federation and the American Labor Movement 1900–1925* (Washington, D. C., 1956), is useful for the period after 1900. Alfred P. James, "The First Convention of the American Federation of Labor, Pittsburgh, Pennsylvania, November 15th–18th, 1881: A Study in Contemporary Local Newspapers as a Source," *Western Pennsylvania Historical Magazine*, VI (October, 1923), 201–33, VII (January, 1924), 29–56, (April, 1924), 106–20, is useful for the establishment of the Federation of Organized Trades and Labor Unions.

Some of the early publications of the A.F. of L. and its leaders are of help in understanding the trade-union movement of this period. In this category are William Trant, *Trade Unions, Their Origin and Objects, Influence and Efficacy; With an Appendix Showing the History and Aims of the American Federation of Labor* (8th ed: Washington, D. C., 1899); Dyer D. Lum, *Philosophy of Trade Unions* (New York, 1892); Frank K. Foster, "The Condition of the American Working-Class: How Can it be Benefited?," *Forum*, XXIV (February, 1898), 711–22; *Official Book of the American Federation of Labor Issued for the 10th Annual Convention . . . 1890* (New York, 1890); *Official Book of the American Federation of Labor Issued for the Eleventh Annual Convention . . . 1891* (n.p., 1891); *Official Book of the American Federation of Labor Issued for the Twelfth Annual Convention . . . 1892* (New York, 1892).

For the attitude of the A.F. of L. toward legal injunctions see the House Judiciary Committee, *Hearing on Conspiracies and Injunctions*, 56th Congress, 1st Session, H.R. 8917 (Washington, D. C., 1900), and for a general discussion

Charles O. Gregory, *Labor and the Law* (rev. ed: New York, 1949). Background material on the A.F. of L. and strikes is provided in Samuel Yellen, *American Labor Struggles* (New York, 1936), and Almont Lindsey, *The Pullman Strike* (Chicago, 1942).

Much of the early history of the A.F. of L. revolves around the crucial figure of Samuel Gompers. Gompers' own autobiography, *Seventy Years of Life and Labor* (2 vols: New York, 1925), is an indispensable source despite its partisanship. Some of Gompers' speeches and writings have been conveniently collected in *Labor and the Common Welfare* (New York, 1919), and *Labor and the Employer* (New York, 1920). See also Gompers, "The Lesson of the Recent Strikes," *North American Review*, CLIX (August, 1894), 201–06; Gompers, "Strikes and the Coal-Miners," *Forum*, XXIV (September, 1897), 27–33; *Address of Samuel Gompers . . . Before the Arbitration Conference, Held at Chicago, Ill., December 17, 1900, Under the Auspices of the National Civic Federation* (Washington, D. C., 1901) ; Gompers, "The Limitations of Conciliation and Arbitration," *American Academy of Political and Social Science, Annals,* XX (July, 1902), 27–34. There is no adequate biography of Gompers. Rowland H. Harvey, *Samuel Gompers: Champion of the Toiling Masses* (Stanford University, California, 1935), is based largely on Gompers' own autobiography. Louis S. Reed, *The Labor Philosophy of Samuel Gompers* (New York, 1930), is a hostile study based solely on printed sources, while Hermann Lufft, *Samuel Gompers: Arbeiterschaft und Volksgemeinschaft in den Vereinigten Staaten von Amerika* (Berlin, 1928), is again a paraphrasing of Gompers' autobiography. Florence Calvert Thorne, *Samuel Gompers—American Statesman* (New York, 1957) is by Gompers' research assistant and expresses her admiration for him. John R. Commons, "Karl Marx and Samuel Gompers," *Political Science Quarterly*, XLI (June, 1926), 281–86, is a provocative and favorable interpretation of Gompers' career. Bernard Mandel, who is working on a full-length biography of Gompers, has also published two articles, "Gompers and Business Unionism, 1873–90," *Business History Review*, XXVIII (September, 1954), 264–75, and "Samuel Gompers and the Establishment of American Federation of Labor Policies," *Social Science*, XXXI (June, 1956), 165–76, but his work, written from a Marxian viewpoint, is marked by an implacable hostility toward Gompers. Benjamin Stolberg, "What Manner of Man was Gompers?," *Atlantic Monthly*, CXXXV (March, 1925), 404–12, is also critical of Gompers. Clifton K. Yearley, Jr., "Samuel Gompers: Symbol of Labor," *South Atlantic Quarterly*, LVI (Summer, 1957), 329–40, presents a sober and judicious assessment of Gompers.

V. SOCIALISM, POPULISM, POLITICS, AND THE LABOR MOVEMENT

The history of American socialism has been receiving close attention by historians in recent years. For many years Morris Hillquit, *History of Socialism in the United States* (rev. ed: New York, 1910), was the standard work. Although superseded by recent studies, it still retains value because of Hillquit's participation in the socialist movement. Two works of major importance upon American socialism are Donald D. Egbert and Stow Persons, eds., *Socialism and American Life* (2 vols: Princeton, 1952), of which the second volume is devoted to a critical bibliography of socialism, and Howard H. Quint, *The Forging of Amer-*

ican Socialism: Origins of the Modern Movement (Columbia, South Carolina, 1953). David A. Shannon's *The Socialist Party of America: A History* (New York, 1955), deals primarily with the period since 1900, while Ira Kipnis, *The American Socialist Movement 1897–1912* (New York, 1952), is marred somewhat by the author's prejudices. The ideological background of this period is brilliantly treated in Chester M. Destler's *American Radicalism 1865–1901* (New London, Connecticut, 1946), and Sidney Fine's *Laissez Faire and the General-Welfare State: A Study of Conflict in American Thought 1865–1901* (Ann Arbor, Michigan, 1956). Henry David, *The History of the Haymarket Affair* (New York, 1936), is a masterful study of an important event.

The commentaries of Marx and Engels often contain insights into the American scene. See especially Leonard E. Mins, transl. and ed., "Unpublished Letters of Karl Marx and Friedrich Engels to Americans," *Science & Society*, II (Spring, Summer, 1938), 218–31, 348–75; Karl Marx and Frederick Engels, *Selected Correspondence 1846–1895* (New York, 1942), and *Letters to Americans 1848–1895: A Selection* (New York, 1953). Many Europeans, especially socialists, were fascinated by the fact that one of the most advanced industrialized nations in the world also had the weakest socialist movement. For some explanations see the following: A. Sartorius Freiherrn von Walterhausen, *Der Moderne Sozialismus in den Vereinigten Staaten von Amerika* (Berlin, 1890), and *Die Nordamerikanischen Gewerkschaften Unter dem Einfluss der Fortschreitenden Productionstechnik* (Berlin, 1886); Edward and Eleanor Marx Aveling, *The Working-Class Movement in America* (2nd ed: London, 1891); Werner Sombart, *Warum gibt es in den Vereinigten Staaten keinen Sozialismus?* (Tübingen, 1906), "Study of the Historical Development and Evolution of the American Proletariat," *International Socialist Review*, VI (September, 1905), 129–36, (November, 1905), 293–301, (December, 1905), 358–67, and "Studien zur Entwicklungsgeschichte des nordamerikanischen Proletariats," *Archiv für Sozialwissenschaft und Sozialpolitik*, XXI (1905), 210–36, 308–46, 556–611.

For specific treatments of the American socialists and their relationships with the labor movement see Hermann Schlüter, *Die Internationale in Amerika* (Chicago, 1918); David J. Saposs, *Left Wing Unionism: A Study of Radical Policies and Tactics* (New York, 1926); James W. Sullivan, *Socialism as an Incubus on the American Labor Movement* (New York, 1909); Philip Taft, "Attempts to 'Radicalize' the Labor Movement," *Industrial and Labor Relations Review*, I (July, 1948), 580–92; Louis Levine (Lorwin), "The Development of Syndicalism in America," *Political Science Quarterly*, XXVIII (September, 1913), 451–79; Sidney Fine, "Is May Day American in Origin?," *The Historian*, XVI (Spring, 1954), 121–34. Ray Ginger, *The Bending Cross: A Biography of Eugene Victor Debs* (New Brunswick, New Jersey, 1949), is a sympathetic study that is marred somewhat by the author's dislike of trade-union leaders. Two useful reminiscences by prominent socialists are Morris Hillquit, *Loose Leaves From a Busy Life* (New York, 1934), and John Spargo, *Americanism and Social Democracy* (New York, 1918). There is no adequate study of Daniel DeLeon, but see J. B. Stalvey, "Daniel De Leon: A Study of Marxian Orthodoxy in the United States," unpublished Ph.D. dissertation, University of Illinois, Urbana, Illinois, 1946, and Leonid G. Raisky, *Daniel De Leon: The Struggle Against Opportunism in the American Labor Movement* (New York, 1932). DeLeon's own writings are revealing. See especially *What Means This Strike?* (New York, 1898); *Reform or*

Revolution: Address Delivered . . . Eighteen Ninety Six (New York, 1918);
The Burning Question of Trades Unionism (New York, 1904); *A Debate on the
Tactics of the S.T. & L.A. Toward Trade Unions Between Daniel DeLeon . . .
and Job Harriman . . . November 25, 1900* (n.p., n.d.).

The struggle between the socialists and trade unionists in the A.F. of L. can
be clearly followed in the debates at the conventions of the Federation in 1890
and 1894. These debates were reprinted as *An Interesting Discussion at the
Tenth Annual Convention of the American Federation of Labor Held at Detroit, Michigan, December 8–13, 1890* (New York, 1891), and *A Verbatim Report of the Discussion on the Political Programme, at the Denver Convention
of the American Federation of Labor, December 14, 15, 1894* (New York, 1895).

There is as yet no general history of the political activities of American labor
during the nineteenth century. Edward T. James, "American Labor and Political Action, 1865–1896: The Knights of Labor and Its Predecessors," unpublished
Ph.D. dissertation, Harvard University, Cambridge, Massachusetts, 1954, is a
good beginning. Useful information on labor's political uprising in 1886 can be
found in Charles A. Barker, *Henry George* (New York, 1955), and Peter
A. Speek, *The Singletax and the Labor Movement* (Madison, Wisconsin, 1917).
Marc Karson, *American Labor Unions and Politics 1900–1918* (Carbondale,
Illinois, 1958), deals largely with a later period, and gives a generally unfav-
able picture of Gompers and the Federation. Gerald N. Grob, "The Knights of
Labor, Politics, and Populism," *Mid-America*, XL (January, 1958), 3–21,
briefly evaluates the reform political activities of the Knights. Mollie R. Carroll,
*Labor and Politics: The Attitude of the American Federation of Labor Toward
Legislation and Politics* (Boston, 1923), is based solely on published sources.
See also Harwood L. Childs, *Labor and Capital in National Politics* (Columbus,
Ohio, 1930); Robert Hunter, *Labor in Politics* (Chicago, 1915); Edward B. Mit-
telman, "Chicago Labor in Politics 1877–96," *Journal of Political Economy*,
XXVIII (May, 1920), 407–27; W. Macarthur, "Political Action and Trade-Un-
ionism," American Academy of Political and Social Science, *Annals*, XXIV
(September, 1904), 32–4.`.

Nathan Fine, *Labor and Farmer Parties in the United States 1828–1928* (New
York, 1928), and John D. Hicks, *The Populist Revolt* (Minneapolis, 1931),
serve as introductions to the relationship between the farmers and workers during the latter quarter of the nineteenth century. Gompers' hostile attitude toward the Populist movement can be gleaned from his article, "Organized Labor
in the Campaign," *North American Review*, CLV (July, 1892), 91–96, and Irving Bernstein, ed., "Samuel Gompers and Free Silver, 1896," *Mississippi Valley
Historical Review*, XXIX (December, 1942), 394–400. See also James Peterson,
"The Trade Unions and the Populist Party," *Science & Society*, VIII (Spring,
1944), 143–60, and John Lee Coulter, "Organization Among the Farmers of
the United States," *Yale Review*, XVIII (November, 1909), 273–98.

VI. EIGHT HOURS

The only general account of the eight-hour movement is Marion C. Cahill,
Shorter Hours: A Study of the Movement Since the Civil War (New York,
1932). For the influence of Ira Steward, the intellectual father of the movement,
see Ira Steward, *Poverty* (Boston, 1873); Hyman Kuritz, "Ira Steward and the

Eight Hour Day," *Science & Society*, XX (Spring, 1956), 118–34; Dorothy W. Douglas, "Ira Steward on Consumption and Unemployment," *Journal of Political Economy*, XL (August, 1932), 532–43; Frederic Meyers, "Underconsumption: A Rationalization for Trade Unionists," *Southwestern Social Science Quarterly*, XXX (March, 1950), 237–45. For Powderly's views on eight hours see his article "The Plea for Eight Hours," *North American Review*, CL (April, 1890), 464–69. Material on the A.F. of L. and eight hours can be found in Sidney Fine, "The Eight-Hour Day Movement in the United States, 1888–1891," *Mississippi Valley Historical Review*, XL (December, 1953), 441–62, and Henry R. Mussey, "Eight-Hour Theory in the American Federation of Labor," in Jacob H. Hollander, ed., *Economic Essays Contributed in Honor of John Bates Clark* (New York, 1927), pp. 229–43. The following pamphlets published by the A.F. of L. are also revealing: Lemuel Danryid, *History and Philosophy of the Eight-Hour Movement* (New York, 1889); George Gunton, *The Economic and Social Importance of the Eight-Hour Movement* (Washington, D. C., 1889); George E. McNeill, *The Eight Hour Primer* (New York, 1889); Samuel Gompers, *The Eight-Hour Workday: Its Inauguration, Enforcement and Influences* (Washington, D. C., 1897).

VII. WOMEN AND NEGRO LABOR

Material on women in the labor movement is relatively scarce. John B. Andrews and W. D. P. Bliss, *History of Women in Trade Unions*, 61st Congress, 2d Session, *Senate Document 645*, Vol. X (Washington, D. C., 1911), Edith Abbott, *Women in Industry* (New York, 1915), and Eleanor Flexner, *Century of Struggle: The Woman's Rights Movement in the United States* (Cambridge, Massachusetts, 1959), are useful introductions.

Material on the Negro is abundant. General introductions to the subject include Charles H. Wesley, *Negro Labor in the United States 1850–1925* (New York, 1927); Sterling D. Spero and Abram L. Harris, *The Black Worker: The Negro and the Labor Movement* (New York, 1931); Rayford W. Logan, *The Negro in American Life and Thought: The Nadir 1877–1901* (New York, 1954); W. E. Burghardt Du Bois, ed., *The Negro Artisan* (Atlanta, Georgia, 1902); Herbert Aptheker, ed., *A Documentary History of the Negro People in the United States* (New York, 1951); John Hope Franklin, *From Slavery to Freedom* (New York, 1947); National Urban League, *Negro Membership in American Labor Unions* (New York, n.d.); Gerald N. Grob, "Organized Labor and the Negro Worker, 1865–1900," *Labor History*, I (Spring, 1960), 164–76; George S. Mitchell, "The Negro in Southern Trade Unionism," *Southern Economic Journal*, II (January, 1936), 26–33; Herman D. Bloch, "Craft Unions and the Negro in Historical Perspective," *Journal of Negro History*, XLIII (January, 1958), 10–33. Sumner E. Matison, "The Labor Movement and the Negro During Reconstruction," *Journal of Negro History*, XXXIII (October, 1948), 426–68, treats the Negro during the period of the National Labor Union, while Sidney H. Kessler, "The Negro in Labor Strikes," *Midwest Journal*, VI (Summer, 1954), 16–35, and "The Organization of Negroes in the Knights of Labor," *Journal of Negro History*, XXXVII (July, 1952), 248–76, covers the period of the 1880's. Bernard Mandel, "Samuel Gompers and the Negro Workers, 1886–1914," *Journal of Negro History*, XL (January, 1955), 34–60, though based on extensive research, is marked by a Marxian dogmatism that results in an inaccurate treatment of an important topic.

VIII. THE LABOR MOVEMENT AND IMMIGRATION

Charlotte Erickson, *American Industry and the European Immigrant, 1860–1885* (Cambridge, Massachusetts, 1957), minimizes the importance of contract skilled labor from abroad. John Higham, *Strangers in the Land: Patterns of American Nativism, 1860–1925* (New Brunswick, New Jersey, 1955), is a masterful discussion of American nativism since the Civil War.

Nicholas A. Somma, "The Knights of Labor and Chinese Immigration," unpublished M.A. thesis, Catholic University of America, Washington, D. C., 1952, is an adequate introduction to the subject. The Chinese Massacre in Wyoming Territory in 1885 is treated in Paul Crane and Alfred Larson, "The Chinese Massacre," *Annals of Wyoming,* XII (January, 1940), 47–55, (April, 1940), 153–61; Isaac H. Bromley, *The Chinese Massacre at Rock Springs, Wyoming Territory, September 2, 1885* (Boston, 1886); *The Chinese Question,* 49th Congress, 1st Session, *House Executive Document 102* (Washington, D. C., 1886). For the position of the A.F. of L. see A.F. of L., *Some Reasons for Chinese Exclusion* (Washington, D. C., n.d.), and Arthur Mann, "Gompers and the Irony of Racism," *Antioch Review,* XIII (June, 1953), 203–14.

Index

213

Social Science

E. Digby Baltzell. *Philadelphia Gentlemen.* (QP236)
Abraham S. Blumberg. *Criminal Justice.* (QP227)
Donald R. Cressey. *Crime and Criminal Justice.* (NYTimes Book, QP233)
Shalom Endleman. *Violence in the Streets.* (QP215)
Nathan Glazer. *Cities in Trouble.* (NYTimes Book, QP212)
William J. Goode. *The Contemporary American Family.* (NYTimes Book, QP223)
George and Eunice Grier. *Equality and Beyond.* (QP204)
F. William Howton. *Functionaries.* (QP232)
Morris Janowitz. *Political Conflict.* (QP226)
Michael B. Kane. *Minorities in Textbooks.* (QP231)
Kurt Lang and Gladys Engel Lang. *Politics and Television.* (QP216)
Charles O. Lerche, Jr. *Last Chance in Europe.* (QP207)
Raymond W. Mack. *Prejudice and Race Relations.* (NYTimes Book, QP217)
Harry T. Marmion. *The Case Against a Volunteer Army.* (QP234)
David Mitrany. *A Working Peace System.* (QP205)
Earl Finbar Murphy. *Governing Nature.* (QP228)
H. L. Nieburg. *In the Name of Science.* (QP218)
Martin Oppenheimer. *The Urban Guerrilla.* (QP219)
Martin Oppenheimer and George Lakey. *A Manual for Direct Action.* (QP202)
James Parkes. *Antisemitism.* (QP213)
Fred Powledge. *To Change a Child.* (QP209)
Lee Rainwater. *And the Poor Get Children.* (QP208)
The Rockefeller Report on the Americas. (QP214)
Ben B. Seligman. *Main Currents in Modern Economics.* (3 vols, QP237, 238, 239)
Ben B. Seligman. *Molders of Modern Thought.* (NYTimes Book, QP224)
Ben B. Seligman. *Permanent Poverty.* (QP229)
Clarence Senior. *The Puerto Ricans.* (QP201)
Harold L. Sheppard. *Poverty and Wealth in America.* (NYTimes Book, QP220)
Arthur L. Stinchcombe. *Rebellion in a High School.* (QP211)
Edward G. Stockwell. *Population and People.* (QP230)
Harry M. Trebing. *The Corporation in the American Economy.* (NYTimes Book, QP221)
Michael Walzer. *Political Action.* (QP235)
David Manning White. *Pop Culture in America.* (NYTimes Book, QP222)
Harold Wolozin. *American Fiscal and Monetary Policy.* (NYTimes Book, QP225)

Philosophy

F. H. Bradley. *The Presuppositions of Critical History.* (QP108)
E. M. Cioran. *The Temptation to Exist.* (QP119)
William Earle. *Objectivity.* (QP109)
James M. Edie, James P. Scanlan, Mary-Barbara Zeldin, George L. Kline. *Russian Philosophy* (3 vols, QP111, 112, 113)
James M. Edie. *An Invitation to Phenomenology.* (QP103)
James M. Edie. *New Essays in Phenomenology.* (QP114)
James M. Edie. *Phenomenology in America.* (QP105)
R. O. Elveton. *The Phenomenology of Husserl.* (QP116)
Manfred S. Frings. *Heidegger and the Quest for Truth.* (QP107)
Moltke S. Gram. *Kant: Disputed Questions.* (QP104)
James F. Harris, Jr., and Richard Severens. *Analyticity.* (QP117)
E. D. Klemke. *Studies in the Philosophy of G. E. Moore.* (QP115)
Lionel Rubinoff. *Faith and Reason.* (QP106)
Stuart F. Spicker. *The Philosophy of the Body.* (QP118)
Pierre Thévenaz. *What Is Phenomenology?* (QP101)
Paul Tibbetts. *Perception.* (QP110)
Robert E. Wood. *The Future of Metaphysics.* (QP120)